Moral Motivation through the Life Span

Volume 51 of
the Nebraska Symposium
on Motivation

University of Nebraska Press
Lincoln and London

Volume 51 of the Nebraska Symposium on Motivation

Moral Motivation through the Life Span

Richard A. Dienstbier — *Series Editor*
Gustavo Carlo
Carolyn Pope Edwards — *Volume Editors*

Presenters

Gustavo Carlo — *Associate Professor in Developmental Psychology, University of Nebraska–Lincoln*

Carolyn Pope Edwards — *Professor of Psychology and Family and Consumer Sciences, University of Nebraska–Lincoln*

Nancy Eisenberg — *Professor of Psychology, Arizona State University*

Daniel Hart — *Professor of Psychology, Rutgers University*

Jerome Kagan — *Research Professor Emeritus, Harvard University*

Darcia Narvaez — *Associate Professor of Psychology, University of Notre Dame*

F. Clark Power — *Professor of Psychology, Notre Dame University*

Ervin Staub — *Professor of Psychology, University of Massachusetts, Amherst*

Moral Motivation through the Life Span is Volume 51 in the series
CURRENT THEORY AND RESEARCH
IN MOTIVATION

Manufactured in the United States of America
International Standard Book Number
ISBN-13: 978-0-8032-1549-8 (Clothbound)
ISBN-10: 0-8032-1549-5 (Clothbound)

The Library of Congress has cataloged
this serial publication as follows:
Nebraska Symposium on Motivation.
Nebraska Symposium on Motivation.
[Papers] v. [1]–1953–
Lincoln, University of Nebraska Press.
v. illus., diagrs. 22cm. annual.
Vol. 1 issued by the symposium under
its earlier name: Current Theory and
Research in Motivation.
Symposia sponsored by the Dept. of
Psychology of the University of Nebraska.
1. Motivation (Psychology)
BF683.N4 159.4082 53–11655
Library of Congress

Preface

With this 51st edition of the Nebraska Symposium on Motivation, we happily begin the second half century of the longest continuously running symposium series in psychology.

The volume editors for the 51st edition of the symposium are Professors Gustavo Carlo and Carolyn Pope Edwards, who worked as equal partners in creating both the sessions of the symposium and this book. They planned the volume by selecting the theme of this symposium, and they then invited the contributors and coordinated all aspects of the editing. This year Professors Carlo and Edwards performed those many roles with dispatch and dedication. I extend thanks to them and to our contributors for the timely production of these chapters.

As with symposium sessions of the last several years, in order to allow other scholars to travel to the symposium as participants, we invited posters relevant to the main theme of moral development. The contributions of these participants enhanced the symposium's quality and value. Since this is a tradition that we will continue, we urge you, our readers, to consider such poster submissions when you receive future symposium announcements.

This symposium series is supported largely by funds donated in the memory of Professor Harry K. Wolfe to the University of Nebraska Foundation by the late Professor Cora L. Friedline. This symposium volume, like those of the recent past, is dedicated to the memory of Professor Wolfe, who brought psychology to the University of Nebraska. After studying with Professor Wilhelm Wundt, Professor Wolfe returned to this, his native state, to establish the first undergraduate laboratory of psychology in the nation. As a student at the university, Professor Friedline studied psychology under Professor Wolfe.

We are grateful to the late Professor Friedline for this bequest as well as to the University of Nebraska Foundation for continued financial support for the series. For the 50th anniversary year, and for subsequent years, the amount of funding granted by the foundation has been increased. We are particularly grateful to Vice Chancellor for Academic Affairs Richard Edwards for assistance in securing that increase.

It is time to give a special thanks to Claudia Price-Decker, who regularly helps with the coordination of the sessions themselves, overseeing the many details that must be considered for the symposium to run smoothly. Claudia's great skills and competence are greatly appreciated, and the Department of Psychology has come to take smooth running of the symposium for granted. Others who assisted and also deserve thanks include Becki Barnes, who has been helping for years, and Joy Menke, who has joined this effort more recently.

Richard A. Dienstbier
Senior Editor

Contents

ix Carolyn Pope Edwards and Gustavo Carlo — *Introduction: Moral Development Study in the 21st Century*

1 Jerome Kagan — *Human Morality and Temperament*

33 Ervin Staub — *The Roots of Goodness: The Fulfillment of Basic Human Needs and the Development of Caring, Helping and Nonaggression, Inclusive Caring, Moral Courage, Active Bystandership, and Altruism Born of Suffering*

73 Nancy Eisenberg — *The Development of Empathy-Related Responding*

119 Darcia Narvaez — *The Neo-Kohlbergian Tradition and Beyond: Schemas, Expertise, and Character*

165 Daniel Hart — *The Development of Moral Identity*

197 F. Clark Power — *Motivation and Moral Development: A Trifocal Perspective*

251 Contributors

257 Subject Index

265 Author Index

Introduction: Moral Development Study in the 21st Century

Carolyn Pope Edwards
and Gustavo Carlo
University of Nebraska–Lincoln

Questions of right and wrong, good and bad, lawful and unlawful, have been debated by philosophers, theologians, scholars, and ordinary people since ancient times. The moral domain represents humanity's answers to three questions: What is the right thing to do? How is the best state of affairs achieved? What qualities make for a good person? However, the scientific investigation of the moral life has a much shorter intellectual history than does philosophical and religious reflection; nevertheless, it is not new. Moral development theory and research emerged as a critical topic over 100 years ago, at the beginning of the 20th century. Thus, given this deep background, it may surprise readers to learn that this is the very first time that the Nebraska Symposium on Motivation has served as a forum to reflect on what we know about moral development and motivation and to integrate theory and research with practical implications for schools, communities, and childrearing. This book presents the products of the 51st Nebraska Symposium on Motivation: "Moral Development through the Life Span: Theory, Research, and Applications." The symposium was held in Lincoln, Nebraska, in April 2003.

Interest in moral development and motivation has been prominent in the field of psychology since Sigmund Freud's theory about the Oedipus complex and the formation of the superego. Indeed, during certain earlier decades, especially the 1970s and 1980s, moral development was a hot and contentious topic among social and behavioral scientists. Various proponents of behavioral versus structural theories, such as Lawrence Kohlberg and Jacob Gewirtz, enjoyed squaring off in public and professional debates. Some important books, such as Lickona (1976), Kurtines and Gewirtz (1984), and Eisenberg, Reykowski, and Staub (1989), grew out of those debates, and, even today, these sources are useful for reading clear statements of the alternative theoretical perspectives, which are presented as competing approaches to the study and interpretation of moral development. However, following that lively but contentious period, the 1990s represented a quieter time of solid and steady gains in research study of moral development and prosocial behavior as well as a period of serious attempts at theoretical reconciliation and bridge building.

This volume presents some of the most significant fruits of that labor by distinguished and well-known researchers in the field. It is intended to summarize what we now know about moral motivation theory, research, and application across the life span. Although not all major theoretical or empirical traditions are covered here, the authors represent diverse theoretical orientations and methodologies that address many of the important issues in moral motivation. Various themes run throughout the chapters, and each chapter summarizes work that adds to our existing knowledge regarding moral development.

The Historical Background to Current Research

To understand our existing scientific knowledge of moral motivation, it is necessary first to consider some aspects of the historical, cultural, and contextual underpinnings of the major research going on in this field today. There is now a long and storied tradition of scholarly advances in the study of moral development. The first large systematic study of children's cheating, lying, obedience, and other "good" behavior was conducted by Hartshorne, May, and Shuttleworth (1930). James Mark Baldwin (1897), a developmental psychologist, and John Dewey (1930), a philosopher and educator, were two other Americans who did important foundational writing about the ways in which moral thinking unfolds in childhood, but they did not test or document their theories with empirical research. Jean Piaget in Geneva, Switzerland, drew partly on the work of Baldwin when he invented new and productive ways to observe and interview children and then construct a framework with which to understand children's conceptions of games, rules, punishment, and justice and fairness (Piaget, 1932/1977).

Schooled in these early theoretical speculations and bodies of findings as well as in the sociological theories of George Herbert Mead (1967) and Emile Durkheim (1979), Lawrence Kohlberg initiated the contemporary era of systematic empirical research when, in the 1960s, he formulated his "cognitive-developmental" stage theory of moral judgment (Kohlberg, 1981, 1984; Kohlberg, Levine, & Hewer, 1983) in the form of strong claims and invited the field to engage in dialogue on the basis of argument and empirical evidence. At Harvard University, Kohlberg worked with a series of colleagues and students who went on to refine, elaborate, or critique and revise his theory in major ways, extending its reach into such areas as domain theory and social conventions (Turiel, 1983), social perspective taking (Selman, 1980), ego development (Kegan, 1982), distributive justice concepts (Damon, 1977), sociomoral reflection (Gibbs, Basinger, & Fuller, 1992), women's "way of knowing" (Belenky, 1986; Gilligan, 1982), and cross-cultural studies (Edwards, 1979, 1985; Snarey, 1985). Methodological issues (measurement, reliability, validity) were central, and Ann Colby and Kohlberg (1987) published a manual to aid systematic methods of coding and scoring moral judgment interviews. James Rest at the University of Minnesota established a center devoted to research on moral development using a paper-and-pencil questionnaire based on Kohlberg's theory of moral development (the Defining Issues Test; Rest, 1979; for more discussion, see Narvaez, in this volume). Kohlberg was always deeply committed to making positive changes in human life and society and, with such colleagues as Clark Power and Ann Higgins (Power, Higgins, & Kohlberg, 1989), innovated methods of stimulating the development of moral reasoning and attitudes in school and prison settings.

Meanwhile, the theory aroused passionate debate and criticism (e.g., Gilligan, 1982; Kurtines & Grief, 1974). Not only were more behaviorally oriented psychologists eager to establish alternative methods for systematically studying prosocial values and behavior (see, e.g., Eisenberg et al., 1989; Staub, 1978), but also educators moved quickly to establish alternative ways of promoting "character education" in schools as a way of fostering the development and practicing of attitudes and behaviors creating respect for others, caring attitudes, empathy, and appropriate cooperation with authority (see also Noddings, 1984). Many of these programs have thrived and become influential models (e.g., Battistisch, Watson, Solomon, Schaps, & Solomon, 1991). Thus, the controversies stimulated a rising and vital field of study and helped set the agenda (pro and con) for much of the ensuing research and practice regarding moral development and education.

Since Kohlberg's death in 1987, moreover, the field of moral development and education has continued to evolve and change. Its theoretical foundations have undergone important transformations, perhaps as the almost inevitable consequence of over 4 decades of accumulating empirical study as well as the sustained, extensive scholarly debate. In this volume, we present the views of six noted scholars concerning the most important recent findings. Our contributors synthesize work that has had, or is expected to have, a significant impact on moral development theory, research, and application.

The varied research traditions in moral development and motivation are linked to crucial differences in underlying metatheoretical assumptions. These philosophical and scientific assumptions are inherent to their perspectives, and they affect how each scholar both interprets observed moral phenomena and selects his or her research methods. In simplified terms, the issues can be considered by addressing a series of critical questions. (1) What *motivates* moral thinking and behavior? While emotions, intellect, and values may all be part of the story, what is most important for the researcher to study and describe? (2) Are *objective* standards or validating criteria (such as religious commandants or approval by society) necessary to judge and justify a person's actions? Or, instead, are matters of right and wrong (good and bad) dependent on human beings' *subjective choices*, which cannot be externally validated? (3) Are any moral rules or principles *universal* to all times and places, in the sense that they ought to be recognized by all human societies, or are moral issues necessarily specific and *relative* to cultural and historical contexts and circumstances? (4) What is the *nature of human beings* who make choices and engage in moral or immoral actions? Are they *active* and *autonomous* moral agents or, instead, *passive* persons whose behavior is (fully) explained by processes of socialization/social influence or by unconscious emotions beyond individual control? (5) What is the place of *spirituality* or *faith* in moral development as well as in research? Can nonrational processes like the spiritual dimension of moral decisionmaking be investigated by moral researchers? Does *spiritual* development have a legitimate place in public school or community service programs that seek to promote moral development? (6) What scientific *methodologies* should be employed and what kinds of evidence brought forward to study moral motivation and development? Should *affective* or *cognitive* processes be the focus of attention? What kind of evidence about *actions*, or *observed behaviors*, is required to substantiate a research program? (7) Finally, what is the relation between moral development research and *childrearing and education*? That is, what can (and should) be fostered through processes of socialization or programs of therapy, reconciliation, and education? Are such efforts primarily intended to foster changes in people's *ideas* and *expertise* in rational decisionmaking, or, instead, are they directed toward creating changes in people's *emotions*, *feeling capacities*, and *sphere of concern*?

Because the philosophical, scientific, and educational issues that lie behind and drive each scholar's program of research make for interesting contrasts, we provide a preview of the volume and its dominant themes by considering what the authors have to say about each of these key questions. Readers will, we believe, find that the chapters provide stimulating and provocative reflections on some of the most important and timely issues of our day. The authors represent some of the sophisticated and up-to-date theories, research, and applications in knowledge about moral development across the life span.

What Motivates Morality?

Moral behavior is *intentional* behavior, but what motivates it? Kagan describes two essential motives as the foundation of moral behavior: first, an emotional motivation to gain sensory pleasure (and avoid pain); second, a cognitive motivation to confirm that one's behaviors, thoughts, or feelings are in accord with one's concepts or representations of what is good. Eisenberg focuses on the influence of empathy-related responding in motivating behavior. Although the primary focus of her research in graduate school was moral reasoning, over time she became convinced that affective responses (empathy, sympathy, and personal distress) are as important as or more important than rationality (moral reasoning) in predicting both prosocial and antisocial behavior. Power and Narvaez seem to agree that moral motivation is an explicit yearning or desire to *be* good (virtuous, righteous) and to *do* good for self and others. Narvaez describes four processes fundamental to a moral orientation: moral sensitivity; judgment; motivation; and action. Power's model delineates cognitive, environmental, and spiritual conditions or experiences that push individuals to seek the good. Hart, a personality theorist, is interested in moral identity as a source of motivation. Identity is composed of experiences related to self-awareness, continuity through time and place, the self in relation to others, and the self as the basis for strong evaluations. It includes the important plans, goals, and values that form a basis for the individual's perceiving, judging, and acting. Hart acknowledges that personality attributes influence moral responses but reminds us of the social forces (community conditions) that can facilitate or mitigate those behaviors.

Finally, Staub provides the most elaborated discussion of moral motivations. He emphasizes a core set of basic human *needs*, such as needs for nurturance, affection, and guidance in childhood. Emotional deprivation and difficult and challenging environments usually frustrate the individual and lead to negative emotions, such as anger, envy, hostility, and aggression. Staub lays out a typology of moral motivations: (1) beliefs or principles, such as enlightened self-interest, the golden rule, or the sanctity of life; (2) altruism, which arises out of empathy, sympathy, compassion, and, occasionally, suffering; and (3) prosocial value orientation, which refers to a positive view of humans and a sense of responsibility for others' welfare. "Inclusive caring" (as opposed to in-group caring), moral courage, and positive bystandership are forms of moral motivation especially important to Staub.

Is Morality Objective or Subjective?

All researchers on moral development make some assumptions regarding the objectivity versus subjectivity of basic moral principles. Certainly, ethicists have debated questions about the truth basis of morality and ethical decisionmaking for thousands of years without coming to a consensus. Scientists, too, make different judgments, having responded in contrasting ways to the complex issues involved. On the one hand, as moral researchers, they participate in the Western community of science, which inherits an ancient intellectual legacy of notions about truth seeking that is rooted in Greek philosophy, for instance, Platonic notions about moral "ideals" that can be and should be rediscovered by the rational mind. The Platonic tradition has endured in the influential works of philosophers such as Immanuel Kant (1785/1993) and, more recently, John Rawls (1971, 2001). Along that same line, most moral researchers are descendants of cultural-religious traditions that affirm some objective and universal basis to certain moral principles, all the major world religions (Christianity, Judaism, Islam, Hinduism) recognizing basic ethical laws or moral commandments.

On the other hand, contemporary moral researchers undergo training that immerses them in psychological concepts of consciousness and the self. They are exposed to developmental theories concerning childhood socialization and enculturation along with social-psychological theories about interpersonal influence that heighten recognition of the conscious and unconscious sources of individual decisionmaking and the influence of context. Along this same line, moral researchers as social scientists learn to appreciate the difficulty of choosing one single "correct" overarching theory that explains all aspects of human development, and they are trained in descriptive and predictive statistical analytic techniques based on probabilistic determinism. All these influences incline researchers to question whether moral decisionmaking can be truly objective.

Perhaps as a result of their scientific training, many moral developmental psychologists currently take the view that moral phenomena are interpreted and processed in unique ways by each individual, as stated by Narvaez in her chapter. For example, both Kagan and Staub devote major portions of their chapters to summarizing what they see as the most important and general cognitive mechanisms and developmental processes that can help account for the incredibly wide range of human moral choices and phenomena. Kagan suggests that there is a "good" to which human beings aspire, and he identifies a developmental cascade of processes that help account for individual and group differences in moral actions, yet he explicitly rejects an objective basis to morality. At the Nebraska symposium, he sparked lively debate when he declared that there is no objective way to call immoral even the acts of people (e.g., terrorists) who destroy others in the service of moral ideals. While Staub also focuses on the life-cycle events that tend to promote the development of moral conscience and prosocial behavior, he differs from Kagan in believing that underlying the diversity of human judgments about morality is the basic perception that moral action is about not doing harm or injury to the self or others. Therefore, Staub comes closer than does Kagan to affirming an objective notion of morality.

Eisenberg emphasizes subjectivism when she describes how processes such as empathy-related responding, affectivity, and affect regulation powerfully motivate prosocial and discourage antisocial actions. She defines *prosocial behavior* as voluntary behavior intended to benefit another person and *altruistic behavior* as prosocial behavior primarily motivated by other-oriented, moral values and emotions rather than egoistic or pragmatic concerns. In other words, she asserts that prosocial behaviors might have many different motives but that altruistic behaviors have a much more specific underlying motive.

Hart takes a pragmatic approach and focuses on the intrapersonal and environmental influences of moral character development. Hart applies the notion of *moral luck,* which refers to the positive opportunities available in certain kinds of environments, to his conception of morality. He suggests that moral behaviors are contingent on social circumstances and opportunities as much as on personal qualities. Thus, the moral qualities of individuals can be fostered or hampered by experiences and opportunities in their environment.

In contrast to the others, Power takes the position closest to objectivism by holding to the central Kohlbergian insight that a sense of justice as fairness does, and should, underlie mature and principled moral reasoning. Narvaez, also a cognitive-developmentalist in the James Rest tradition, has moved away from Kohlbergian notions of principled moral reasoning to the extent of viewing mature moral reasoning as the product of "expertise." The objectivist orientations that are reflected in Staub's, Power's, and Narvaez's perspectives provide some contrast to the subjectivist orientations that are reflected in Eisenberg's, Hart's, and Kagan's perspectives.

Are Moral Truths Universal?

The tension between objective and subjective moral ideals becomes especially apparent when moral scholars debate the universal versus relative nature of moral values and judgments (e.g., Wong, 1984). In the present volume, most of the authors present paradigms that oppose extreme cultural relativism. Kagan is the exception. He argues that cultures with integrity have promoted very different a priori moral standards as moral ideals and that no one can be considered altruistic or prosocial without specifying the agent, the target, and the context of the action.

Leaving aside the issue of whether there are any cultural universals in the content of morality, all six contributors argue for some universal elements of moral motivation or moral development. Kagan posits a universal developmental sequence for the separate components of morality: an initial concept of prohibited acts; an ability to infer the thoughts of another; the acquisition of the value of the semantic concepts *good* and *bad*; the ability to relate past to present; and a recognition of social identity categories to which self belongs. Likewise, Staub, Eisenberg, Narvaez, and Hart claim that there are general cognitive *mechanisms* and emotional *processes* that underlie moral development around the world.

Power goes farther and suggests that these universal formal processes imply a culturally universal basis to the *content* of the human recognition of the good. For example, Power argues that desire for good is tied closely to a desire for truth, justice, and happiness, and he attempts to describe "the categorical, universal, and prescriptive features of the moral domain" (p. 199). Furthermore, Power notes the lack of focus by most researchers on the spiritual aspects of morality, and he asserts that, at the highest stages of moral development, there is transcendent understanding and appreciation of human existence.

It is important to note that the authors' perspectives on the generality of moral processes are not necessarily incompatible with other evidence on the culturally specific aspects of moral decisionmaking (Carlo, Koller, Eisenberg, Da Silva, & Frohlich, 1996; Shweder, Mahapatra, & Miller, 1987; Tietjen, 1986; Whiting & Edwards, 1988). For example, Eisenberg notes that her research suggests that cross-cultural differences in prosocial traits (e.g., moral reasoning) exist. Narvaez agrees but notes that the use of the Defining Issues Test reveals larger within-group than between-group differences, after controlling for age and education. Staub (1989, 2003), who studies genocide and works to promote reconciliation and healing, is especially interested in societal-level forces and historical conditions that incline whole groups of people to accept authoritarian regimes or commit mass harm to others (see also Moshman, 2004).

One key to reconciling the different perspectives is to examine the multiple sources of between- and within-group variance and consider both additive and interactive effects (Carlo, Roesch, Knight, & Koller, 2001). Acknowledging the additive and multiplicative influences of moral outcomes would reflect the multidimensional, real-life complexity of individuals and enhance the ecological validity of moral development theories. Furthermore, beyond simply documenting individual differences, it is critical to understand them. Many or most aspects of normative moral thinking and behavior grow out of specific cultural contexts for which they may be generally *adaptive* (i.e., they allow people to function together in social settings, manage and control aggression, and negotiate individual striving; LeVine, 1994). For example, working in Kenya, Edwards (1979, 1985; Harkness, Edwards, & Super, 1981) documented that differences in the adult stage of moral reasoning among respected adults and elders (as measured by Kohlberg's structural system) were closely related to the context of daily living: whether conflict resolution was situated within the close setting of a face-to-face community (rural village) or, instead, within the impersonal institutions of a complex society with competing elites. However, adaptation is not the whole story of moral functioning. Any set of normative values or cognitive schemata can quickly become *maladaptive* and reactionary in the face of disequilibrating forces (overpopulation, famine, war, disease) or rapid transformations of economy, education, and technology that outpace individual and group capacities to adapt smoothly. Without attention to the possible impact of historical and societal conditions, there is a danger of overestimating the homogeneity of moral development in diverse social contexts.

Are Human Beings Active Moral Agents?

One of the common themes throughout the volume is the acknowledgment of individuals as active moral agents who have the capacity to control their actions. Whereas some prior theories of moral conduct (e.g., radical behaviorist theories; Skinner, 1971) might have posited the individual as a relatively passive agent, most contemporary theories of moral motivation seem to adopt an interactionist perspective that acknowledges the individual as an active or autonomous agent. Interestingly, however, each theory may differ in terms of the specific impact accorded the environment and the degree to which individuals can modify or select their environment.

The chapters by Power and Narvaez provide examples of theories that emphasize the active role of the moral agent through cognitive and social information processes. Individuals are posited to respond to moral situations on the basis of their own unique perceptions, which make their action choices dynamic and unpredictable. Both Hart and Power acknowledge the role of the "moral self" as an agent of morality—and, hence, self-concept development is an integral part of moral development. Hart places the self inside the community when he discusses "moral luck," or the socioeconomic community into which the child is born and how poverty and other adverse conditions can overwhelm a community's capacity to provide its young people with adequate opportunities for public service. Eisenberg and Kagan offer a somewhat different but compatible conception of the active role of the moral agent via the individual's affective tendencies. According to them, affectivity and affective regulation processes influence both cognitive processes and moral action choices. Two central issues in their scheme are the degree to which individuals are aware of their influence and the degree to which those processes are under individuals' willful control. In a different but not necessarily incompatible perspective, Staub's chapter provides the most elaborate account of the interaction between agent and environment.

What Is the Role of Spirituality in Moral Development?

Many theorists of moral development do not explicitly acknowledge the role of spirituality, but Power addresses this topic in depth. Power begins his chapter by referring to Kohlberg's (1973) proposed "stage 7" (existential stage). The idea of moral development beyond stage 6 was speculative (and, therefore, usually neglected in current textbook descriptions of Kohlberg's moral stage theory). In his paper on stage 7, Kohlberg hypothesized that the developing person may seek a kind of cosmic insight or understanding that goes beyond the advanced and principled understanding of justice and welfare encoded in the postconventional moral judgment stages. Although Kohlberg was tentative in his hypotheses, Power has picked up on the invitation to speculate about cosmic or spiritual awareness as part of moral development. Power believes that individuals who have attained a sophisticated level of moral reasoning sometimes also thirst for a mystical and personal understanding of the relation between their moral self and the natural or supernatural universe. Their sense of transcendence and spiritualism can be a source of moral inspiration and motivation. Unfortunately, there is little empirical evidence to support this notion, but Power provides compelling anecdotal descriptions of how deep spiritual convictions and commitment interplay with moral understanding and lead to moral actions and self-sacrifice (but see Colby & Damon, 1992; Oliner & Oliner, 1982). Furthermore, Hart studies young people nominated as "care exemplars," and he discusses findings that suggest that most of the adolescents became involved in their moral commitments through social institutions such as churches, service agencies, and schools. Clearly, this is an area that deserves more attention from future researchers.

What Methods Should Be Used to Investigate Moral Development?

It is evident from our discussion of the various metatheoretical assumptions that the experts contributing to this volume have employed different methodological techniques in their research. However, arguments about methodology did not dominate the discussion at the 51st Nebraska symposium. Perhaps this should not be surprising since debates that took place in the field 20 years ago about the superiority of different research strategies (e.g., clinical interview format, paper-and-pencil questionnaires, experimental observations of prosocial behavior, physiological measures of affective responding) have given way in recent years to a general acknowledgment of the potential benefits of using multiple methodologies. This transformation has yielded a rich pool of new information that promises to converge to provide a complex and differentiated conceptualization of moral development. We are moving toward a more integrated understanding that includes cognitive and emotional dimensions, micro and macro levels of analysis, and proximal and distal causal factors.

Power and Narvaez, who emphasize cognitive-developmental and information-processing approaches, use a combination of traditional and innovative methodologies to assess the cognitive components of moral development. Kagan, in contrast, is particularly interested in temperamentally based reactions to unfamiliar events and situations, and, therefore, he advocates longitudinal research on the interaction of physiological predispositions (reactivity) and emotional dispositions relevant to moral development (such as shame and guilt). Eisenberg provides a synopsis of her multimethod approach, which relies heavily on physiological markers, self-report and multiple-reporter measures, and observational techniques. In her chapter, she argues for the importance of carefully distinguishing different kinds of empathy-related responses and measuring them separately. Each affect—defined as *empathy*, *sympathy*, and *personal distress*—has different predictors and outcomes. For example, sympathy is associated with enhanced prosocial responding toward needy or distressed individuals, whereas personal distress reactions sometimes are negatively related to helping and sharing. Similarly, Staub relies on research findings from various methodologies but extends his analysis by reflecting on case studies of individuals and societal-level events. In contrast, Hart uses a case study approach and also borrows heavily from personality traditions in using large, archival data sets to examine the personality by situation interactions that predict moral functioning.

How Are Theory and Research Linked to Applications?

Questions regarding moral motivation become most significant when we begin to develop programs aimed at promoting and fostering moral development. Each of the chapters offers insights into the various sources of moral motivation and implications for childrearing or education. For example, Eisenberg's chapter indicates the heuristic value of distinguishing between several categories of empathy-related responses (empathy, sympathy, and personal distress) because each appears to be positioned differently along the pathways linking socializing events and long-term prosocial outcomes. High levels of sympathy and empathy are linked to more positive outcomes, whereas high levels of personal distress (e.g., discomfort in the presence of someone needing help or comfort) tend to predict more negative outcomes such as low levels of prosocial behavior (e.g., avoidance). Kagan's chapter likewise suggests the vulnerability of highly anxious people to uncomfortable levels of guilt and shame. Although not discussed at length in the present volume, programs designed to foster empathic responding or to regulate emotional responding have been the focus or part of many prevention and intervention programs (e.g., Battistisch et al., 1991).

The chapters by Power, Narvaez, Hart, and Staub go farthest in elaborating links between theory, research, and application. Power identifies three social contexts for promoting moral development: schools; prisons; and sports. Based on Kohlberg's theory, the *just-community approach* provided a rich source of innovation in moral education (Power et al., 1989). Power makes a persuasive argument that, although the just-community program was originally designed to foster moral judgment and reasoning through discussion and reflection, it actually affected behavior and motivation as well and involved changes in the moral atmosphere of the school, prison, or community program toward becoming a democratic and respectful community. Power's reflection on the impact of those pioneering projects provides compelling evidence on the links between moral cognitions, emotions, and behaviors.

In recent years, Power has turned his attention to implementing moral development through sports activities and participation. Similarly, Hart and his colleagues have developed a program designed to promote social responsibility and care through sports. The Sports Teaching About Responsibility and Respect (STARR) program is an exemplar of programs that can work under some of the most adverse social circumstances, given the unique potential of sports to attract and motivate young children and adolescents in situations where other approaches to character education may fail. These research-based, systematic ventures into changing moral character through participation in team sports will undoubtedly become the subject of much discussion and analyses by future moral developmental scholars.

Narvaez provides the most in-depth discussion of the application of moral education programs in schools. She summarizes in her chapter various techniques that practitioners, teachers, and professionals (and parents) can use to promote moral development in children. Based on a program developed for schools in Minnesota, Narvaez's approach is comprehensive and multidimensional and designed to address the four components of morality (Rest, Narvaez, Bebeau, & Thoma, 1999).

Hart's chapter, as noted above, addresses how and why some adolescents come to have relatively more moral elements in their identity. Hart is interested in how identity comes to be invested in moral lines of action through opportunities to join with others in the activity or to be called to the activity by others. His work suggests the importance of community service for developing adolescents.

Finally, Staub's chapter focuses on raising caring and nonviolent children but also includes reflections on significant societal-level moral needs and challenges. Staub has long been interested in promoting active caring and helping, and he has helped create training programs for teachers, police, and others to reduce violence, racism, and the passivity of bystanders. He is also an expert on the roots of collective violence and genocide (Staub, 1989) and has spearheaded a project in Rwanda and worked with world leaders to promote healing, forgiveness, and reconciliation. His chapter finds echoes throughout the volume when he describes what we know about raising children to be "inclusively" caring, that is, children who care about all human beings. The theme of *moral courage*—going beyond the expected in the face of adversity—was important to all the contributors and participants at the 51st Nebraska Symposium on Motivation.

In conclusion, this volume represents a set of chapters equally guided by respect for diverse theoretical perspectives, for experimental as well as observational and interview methodologies, and for traditional as well as innovative approaches for studying the physiological, emotional, cognitive, and even spiritual sources of moral motivation and behavior.

We hope that the integrations, analyses, and speculations offered here will be provocative and that they will inspire a renewed interest in moral development theory and research as well as renewed optimism about their potential to be implemented at individual and collective levels of moral education.

Acknowledgments

The volume editors would like to acknowledge the contributions and assistance of the numerous people who made this work possible, including Dick Dienstbier, Claudia Price-Decker, Gretchen Walker, Richard Edwards, the NU Foundation, the University of Nebraska Press, Jamie Longwell, Becki Barnes, and Joy Mehnke. Others who participated and contributed to the discussions and/or poster session at the symposium included the developmental psychologists Mary Eberly, John Gibbs, Robert Lazarre, David Moshman, Brandy Randall, Ken Rotenberg, and Ross Thompson. We are especially grateful to our present and recent students Myesha Alberts, Rebecca Goodvin, Cherry de Guzman, Sam Hardy, Dr. Asiye Kumru, Laura Padilla-Walker, and Dr. Brandy Randall, who provided invaluable editorial feedback.

References

Baldwin, J. M. (1897). *Social and ethical interpretations in mental development: A study in social psychology*. New York: Macmillan.

Battistisch, V., Watson, M., Solomon, D., Schaps, E., & Solomon, J. (1991). The Child Development Project: A comprehensive program for the development of prosocial character. In W. M. Kurtines & J. L. Gewirtz (Eds.), *Handbook of moral behavior and development: Vol. 3. Application* (pp. 1–34). New York: Erlbaum.

Belenky, M. F. (1986). *Women's ways of knowing: The development of self, voice, and mind*. New York: Basic.

Carlo, G., Koller, S. H., Eisenberg, N., Da Silva, M. S., & Frohlich, C. B. (1996). A cross-national study on the relations among prosocial moral reasoning, gender role orientations, and prosocial behaviors. *Developmental Psychology, 32*, 231–240.

Carlo, G., Roesch, S. C., Knight, G. P., & Koller, S. H. (2001). Between- or within-culture variation? Culture group as a moderator of the relations between individual differences and resource allocation preferences. *Journal of Applied Developmental Psychology, 22*, 559–579.

Colby, A., & Damon, W. (1992). *Some do care: Contemporary lives of moral commitment*. New York: Free Press.

Colby, A., & Kohlberg, L. (1987). *The measurement of moral judgment*. New York: Cambridge University Press.

Damon, W. (1977). *The social world of the child*. San Francisco: Jossey-Bass.

Dewey, J. (1930). *Human nature and conduct*. New York: Modern Library.

Durkheim, E. (1979). *Durkheim: Essays on morals and education* (W. S. F. Pickering, Ed.; H. L. Sutcliffe, Trans.). Boston: Routledge & Kegan Paul.

Edwards, C. P. (1979). The comparative study of the development of moral judgment and reasoning. In R. Munroe, R. L. Munroe, & B. B. Whiting (Eds.), *Handbook of cross-cultural human development* (pp. 501–527). New York: Garland.

Edwards, C. P. (1985). Rationality, culture, and the construction of "ethical discourse": A comparative perspective. *Ethos: The Journal of Psychological Anthropology, 13,* 318–339.

Eisenberg, N., Reykowski, J., & Staub, E. (Eds.). (1989). *Social and moral values: Individual and societal perspectives.* Hillsdale NJ: Erlbaum.

Gibbs, J. C., Basinger, K. S., & Fuller, D. (1992). *Moral maturity: Measuring the development of sociomoral reflection.* Hillsdale NJ: Erlbaum.

Gilligan, C. (1982). *In a different voice: Psychological theory and women's development.* Cambridge: Harvard University Press.

Harkness, S., Edwards, C. P., & Super, C. (1981). Social roles and moral reasoning: A case study in a rural African community. *Developmental Psychology, 17,* 595–603.

Hartshorne, H., May, M. A., & Shuttleworth, F. K. (1930). *Studies in the nature of character.* New York: Macmillan.

Kant, I. (1993). *Grounding for the metaphysics of morals* (J. W. Ellington, Trans.). Indianapolis: Hackett. (Original work published 1785.)

Kegan, R. (1982). *The evolving self: Problem and process in human development.* Cambridge: Harvard University Press.

Kohlberg, L. (1973). Stages and aging in moral development: Some speculations. *Gerontologist, 13,* 497–502.

Kohlberg, L. (1981). *The philosophy of moral development: Moral stages and the idea of justice.* San Francisco: Harper & Row.

Kohlberg, L. (1984). *The psychology of moral development: The nature and validity of moral stages.* San Francisco: Harper & Row.

Kohlberg, L., Levine, C., & Hewer, A. (1983). *Moral stages: A current formulation and a response to critics.* New York: Karger.

Kurtines, W. M., & Gewirtz, J. L. (1984). *Morality, moral behavior, and moral development.* New York: John Wiley.

Kurtines, W. M., & Grief, E. B. (1974). The development of moral thought: Review and evaluation of Kohlberg's approach. *Psychological Bulletin, 81,* 453–470.

LeVine, R. A. (1994). *Child care and culture: Lessons from Africa.* New York: Cambridge University Press.

Lickona, T. (1976). *Moral development and behavior: Theory, research, and social issues.* New York: Holt, Rinehart & Winston.

Mead, G. H. (1967). *Mind, self, and society: From the standpoint of a social behaviorist.* Chicago: University of Chicago Press.

Moshman, D. (2004). False moral identity: Self-serving denial in the maintenance of moral self-conceptions. In D. K. Lapsley & D. Narvaez (Eds.), *Moral development, self, and identity* (pp. 83–109). Mahwah NJ: Erlbaum.

Noddings, N. (1984). *Caring*. Berkeley and Los Angeles: University of California Press.

Oliner, S. P., & Oliner, P. M. (1988). *The altruistic personality: Rescuers of Jews in Nazi Europe*. New York: Free Press.

Piaget, J. (1977). *The moral judgment of the child* (Marjorie Gabain, Trans.). London: Penguin. (Original work published 1932)

Power, F. C., Higgins, A., & Kohlberg, L. (1989). *Lawrence Kohlberg's approach to moral education*. New York: Columbia University Press.

Rawls, J. (1971). *A theory of justice*. Cambridge: Belknap/Harvard University Press.

Rawls, J. (2001). *Justice as fairness: A restatement* (Erin Kelly, Ed.). Cambridge: Harvard University Press.

Rest, J. (1979). *Development in judging moral issues*. Minneapolis: University of Minnesota Press.

Rest, J., Narvaez, D., Bebeau, M. J., & Thoma, S. J. (1999). *Postconventional moral thinking: A neo-Kohlbergian approach*. Mahwah NJ: Erlbaum.

Selman, R. L. (1980). *The growth of interpersonal understanding: Developmental and clinical analyses*. New York: Academic.

Shweder, R. A., Mahapatra, M., & Miller, J. (1987). Culture and development. In J. Kagan & S. Lamb (Eds.), *The emergence of morality in young children* (pp. 1–82). Chicago: University of Chicago Press.

Skinner, B. F. (1971). *Beyond freedom and dignity*. Toronto: Bantam.

Snarey, J. (1985). The cross-cultural universality of sociomoral development: A critical review of Kohlbergian research. *Psychological Bulletin, 97*, 202–232.

Staub, E. (1978). *Positive social behavior and morality*. New York: Academic.

Staub, E. (1989). *The roots of evil: The origins of genocide and other group violence*. New York: Cambridge University Press.

Staub, E. (2003). *The psychology of good and evil: Why children, adults, and groups help and harm others*. New York: Cambridge University Press.

Tietjen, A. (1986). Prosocial moral reasoning among children and adults in Papua New Guinea society. *Developmental Psychology, 22*, 861–868.

Turiel, E. (1983). *The development of social knowledge: Morality and convention*. New York: Cambridge University Press.

Whiting, B. B., & Edwards, C. P. (1988). *Children of different worlds: The formation of social behavior*. Cambridge: Harvard University Press.

Wong, D. B. (1984). *Moral relativity*. Berkeley and Los Angeles: University of California Press.

Human Morality and Temperament

Jerome Kagan
Harvard University

Most human actions are motivated by two different desires: to gain sensory pleasure and to produce evidence indicating that one's behaviors, thoughts, or feelings are in accord with a representation that the agent regards as good. Few persons confuse the state that accompanies the sweetness of chocolate with the sense of virtue that follows a nurturant act toward someone in need. Further, children build sand castles and adults climb mountains because implementing actions that are guided by an idea of perfection is as clearly a biologically prepared disposition as seeking sweet tastes and avoiding pain. The pursuit, and eventual capture, of power, status, wealth, romance, and 20-year-old brandy, which contemporary Western society treats as pleasures, can, on occasion, be strategies to affirm one's virtue. In societies where frugality is prized, as in Puritan New England, individuals hide their wealth. In societies where wealth is a sign of virtue, as in contemporary America, individuals are obligated to display it. A winter holiday in the Caribbean can serve as a motive to do what one ought to do as frequently as it serves the wish to avoid January blizzards. "I am doing what I should be doing" is often the silent voice behind the louder declaration, "I am doing what I enjoy." The

Preparation of this paper was supported, in part, by a grant from the Bial Foundation.

argument that moral standards are derived from sensory pleasure and the reduction of pain cannot explain the universal fact that people become angry when they see others violate standards that they believe are right. One reason why most individuals become upset when they see a stranger lie to a tourist, even when their own circumstances are unaffected by the act, is that asocial behavior by a stranger violates the observer's personal ethic, leading him to question the moral correctness of his beliefs. Because these beliefs are essential to each day's decisions and conduct, their violation, even by a stranger, threatens the foundation of the observer's reason for loyalty to his ethical code.

The content of every moral standard is tied to a particular time and place (Edwards, 1987; Shweder, Much, Mahaptra, & Park, 1997). Fourteenth-century Europeans regarded lending money on interest, marital infidelity, and homosexuality as cardinal sins; none is so regarded by contemporary Europeans. Four significant changes in Western ethical assumptions over the past 1,000 years are captured in four currently popular beliefs: there is no absolutely evil act independent of circumstances; all humans are of equal virtue and entitled to equal dignity; human will is weak and is expected to yield to strong temptations; and, finally, people should not be overly concerned with the evaluations that others might entertain about them—to thine own self be true. Readers familiar with Japanese culture recognize that this last premise violates the traditional notion of *omoiyari*, which requires each individual to be continually sensitive to the feelings of others and never to perturb another's psyche. Contemporary Japanese adolescents report that being inconsiderate to another is a frequent source of a subjectively felt guilt (Arimitsu, 2002).

Many animal species are distinguished from their close genetic relatives by one or more distinct properties. Spiders weave webs, bees do not; snakes shed their skin, crocodiles do not; prairie voles pair bond, montane voles do not. Some of the distinctive qualities of humans, compared with chimpanzees, are an opposable thumb and forefinger, a generative language, the ability to retrieve details of events in the distant past, the ability to anticipate desired goals in the distant future, consciousness of the self's states and properties, and an omnipresent symbolic evaluation of all events as proper or improper, which defines an essential feature of morality.

Meanings of *Moral*

Discussions of morality engage three different questions. The first, philosophical in tone, asks whether it is possible to defend, on a priori grounds, a particular set of human states, actions, or intentions as moral or immoral. For example, are the protection of human life, personal liberty, and justice for the oppressed moral imperatives that should be applied universally? The problem with this position is that some cultures with integrity promote different a priori standards as moral ideals. The ancient Greeks made loyalty to the polis an imperative and were not troubled by the fact that slaves in Athens enjoyed neither freedom nor justice.

The second question asks whether the subjective judgment of the agent is sufficient to justify a person's actions or whether the view of others or an a priori criterion takes precedence. Although a majority of Americans and Europeans believe that a suicide bomber who kills innocent civilians violates a fundamental moral standard, a pregnant woman who becomes a suicide bomber because she believes in the Palestinian cause and is certain that her action will permit access to heaven regards herself as morally pure. Many Northern soldiers who ravaged Savannah, Georgia, during the Civil War believed that their actions served the praiseworthy ideal of abolishing slavery; the citizens of that city did not.

The third question asks whether it is useful to contextualize all moral actions. An answer to this question provides a possible solution to the problems raised by the differences between the subjective judgment of what is moral and the judgment of others or a priori standards. The proposed solution requires specifying the agent, the target, and the context of the action. That is, if the moral judgment is made on the combination of the agent, the action, and the target of the behavior, much, but perhaps not all, of the conflict is resolved.

Nazi soldiers killed in order to impose a dictatorial government on populations that did not wish to live in a society controlled by Hitler's values. Hence, they had a weak moral argument. By contrast, the American troops who killed Germans were protecting the liberty of Americans and Europeans; this rationale has more persuasive moral credibility. Once we specify the agent, target, and context in which killing occurs and cease brooding over whether all killing is morally sanctioned, a great deal of tension is reduced.

One problem with contemporary research on morality and its development is that concepts like *prosocial, empathic,* and *altruistic* are used as descriptors for humans without specifying the occasions and targets of the actions. No human is altruistic or prosocial in all contexts and toward all targets. The Australian authorities in 1930 felt altruistic toward the half-caste children of the illiterate aboriginal population who lived under primitive conditions and wanted to help them become educated citizens who would participate in Australian society. Hence, they removed them from their parents and took them to camps miles away, even though both children and parents were unhappy with this practice. One can question the morality of the altruism of the Australians because the aboriginals did not want this prosocial gift. The morality of a prosocial behavior must be judged in the light of the agent and the recipient and not only the intentions of the benevolent agent.

It is also relevant to note that, if the recipients of altruism cannot reciprocate, they can feel shame, psychological impotence, or denigration by receiving the nurture. When these are the emotional consequences of someone's altruism, it is reasonable to question the morality of those who implement such acts.

One reason why social science writing about morality decontextualizes moral concepts is that many theorists approach this problem with a philosophical perspective that seeks truth through semantically coherent arguments. This criterion of truth differs from that adopted by natural scientists, who regard correspondence between statement and evidence as the sole basis for judging the truth of a proposition. Because empirical data usually reveal low correlations in a sample of subjects for prosocial acts across very different contexts, it seems useful to reject the decontextualized descriptors *prosocial, altruistic,* and *empathic* and insist that moral arguments specify the contexts.

Thus, it is useful to begin with the specific phenomena named by the abstract word *moral,* rather than assume a unitary or consensual meaning. There are at least four meanings of the concept *moral* when used as an adjective to describe a person. Although some speakers use this adjective to describe behaviors, institutions, events, cultures, laws, and even apes, the usual referent is a human agent.

One meaning refers to a person whose behaviors conform to the standards of the community or, in the case of a young child, to those of the family. A second meaning applies to those whose intentions are to help others in need, to be fair in interactions, to perform as well as one is able, and to seek understanding of what is right. This definition is close to Kant's view. Dostoyevsky was imprisoned for 5 years in an isolated Siberian outpost with peasant convicts who rejected him because of his middle-class origins and moral premises. Although it would have been expedient for Dostoyevsky to adopt, temporarily, the values of his debauched fellow prisoners, he continued to honor the moral standards that he brought to that harsh setting. Kant would have understood his inability to act in ways he believed were immoral.

A third definition applies to individuals who experience the emotions of empathy with the distress of another and shame and guilt following intentions to violate a standard or following a violation. The fourth, synthetic definition applies to persons who meet the criteria for all three of the above meanings. It is important to appreciate that a person could fit the definition 1 of *morality* but fail definitions 2 and 3, fit definition 2 but not definitions 1 and 3, or fit definition 3 but not definitions 1 and 2.

Developmental Stages

There seems to be a universal developmental sequence for the separate components of morality.

1. The first stage in the development of a moral agent, usually observed by the first birthday, is defined by the selective suppression of actions being socialized by the family. This phenomenon exploits the power of discrepant experience to alert the child. A mother who has just seen her 14-month-old spill milk on the tablecloth says in a voice louder and with a face sterner than usual, "Don't do that." The unexpected parental behavior creates a state of uncertainty that is assimilated to the schematic category for other hedonically unpleasant experiences, like pain, hunger, and cold. The child quickly learns that spilling food is usually followed by a similar chastisement and a feeling of uncertainty and, as a result, inhibits such acts. It is probably impossible for any parent to raise a child without interrupting some child actions that are potentially harmful or violate a family standard.

The child's schematic representations of the prohibited actions (always associated with a context), the parental disciplinary reaction, and the feeling of uncertainty become linked to create a conditioned reaction of uncertainty whenever the child is in a situation that has been associated with parental discipline. This first stage of moral development can be likened to the state of a puppy who has been trained to lie down in response to a command.

2. The next stage, usually observed by the end of the second year, is marked by the anticipatory display of facial expressions or bodily postures implying uncertainty in contexts where no punishments for violations have occurred in the past, suggesting that the child possesses a schematic concept for prohibited actions. Most 3-year-olds hesitate, or do not perform at all, if a parent or an examiner asks them to display a response that would violate a family norm—for example, to pour cranberry juice on a clean tablecloth or to scribble with crayon on a clean page of a new book—even though they have never displayed these behaviors and, therefore, have not been punished (Kagan, 1981). The refusal implies that the child possesses a concept of *prohibited actions* that includes novel behaviors that have not been prohibited in the past.

This category is applied to objects whose integrity has been flawed. For example, 2-year-olds will point to a small hole in a shirt, a missing button, or an ink spot on a chair and, in a serious tone of voice, say, "Boo-boo," indicating that they regard the flaw as improper. When 14- and 19-month-old children were brought to a laboratory playroom that contained many toys, some of which were purposely torn or flawed, not one of the younger children but over half the older ones showed obvious preoccupation with the damaged toy. They would bring the flawed toy to the mother, point to the damaged part, and, if they had language, indicate that something was wrong by saying "fix" or "yucky." The recognition of a flaw implies that the child has an initial notion of the proper form or state for an event. I once observed a 2-year-old girl who was upset because she was holding a small doll and a large toy bed and could not find a small bed that was more appropriate for the small doll. This girl possessed a schema for the most appropriate bed for the doll.

3. A state of empathy with a person or an animal in distress is also observed at the end of the second year (Lamb, 1988; Zahn-Waxler,

Radke-Yarrow, & King, 1979). Empathy requires the ability to infer the thoughts and/or feelings of another. Two-year-olds are capable of inference: by the middle of the second year, they will infer that a nonsense word—*zoob*, for example—might be the name of an unfamiliar object, and their speech implies an ability to infer the private feeling states of others. Two-year-olds have experienced the unpleasant state that follows criticism, aggression, and teasing and can infer these psychological states in others. As a result children now restrain behaviors that harm another. This restraint will be acquired even if the child had never been aggressive and aggressive actions had never been punished.

The capacity for inference also explains why children will refuse to attempt tasks that are too difficult for them to master. When an examiner modeled three coherent actions with props and then said, "It is your turn to play," many 2-year-olds cried because they inferred that the adult wanted them to imitate the same acts and they sensed their inability to do so (Kagan, 1981). The distress implies that the child inferred that failure to perform correctly would evoke adult disapproval. This inference requires some comprehension of the meaning of *ought* and a category of improper actions.

Parents from diverse cultures recognize that, before the third birthday, children are aware of standards on prohibited behavior. The Utku Eskimo of Hudson Bay call this awareness *ihuma* (reason), the Fijians *vakayalo* (a sense of what is proper) (Kagan, 1984).

4. Signs of a feeling of shame following a violation of a standard can be observed, sometimes by the end of the second year, but more often during the third year (Lewis, 1992). Shame requires not only an inference of another's thoughts—another person is a entertaining critical evaluation of the self—but also an initial awareness of self. One sign of self-awareness is recognizing one's reflection in the mirror, another is manipulating the behavior of others, and a third is verbal reference to self in productive speech (Kagan, 1981; Lewis & Brooks-Gunn, 1979).

5. The next stage of moral development, which usually occurs in the third year, involves the acquisition and application of the semantic concepts *good* and *bad* to objects, events, actions, people, and self. Although G. E. Moore (1903) argued that the meanings of *good* and *bad*

are given intuitively and cannot be defined objectively, most citizens and philosophers are unhappy with this degree of permissiveness and have tried to defend a definition on rational grounds. I suggest that the semantic term *good* is applied to four related, but nonetheless distinct, states. *Good* refers to (1) the receipt of praise or affection, (2) the avoidance of punishment and feelings of shame or guilt, (3) semantic consistency between an action and a standard, and (4) sensory delight. By contrast, receipt of criticism, anticipation of punishment, semantic inconsistency between actions and standards, and sensory displeasure belong to the semantic category *bad*.

It is important to ask whether the different brain states evoked by the events called *good* (or *bad*) share any feature, or features, that might represent a unitary visceral schema or brain state. Although, theoretically, it is possible that a particular circuit is activated whenever the semantic network for good (or bad) is provoked (and, therefore, a common visceral schema is activated), it is just as likely that there is no common brain state and that the only shared feature is the semantic term.

Children now assume that some intentions, actions, and persons are good or bad because they are part of the semantic network for the concept. Children oscillate with respect to their membership in the categories *good* and *bad*, depending on what has happened in the past few hours or days.

A mother in one of our studies found her 3-year-old boy pinching himself with force. To her request for a reason for the self-inflicted pain, the boy replied, "I don't like myself." This boy was aggressive with children in the neighborhood and was aware that both children and their parents disapproved of him. Many parents have noted that their 4-year-old children deliberately misbehave in order to be punished and then often ask their parents, "Do you love me?" One 4-year-old girl who told her mother she had done something naughty explained that she had a dream in which her infant brother had died after being stung by a bee.

A very small number of children eventually settle on one category for the self. Chronic sexual abuse can persuade a child that she is unredeemably bad. Some sexually abused children feel minimal levels of shame or guilt when they violate a community standard even though they know that the action was bad. A very small proportion become unusually aggressive. Mary Bell, an 11-year-old British girl who murdered two preschool boys, had been sexually abused at an early age by her prostitute mother's male clients and was aware of her father's criminal career (Sereny, 1998). This girl's categorization of self as bad made it easier for her to murder without the passion of anger or the desire for material gain. Fortunately, most children are uncertain about their virtue and dread the onset of shame or guilt.

6. The next stage, usually observed by 3–6 years of age, is characterized by feelings of guilt following an action that violates a personal standard (Kochanska, Gross, Lin, & Nichols, 2002). Guilt differs from shame because it requires the child to be able to relate past to present and to appreciate that an action by self that harmed another could have been suppressed.

Integration of past with present is usually observed by the fourth birthday. One study affirms this claim. An examiner presented a coherent narrative in three separate parts on 3 separate days to two groups of 3- and 4-year-old children. On the first day, the examiner showed the child a puppet called Clem, said that Clem liked to eat frogs, and presented the child with a bright orange toy frog. On the second day, the examiner led the child to a corner of the room containing a small toy house with three locked doors. The experimenter showed the child how to use a red key to open the door in the house in order to find the orange frog seen on the previous day. On the third day, the examiner led the child to a different part of the room, where they found a set of three keys, one of which was the red key used to unlock the door the previous day. Five days later, the examiner returned, produced the puppet, and said, "Clem is hungry. Can you give Clem something to eat?" Two-thirds of the 4-year-olds, but only one-fourth of the 3-year-olds, went immediately to the house that contained the frog. Apparently, the 4-year-olds retrieved their memory of the events that occurred on the second day and integrated it with the present situation; the 3-year-olds were less likely to do so. However, if the entire narrative was presented within the same session, with no delays, 3-year-olds performed as well as 4-year-olds (Loken, Leichtman, & Kagan, 2002).

The automatic habit of relating the present moment to representations of the past motivates the child to wonder about causal connections between events. A seminal feature of the interval between 3 and 6 years is the disposition to assume causal connections. Thus, when children harm a person or damage property, they relate that outcome to a prior intention, or a clumsy or impulsive posture, and are vulnerable to a feeling of remorse because they realize that they could have suppressed the behavior that violated the standard.

The popular distinction between *conventional standards* and *moral standards* captures an important difference in the psychological profile activated in a moral context. Violation of a conventional standard is less likely to be accompanied by guilt because the individual believes that, had society not disapproved of the particular behavior, its display would automatically lose membership in the category *bad*. Two obvious examples for Americans are wearing a hat at the dinner table and eating with one's fingers.

By contrast, most children believe that the imperatives prohibiting unprovoked aggression to another, deceiving a close friend, and failure to care for a sick relative who needs help are binding and not arbitrary. Therefore, their violation usually creates guilt, even if adults in authority positions proclaimed that such behaviors were permissible. Historical events can change a conventional standard to a moral one and vice versa. Most white American college students in 1902 regarded the suppression of insulting racial comments as a conventional ethical standard; large numbers of contemporary American students regard the suppression of bigotry as morally binding. A majority of Americans in 1902 regarded a wife's adulterous affair as a violation of a moral standard; some contemporary American adults regard adultery as a violation of a conventional standard.

A study of adults undergoing fMRI brain scanning while responding to a variety of moral dilemmas that required an agent to act in a way that would harm one person directly, even though the act saved many others, revealed the link between emotions and violations of moral standards. These dilemmas produced greater cerebral blood flow in the medial frontal and posterior cingulate gyrus—two areas that mediate emotion—than did dilemmas in which an agent's behavior did not harm any person directly, even though one victim was harmed and many were saved (Greene, Sommerville, Nystrom, Darley, & Cohen, 2001). It appears that most subjects had a more intense emotional reaction when an agent harmed one person directly in order to save others (e.g., the agent pushed a person in front of a train) than when the agent's action did not harm anyone directly but led to the same outcome.

7. Children between 5 and 10 years gradually acquire an understanding of the concepts of fairness and justice. Obvious examples include the belief that the severity of punishment should match the seriousness of the crime, that the amount of praise should match the quality or benevolence of the act, and that the difficulty of a task assignment should match the competence of the person. The concept of fairness might have a partial origin in the more basic notion of appropriateness for the situation. The latter could have an origin in the frequent instances in which the child must adjust his actions to fit a situation. For example, children have learned that they should speak louder in a noisy environment, exert greater muscle force if an object is heavy, and adjust their effort to fit the difficulty of the task.

8. Young children also feel a moral emotion if they behave in ways that are inconsistent with one of the social categories to which they belong. Children acquire social categories for self, always gender and developmental stage, and, for some, religion and ethnicity as well. As adults, they will add the categories of social class, nationality, vocation, sibling, spouse, parent, and friend. The more distinctive the category (owing, in part, to the fact that large numbers of individuals are not in it), the more likely it will be psychologically salient because humans are exquisitely sensitive to the relative frequency of an event. Thus, social categories that are infrequent possess an automatic salience for those who are members of them as well as for observers. It is likely that this phenomenon is due, in part, to the fact that discrepant and unexpected events activate limbic structures to create a special brain state.

This point warrants some elaboration. Categories vary in their susceptibility to being associated with perceptually distinct events that, on the surface, seem unrelated. *Gender* and *stage of development* are two examples for which there are many symbols, including particular colors, sizes, and animals. For example, most individuals who grew up in Western society associate light colors with a female and dark colors with a male; thick planks of wood with youth and thin planks of wood with old age. By contrast, the categories *vegetable* and *furniture* have much less symbolic elaboration for most Americans.

The category *uncommon*, like gender and developmental stage, links diverse events because they are statistically infrequent. Uncommon events, whether an unusual talent, a special accomplishment, physical attractiveness, or a brutal murder, create a visceral schema with low frequency as one of its distinctive features. Each time a person encounters such a rare event or hears about it, the mind links it to other uncommon events that have a similar evaluative valence (i.e., good vs. bad). As a result, the mind is prone to attribute to a creative artist other rare, desirable properties, like very high intelligence. That is why most are surprised when they learn that a person who is very talented in one domain has acted in a way that reflects irrationality or lack of reflection. For example, Alan Turing was a brilliant English scientist who played an essential role in breaking the Nazi Enigma code during World War II and later invented the basic concept underlying computer software. Surprisingly, he reported to a British magistrate that he had been robbed by a young working-class man with whom he was having a sexual affair at a time when a homosexual act was a criminal offense in Great Britain. As a result, he lost his security clearance and, sometime later, committed suicide.

The mind is also biased to exaggerate the salience of an uncommon trait in others. This bias is a component of what social psychologists call the *attribution error*, which refers to the fact that observers explain an agent's action in a specific context as reflecting a distinctive trait. The agent, by contrast, interprets the same act in a historical context and is aware of the fact that she has behaved differently in that same situation in the past. Thus, she does not regard a particular act of rudeness as definitive of self. An observer, who does not know that history, treats the act, especially if it is infrequent, as a definitive part of the individual's personality. This error is far less likely to occur if the action is frequent. That is, few observers would attribute a strong preference for coffee to someone on seeing that individual order coffee for breakfast in a hotel dining room. This principle has relevance for judging the morality of another because actions that violate ethical standards are always less frequent than actions that do not. Hence, observers are prone to exaggerate an agent's immorality when they note an ethical violation.

Each social category is linked to a set of obligatory actions and intentions. Boys know that they should not wear girls' clothes, even though some boys have never done so and, therefore, have never been punished for such behavior. The relative salience of each category in controlling behavior depends on the local context. The category for gender, for example, is ascendant on the playground; the category for religion is ascendant at a church service.

The ease with which children acquire categories is a distinctive feature of our species. Young infants, without language, detect in trios of syllables the fact that the first and last syllables are identical. Before the second birthday, most children have acquired, in limited form, categories for foods, animals, furniture, and other frequently encountered objects. This competence requires the ability to detect the few features shared by perceptually different events. When language emerges after the first birthday, children attach a semantic label to the schematic representation of the shared characteristics. The shared features can be qualities, actions, or names.

It is easy for children to perceive the physical and behavioral differences between themselves and adults and between girls and boys. Therefore, categories for developmental stage and gender are acquired early. By 5 or 6 years of age, children have acquired categories that are mainly semantic rather than based on perceptual features—religion is one example. And, by 6 or 7 years, they have detected the features that distinguish the economically affluent from the less affluent and those that differentiate their family from other families.

If the child believes that a category is appropriate for self and, in addition, experiences a vicarious affect when a member of that category has an experience with emotional implications, he is regarded as identified with the person or category. However, a child need not be identified with every category that he believes is appropriate for him.

Children wish to maintain semantic consistency between the features of each category to which self belongs and the evaluation of actions that are relevant to that category. Uncertainty may occur if the interpretation of a behavior generates inconsistency with the features of the category. Social psychologists would say that all individuals try to avoid the dissonance created by cognitive inconsistency between beliefs.

This cognitive bias—called the *mutual exclusivity bias*—has an early actualization in the 2-year-old who assumes that a person or an object can have only one semantic name. Although children eventually learn that this bias has exceptions—a mother can be a woman, a parent, and a lawyer—it remains potent. Indeed, in formal logic an event cannot be both A and not-A at the same time. The brain honors this principle for every English-speaking child over 6 or 7 years who will show a negative waveform in the event-related potential at 400 milliseconds on hearing, "The woman is a giraffe." Thus, moral behaviors are maintained, not only by worry over possible criticism or the anticipation of shame or guilt, but also by this new source of uncertainty.

The process described above is extended, over the next half dozen years, to the beliefs, feelings, and intentions that are features of a social category. Youths experience uncertainty following detection of a semantic inconsistency between those private features of a social category and self's beliefs, feelings, thoughts, or intentions. Thus, the comparison at ages 10–12 years is between sets of symbolic representations rather than between representations of the features of the category and self's behavior; the latter is more characteristic of the younger child. This extension is made possible by the talents that Piaget called *formal operations*. Adolescents, but not 8-year-olds, are capable of understanding inconsistencies among propositions that refer to hypothetical events. The detection of an inconsistency can be accompanied by guilt. For example, the recognition of an inconsistency between self's desire to be a good person and disloyal thoughts toward a friend (e.g., hoping that the friend fails an examination) can elicit a moment of guilt.

Individuals who belong to an ethnic or a religious minority are less likely to feel obligated to be loyal to the standards held by the majority and are somewhat freer to act in ways that violate consensual mores. In some cases, this psychological set facilitates original artistic or scientific work; in other cases, it leads to asocial or self-destructive behavior.

The social categories are not a unitary class but consist of two different types. The *nominal class*, with relatively fixed features and functions within a society, appears first in development—gender and developmental stage are examples. Older children add ethnicity, religion, place of residence, and nationality. The ethical obligations of these categories are not tied to a specific person but apply to all others.

The *relational class*, acquired later, is defined by a particular social relationship between self and other (or others). These relational categories include friend, son, daughter, sibling, parent, spouse, lover, and grandparent. The ethical obligations in these cases are to a specific person (or persons) and usually call for loyalty, affection, honesty, and nurture.

The distinction between nominal and relational social categories is an instance of a more general principle in cognitive development. The child's first categorizations are based on observable features and functions shared by a set of objects; animals, food, and furniture are examples. Gender, too, has a set of culturally defined features and functions that young children recognize apply to self. Children must be more mature to understand that the meanings of relational categories, like *left/right* or *bigger/smaller*, vary with the context. A dog is bigger than a mouse but smaller than a lion; the refrigerator is to the right of the sink but to the left of the microwave oven. Similarly, the category *friend* applies to a specific other, and the ethical obligations that apply to one friend may be different from those that apply to another. For example, if the friend is an anxious, social isolate, self will feel an obligation to be gentle and sociable with her. If, on the other hand, the friend is popular, talented, and dominating, self will be obliged to show esteem and follow the other's suggestions. The relational features of nominal categories also develop later. Older children, but not 3-year-olds, recognize that dogs should be loyal to their owner but not to strangers.

Egalitarian societies award greater significance to the ethical directives of relational categories because some nominal ones imply differential status and privilege. The individual can feel proud simply because of membership in a nominal category, independent of self's actual behavior. However, in order to extract pride from a relational category, the individual must implement the obligatory actions. Egalitarian societies wish their members to feel more virtuous because of their acts toward others and not because they are members of a particular group. Priests, physicians, and teachers should feel good at the end of the day because of their benevolent ministrations to others rather than because of their achieved status.

It is likely that loyalty to the obligations of the two categories is based on different processes. Recognition of the obligations attached to the relational category *friend*, for example, is the product of a psychological process that resembles Kant's categorical imperative. If the child wishes her friend to be kind, loyal, protective, and honest toward her—these are the defining features of a friend—then she is obligated to display these same behaviors toward her friend. However, a desire to avoid the dissonance that follows detection of semantic inconsistency motivates loyalty to the obligations linked to gender or developmental stage.

Finally, nominal and relational categories are to be distinguished from categories that refer to personal characteristics with continuous variation (e.g., attractive, competent, or popular). These categories have a much fuzzier set of moral obligations.

The Bases for Ethical Obligations

Two different factors contribute to the moral potency of nominal and relational categories. The young child's first words are for observed objects and events that have relatively fixed features (e.g., *milk, dog, food, eat,* and *fall*). All objects called *dogs* should bark, have fur, and be playful. If not, they are less than ideal dogs.

Thus, when children learn the names for nominal social categories—*boy, girl, adolescent, Catholic, Hispanic*—they are prepared to believe that these words, too, name a set of fixed psychological characteristics that belong to most members of those categories. Boys, for example, should control outward signs of fear and defend against domination by another. Children believe that they "ought" to be loyal to the psychological features that define the categories to which they belong, and they will experience as much dissonance if they stray from these obligations as they would if they saw a four-footed animal without fur that never barked but was called a *dog*.

A different reason for the moral influence of social categories is that membership can enhance the individual's feeling of virtue. Eighteenth-century Puritan New Englanders felt more virtuous than the nearby Indians. Many residents of Boston in the 1830s were proud of their municipal category because Americans regarded their city as the hub of the young nation. With the exception of New England Patriot fans in January 2005, far fewer current Boston residents feel virtuous simply because they live in this urban setting rather than New York or Chicago. More boys in contemporary Latin American homes, compared with boys in American families, extract some virtue from their gender category because parents and teachers communicate an asymmetry of privilege to the sexes. Few American mothers would tell their daughter, "Pick up the glass for your brother"; such requests are common in many South American homes.

Thus, two different psychological processes motivate children and adolescents to be loyal to the ethical requirements that are linked to their social category: the conviction that the category is a real entity whose properties should be preserved and the sense of enhanced virtue that can accompany category membership.

Loss of Moral Persuasion

Some social categories have lost a great deal of their moral power because of a loss of coherence and a dilution of the virtue gained from membership. Each category varies in the degree of feature variation displayed by its members. Hammers and spoons have less variety in their features than do flowers and dogs. The categories *female* and *child* have less variety than do *executive* and *athlete*.

The less varied the members of the social category, the stronger the imperative to be loyal to its ethical constraints. Americans are informed regularly that a small proportion of mothers abandon their children, fathers desert families, teachers and doctors strike, scientists fabricate evidence, workers call in sick, corporate executives lie, priests abuse young boys, and 60-year-olds wearing sneakers and blue jeans divorce their wives of 30 years to marry 25-year-old women. The category *mother* increased its variability when advances in reproductive technology permitted one female's fertilized egg to be carried to term by a different woman. The broad advertisement of these category violations dilutes their coherence and psychological power. A serious change in the understanding of the category *bird* would occur if there were suddenly an increase in the number of birds that neither sang nor flew. One consequence of the loss of coherence is a weakening of the ethical obligations linked to the category.

Second, some social categories have lost their ethical potency because they have lost their ability to award virtue to their members. White Americans are morally bound to acknowledge the dignity of citizens of color; Christians are urged to acknowledge the sacred spirituality inherent in all religions. As a result, the categories *white* and *Christian* have become less potent sources of virtue for their members. The elite class in 19th-century England, which included John Maynard Keynes, felt a moral obligation to serve their society because they recognized their privileged status. This group has far fewer members today.

A parent might resist the ethical imperatives of her category if the role did not enhance her sense of virtue. This state could occur because (*a*) the adult had a rejecting or negligent parent and, therefore, devalued the role; (*b*) a competing category, for example, a professional career, gave greater virtue; or (*c*) the prior experience of raising children was not gratifying because the sons and daughters failed to meet the parent's expectations.

Our society's desire to honor a commitment to an egalitarian ethos, which a majority celebrate, requires a denial of special privilege to some categories that, 2 centuries earlier, were sources of virtue. Nineteenth-century white, Christian males whose parents and grandparents were born in America could reassure the self of its virtue simply because they were members of this category. The rebellion against this reason for self-satisfaction, which accelerated in the 1960s, denied this prize to any social category. All Americans must attain their annual supply of virtue through personal accomplishments.

Because the accumulation of wealth, which usually requires individual effort and talent, seems to be a possibility for most citizens while gaining admission to an elite college or the opportunity to study the cello seems easier for particular class groups, gaining material signs of wealth has become a primary index of virtue in contemporary America.

The hostility to elite nominal categories that characterize egalitarian societies dilutes the sense of moral arrogance that some extract from their social categories. The clash between the mother and the daughter over the father's pomposity in Eugene O'Neill's play *Touch of the Poet* contrasts with the strength that the wife took from her husband's illusion of importance with the daughter's recognition that he was a fraud.

One inevitable consequence of the abandonment of one's social categories as the basis for deciding what to do, and knowing whether self is conducting life properly, is an increased reliance on self's feelings of pleasure and satisfaction, rather than those of another, as the primary criterion for selecting a behavior or goal in the service of enhanced virtue. The culture cooperates by reminding everyone of Jefferson's declaration that happiness is a right, and, by implication, one of life's assignments, and, therefore, a moral obligation. The ascendance of this imperative required a weakening of the ethical constraints linked to the social categories. Although individuals feel freer when social categories lose their power, they remain vulnerable to uncertainty regarding the ethical goals that they should pursue.

Humans require a reason for choosing one goal over another. It took only 5 centuries for Western Europeans to replace enhanced spirituality as the ethical goal to pursue, first with rationality, and later with sensual delight. Although Adam Smith urged self-interest 250 years ago, a careful reading of his writings reveals that he expected all persons to want the approval of others. That assumption guaranteed civility and conformity to social norms. Smith could not have anticipated that many individuals in this century would be indifferent to the attitudes of neighbors and treat the opinions of others as having no constraint on self. Many Americans would smile on learning that Francis Hutcheson, an eminent 18th-century Scottish philosopher, was certain that humans experienced the greatest happiness when they were kind to others.

Moreover, the ethical obligations of the relational categories have been weakened by the biological research and writings of the last century, which, provoked by Darwin's ideas, informed the public that humans are very close relatives of apes—we share 99% of our genes with gorillas. Contemporary adults, unlike 16th-century citizens, believe that they share important psychological features with other animals. The ideological movement called *sociobiology* announces that the facts of evolution imply that humans are prepared, by their genes, to be self-interested and motivated to maximize their status, pleasure, and reproductive potential. However, anyone with a modest knowledge of animal behavior can find examples in nature to support any favored ethical message. Those who wish to sanctify marriage can point to the pair-bonding of gibbons; those who think infidelity is more natural can point to chimpanzees. If one believes that people are naturally sociable, baboons are a good model; if one thinks humans are basically solitary, orangutans are the better example. If one wants mothers to care for infants, cite the behavior of rhesus monkeys; if one prefers the father to be the primary caretaker, refer to titi monkeys; if one believes that surrogate care is closer to nature, point to lionesses. If one is certain that men should dominate harems of beautiful women, point to elephant seals; if one believes that women should be in positions of dominance, point to elephants. Nature has enough diversity to fit almost any ethical taste.

Although scientific evidence has become the arbiter of many moral issues—is an embryo a living human? is violence on television bad for children? does affirmative action have a benevolent effect on the education of college students?—it is an error to assume that any human ethic is an obvious derivative of some class of animal behavior. The concern with right and wrong, the control of guilt, and the desire to feel virtuous are, like the appearance of milk in mammalian mothers, unique events that are discontinuous with what was prior. The continual desire to regard the self as good is a unique feature of our species. Although it has a firm foundation in our genome, it is not an obvious derivative of the competence of apes and monkeys.

Each person holds a number of ethical beliefs that permit him to decide, without too much delay, which action to implement when there is a choice. However, most individuals are silent when asked to provide a foundation for such a decision. The inability to justify moral intuitions with more than "it feels right" generates unease. As a result, any person or group announcing that it can supply an answer to the query, "Why do I believe this is right?" is celebrated. The church was an effective source of justification for Europeans for over 1,500 years until science rose to become the judge. Many contemporary citizens expect the facts of nature to provide a rationale for human ethics. The problem is that humans are selfish and generous, aloof and empathic, hateful and loving, dishonest and honest, disloyal and loyal, cruel and kind, arrogant and humble. However, most feel a little guilt over an excessive display of the first member of each of those seven pairs. The resulting dysphoria is uncomfortable, and humans are eager to have it ameliorated. Confession or psychotherapy is effective for some, especially if the priest or therapist is respected. I suspect that some people feel better when they learn that their less social urges are natural consequences of their phylogenetic history. The current high status of the biological sciences has made it possible for students of evolution to serve as therapists to their community.

In sum, the features of morality described above—the concept of prohibited acts, empathy, shame, guilt, notions of good and bad, justice, and the social categories—emerge from different developmental processes that include (1) conditioning; (2) capacity for inference;

(3) integration of past with present; (4) self-awareness; (5) creation of semantic categories for social roles; (6) Piagetian reversibility; (7) detection of inconsistency among semantic networks; and, finally, (8) acquisition of the concepts of the ideal and fairness. Morality is not a unitary human property.

Temperament and Morality

There is, of course, individual variation in each of the properties that describe a moral agent. Some children acquire a conditioned state of uncertainty more easily than others; some have richer inferences of other's states; some have more elaborated semantic networks; and some experience more frequent feelings of shame, guilt, or uncertainty. The research of Kochanska and her colleagues reveals that infants who show restraint to a maternal request are more compliant in the second year (Kochanska, Tjebkes, & Forman, 1998) and that fearful toddlers show greater signs of conscience at 4 and 5 years than do fearless ones (Kochanska, 1997; see also Kochanska, Coy, & Murray, 2001; and Kochanska et al., 2002). Work in my laboratory on temperamental biases in children is also relevant (Kagan 1984).

Although most children are capable of feeling uncertainty, fear, anxiety, shame, empathy, and guilt, there are individual differences in the frequency and intensity of each of these moral emotions. Some portion of this variation is attributable to the child's temperament, where *temperament* refers to heritable variation in profiles of behavior and mood that emerge early in development (Fowles & Kochanska, 2000; Kochanska, 1997). Kochanska et al. (2002) observed a group of middle-class children from 22 to 56 months of age. The measures of interest were the children's reactions when they unintentionally damaged property in the laboratory. The children who had been more timid and fearful in a special setting designed to measure fearfulness were most likely to show signs of concern after damaging property.

Infants differ on a number of behavioral characteristics; the most obvious are motor activity, irritability, ease of regulating distress, smiling and laughter, and the intensity of a fear reaction to an unfamiliar event. When variation in any of these characteristics is the partial result of inherited biological processes rather than only experience, the disposition is called *temperamental.*

Scientific studies of human temperaments are in an early stage; hence, we do not know the causes of these many biases. I believe that many, but not all, temperamental categories are the result of heritable variation in the concentration of the more than 150 molecules that affect brain function and/or the density and location of their receptors. This fact implies the possibility of many temperaments, for there is a large number of possible neurochemical patterns. Some candidates that could mediate temperamental types include variation in norepinephrine, corticotrophin-releasing hormone, GABA, dopamine, serotonin, and opioids and their receptors. Consider an example. GABA-ergic and serotonergic circuits are usually inhibitory. Hence, infants born with a compromise in either of these circuits should be less able to modulate extreme states of excitation. This hypothesis has some support. The promoter region for the serotonin transporter gene has many alleles, and unusually irritable 2-month-olds differ from relaxed, less irritable ones in one of these alleles. In addition, Japanese and European populations differ in the frequency of this allele, and Japanese infants are far less irritable than European-Caucasian infants.

The two temperamental categories studied most extensively refer to young children's typical reactions to unfamiliar events or situations, whether emotional restraint, caution, and avoidance, on the one hand, or spontaneity and a tendency to approach, on the other. There are two reasons for the interest in these two temperamental types. First, the behaviors that define each are easily quantified. Second, apparently similar variation has been observed within every vertebrate species studied. Intraspecies variation in the tendency to approach or to avoid unfamiliar events or places has been documented in mice, rats, wolves, dogs, cats, cows, monkeys, birds, and fish.

Children who are unusually shy, timid, or avoidant with unfamiliar people, objects, and situations because of an inherited temperamental bias are called *inhibited*. Children who are sociable and approach unfamiliar people and situations because of their temperament are called *uninhibited*. An estimate of the heritability of inhibited and uninhibited profiles, based on a large sample of monozygotic and dizygotic twins, approached 0.5.

My colleagues and I believe that the variation in the excitability of the amygdala, due to neurochemistry, makes a contribution to these two temperaments, for a primary function of the amygdala is responsiveness to unexpected or discrepant events, whether or not they are threatening.

High- and Low-Reactive Infants

My colleagues and I have been studying infant predictors of the behavioral profiles of inhibited and uninhibited children that emerge in the second year. These two categories can be predicted from variation in motor activity and distress to unfamiliar stimuli in 4-month-olds. Because the amygdala is activated by unfamiliar events and is the origin of the projections to structures that potentiate both motor activity and crying, infants born with a neurochemistry that renders the amygdala excitable to unfamiliarity should show higher levels of activity and crying to unfamiliar stimuli (see Figure 1). These infants are biased to become inhibited toddlers. Infants born with a different neurochemistry, one that raises the threshold of the amygdala to unfamiliar events, should show minimal activity and little distress to the same stimuli and become uninhibited children. This hypothesis is supported by the fact that newborns who showed an increased rate of sucking when the liquid that they were receiving through a nipple unexpectedly turned sweet became the most inhibited toddlers 2 years later (LaGasse, Gruber, & Lipsitt, 1989). The unexpected change in taste sensation would excite the amygdala; therefore, the infants who showed the large increase in rate of sucking probably had a lower threshold of excitability in this structure.

We studied a group of 500 healthy Caucasian children born at term to middle-class families who were first observed when the infants were 4 months old. Each infant was classified into one of four temperamental groups based on behavior to a battery of unfamiliar visual, auditory, and olfactory stimuli. Infants who showed a combination of frequent vigorous motor activity and crying were classified as *high reactive* (22% of the sample). Infants who showed an opposite profile of infrequent motor activity and infrequent crying were classified as *low reactive* (40% of the group). Infants who showed low motor activity but a great deal of crying were classified as *distressed* (25%). Infants who showed frequent motor activity but did not cry were classified as *aroused* (10%).

The behavioral reactions of these four groups to unfamiliar peo-

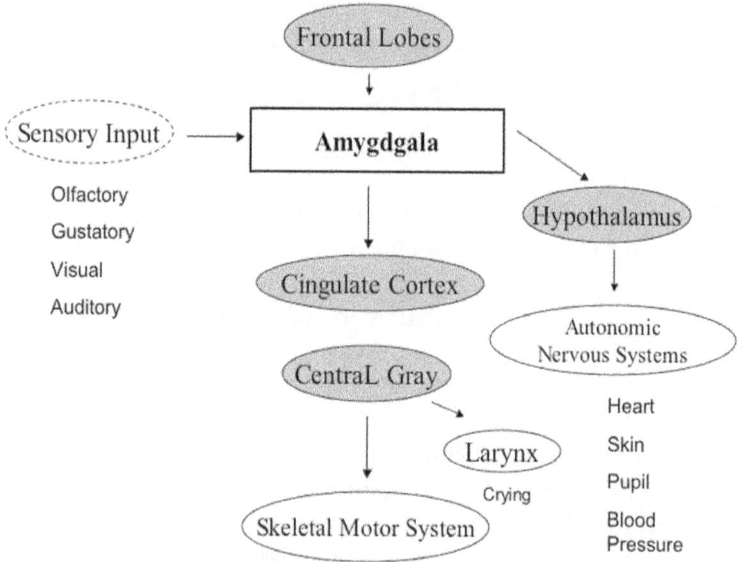

Figure 1. Projections to and from amygdala.

ple and situations were evaluated on two occasions in the second year. The 14- and 21-month-olds who had been categorized as high reactive when they were 4 months old were more likely than other children, but especially more likely than low reactives, to display high levels of fear to these unfamiliar events (see Figure 2). The children were observed again at 4½ years in a play session with two unfamiliar children of the same sex and age while the three mothers sat on a couch in a playroom. The children were classified as either *inhibited, uninhibited,* or *neither* on the basis of their behavior with the other children and their reactions to unfamiliar events that occurred after the play session. The data revealed that many more high than low reactives were inhibited in this setting.

The presence of anxious symptoms—especially extreme shyness, worry about the future, storms, animals, or loud noises, nightmares, and occasional reluctance to go to school—was evaluated when the children were 7½ years old. About one-quarter of the entire sample possessed one or more of these anxious symptoms. However, 45% of the high reactives, but only 15% of the low reactives, possessed anxious symptoms (see Figure 3).

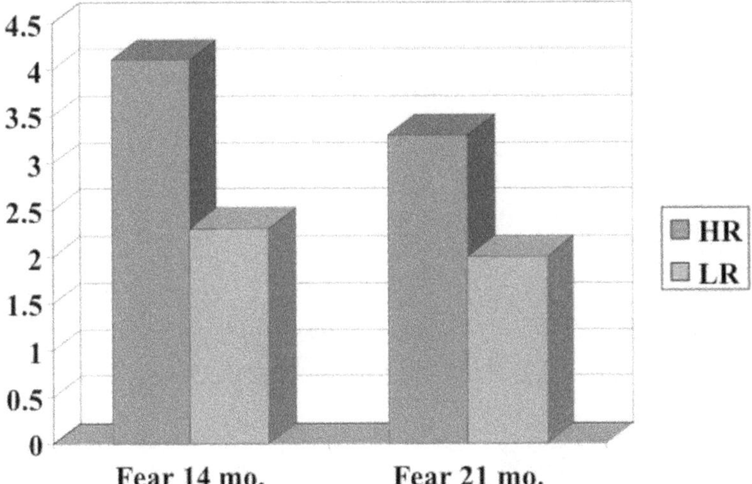

Figure 2. Fear at 14 and 21 months for high- and low-reactive infants. HR = high reactives; LR = low reactives.

These children were evaluated when they were 11 years old with a battery assessing both behavioral and biological variables. Four classes of biological variables, each potentially under the influence of the amygdala, were measured. These variables were (1) asymmetry in the magnitude of desynchronization of alpha frequencies in the EEG; (2) magnitude of the evoked potential from the inferior colliculus to a series of clicks; (3) sympathetic tone in the cardiovascular system; and (4) magnitude of a negative waveform in the event-related potential between 400 and 1,000 milliseconds to discrepant visual scenes.

Children who had been high-reactive infants should show greater EEG activation in the right, compared with the left, hemisphere because states of uncertainty, often due to greater visceral feedback, are usually associated with greater activity in the right amygdala. Because the amygdalar projections to the cortex are ipsilateral, these children should have greater loss of alpha power on the right than on the left side and, therefore, right hemisphere activation.

High reactives should show a larger brain stem–evoked potential from the inferior colliculus—called *Wave 5*—because the amygdala primes the inferior colliculus via the locus ceruleus and the central

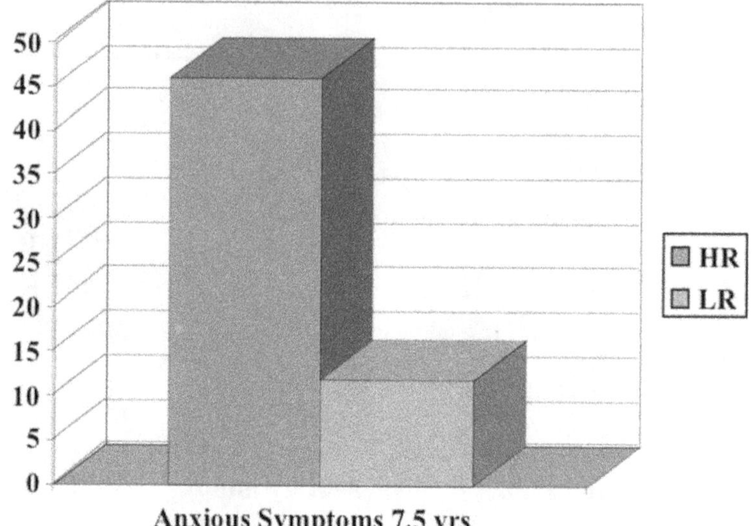

Figure 3. Percentage of high and low reactives with anxious symptoms at 7½ years of age. HR = high reactives; LR = low reactives.

gray. Hence, a more excitable amygdala should be accompanied by a larger Wave 5.

High reactives should show greater sympathetic tone in the cardiovascular system because amygdalar activity enhances sympathetic tone in the heart and circulatory vessels. Finally, high reactives should show a larger event-related potential to discrepant visual scenes because the amygdala, which is responsive to discrepant events, projects to the locus ceruleus and the ventral tegmentum. These brain stem structures send axons to the cortex to enhance synchronization of pyramidal neurons and, as a consequence, produce a larger waveform.

All four predictions were affirmed. The high reactives were more likely than were low reactives to show right parietal activation in the EEG at rest, a larger brain stem–evoked potential from the inferior colliculus to click sounds (called Wave 5); greater sympathetic tone in the cardiovascular system; and a larger EEG waveform between 400 and 1,000 milliseconds to discrepant visual scenes (see Figure 4). In addition, twice as many high as low reactives were extremely shy

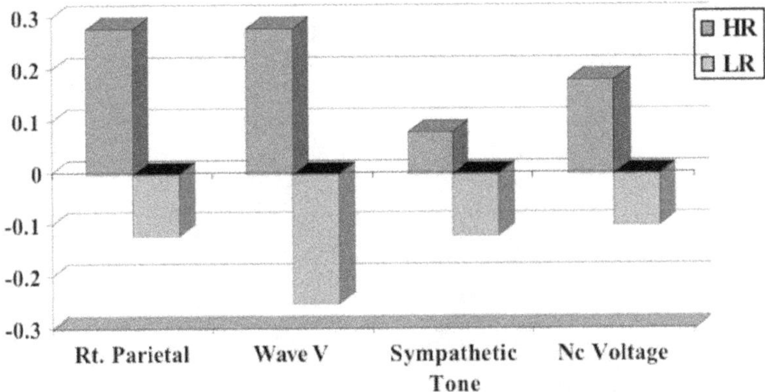

Figure 4. Mean standard score for right parietal activation, Wave 5, sympathetic tone, and magnitude of the event-related potential to discrepant scenes. HR = high reactives; LR = low reactives.

and emotionally subdued as they interacted with the examiner in the laboratory setting (see Figure 5).

About one in four 11-year-olds who had been high-reactive infants, and one in four who had been low-reactive infants, developed a behavioral and biological profile in accord with theoretical expectations for their infant temperament. By contrast, only 1 in 20 infants developed a profile of behavior and biology at age 11 that violated expectations.

Relation of Morality to Temperament

The children who had been high-reactive infants should be more vulnerable than others to bouts of guilt because of greater sympathetic activity and, therefore, greater visceral feedback to the amygdala and the ventromedial prefrontal cortex. However, a verbal report of guilt can occur with or without an appropriate change in physiology at the time of the violation. That is, some children might say that they feel guilty, but this confession might not be correlated with a temperamental vulnerability or accompanied by a physiological reaction at the time the moral failure occurred.

The 11-year-old children were asked in their home setting to rank 20 items descriptive of their personality from most (rank equal to 1) to least (rank equal to 20) characteristic of self. One item was, "I feel

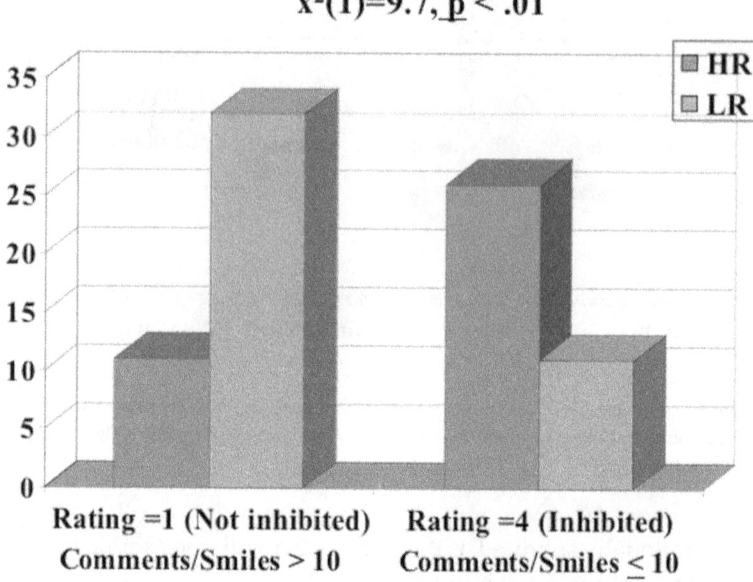

Figure 5. Percentage of high and low reactives who were uninhibited or inhibited with the examiner at 11 years of age. Hr = high reactives; LR = low reactives.

bad if one of my parents says that I did something wrong." There was no difference between high and low reactives in the mean rank assigned this item (mean rank was 10). However, the high reactives who ranked this item as more characteristic of self (a rank less than 10) showed a larger number of indirect signs of amygdalar reactivity than did the low reactives who ranked this item as equally characteristic of self or the high reactives who did not admit to this quality. High reactives who placed this item in ranks 1–9 (48% of the group) had a mean standard score greater than 0.00 across seven biological variables that reflected cortical and autonomic arousal (these seven variables included Wave 5, ERP waveform to discrepant scenes, right hemisphere activation, and sympathetic arousal). The low reactives who admitted to equally frequent feelings of guilt (41%) had a mean standard score less than 0.00 (only 17% of this group of low reactives had a mean standard score greater than 0.00; chi square (1) = 18.7, $p < .001$).

The fact that only high reactives who admitted feeling bad following criticism showed signs of cortical and autonomic reactivity suggests, but does not prove, that these children are especially vulnerable to bouts of guilt. Most children can be socialized to feel shame or guilt following violation of a standard, but a small proportion are especially vulnerable to these emotions because of their temperament.

There was a significant positive correlation among high-reactive girls between the rank assigned to the guilt item, on the one hand, and an index of high sympathetic tone in the cardiovascular system ($r = .38, p < .05$) and the mean standard score across the seven biological variables ($r = .42, p < .01$), on the other. This result implies that high-reactive girls who admit to more frequent bouts of guilt possess a more reactive sympathetic nervous system.

The mothers were asked to rank 28 statements describing their child from most to least characteristic. One item referred to the child's behavior when chastised: "Is sensitive to punishment." The high- and low-reactive girls, but not the boys, differed in the rank given this item. Seventy-three percent of high-reactive, but only 58% of low-reactive, girls were given ranks below the median value of 12, indicating that mothers of high-reactive girls perceived them as more sensitive to criticism. Of greater interest is the fact that the high-reactive girls described as sensitive to punishment showed greater right parietal activation than did high-reactive girls who were less sensitive ($t(28) = 4.92, p < .05$). Right parietal activation was the one biological variable of the seven measures that best differentiated high- from low-reactive girls.

The high-reactive boys described as sensitive to punishment had significantly larger Wave 5 values than did high-reactive boys described as less sensitive ($t(26) = 2.28, p < .05$), and the magnitude of Wave 5 best separated high- from low-reactive boys. Thus, the biological variables that most effectively distinguished high and low reactives (different for each gender) were precisely the measures that differentiated the high reactives described as sensitive to chastisement from those who were less sensitive.

Summary

This chapter has tried to make two points. First, the concept of *morality* refers to a developmental cascade of phenomena whose essential features are (*a*) inhibition of punished acts; (*b*) a representation of prohibited actions; (*c*) the emotions of uncertainty, empathy, shame, and guilt; (*d*) the semantic concepts of *good* and *bad*; (*e*) accepting the moral obligations of social categories; and (*f*) the concepts of *fairness* and *the ideal.*

The inhibition of prohibited actions and the cognitive representation of prohibited behaviors, as well as the affect states that follow violations, appear by the end of the second year of life. The concepts of good and bad appear early in the third year, the experience of guilt and awareness of social categories by 4–6 years, and the notions of fairness, the ideal, and relational social categories during the school years.

Second, some of the variation in the intensity and frequency of the moral emotions is attributable to the child's temperament. Eleven-year-old children who had been high-reactive infants and admitted to feelings of guilt when they violated a family standard were cortically and autonomically more aroused than the low reactives who reported equally frequent experiences of guilt. Further, high reactives who were perceived by their mothers as highly sensitive to punishment were biologically more aroused than high reactives perceived as less sensitive. Both universal developmental phenomena tied to brain maturation and temperamental variation associated with neurochemistry contribute to the complex phenomena that constitute the moral domain.

The role of affect in promoting the adherence to standards remains controversial. Kant believed that people acted morally because acceptance of the categorical imperative required proper behavior—reason was the guardian of social harmony. Peirce and Dewey, by contrast, argued that anticipation of the emotions of anxiety, shame, and guilt motivated loyalty to the community's ethical standards. The fact that adults pay to watch a film that they know will generate a deep feeling of sadness—an emotion most do not seek or welcome in their daily lives—and will remark that they enjoyed the movie warrants an explanation. One possibility is that the experienced emotion affirms their moral values.

The Australian film *The Rabbit Proof Fence* describes three aboriginal sisters who have been taken from their mother to a camp a thousand miles away to be socialized in Australian values. The three girls run away, and most of the film illustrates the hardships that they endure and their close escapes from the authorities who are pursuing them as they walk the thousand miles to reach their home. The audience's empathic sadness for the children affirms their moral belief that children should love their parents and miss their home. I suspect that those in the audience who felt the most intense sadness would praise the film with greater enthusiasm than those who had muted feelings. Because sadness is an emotion that few enjoy or try to attain, there must be another reason for deciding that the film was gratifying. The affirmation of one's moral beliefs could be that source of gratification.

The tension between the importance of a rational and the importance of an affective basis for morality is seen in modern industrialized societies where the balance between the feeling of virtue that follows enhancing another and the pleasure that follows the enhancing of self has shifted toward favoring the latter state. Increasing numbers of Americans do not regard their gender, ethnicity, vocation, place of residence, or friendships or the religion of their parents as distinctive sources of virtue. As a result, they are freed from the moral obligations that were attached to these categories in the past and rely primarily on the anticipation of sensory delight and self-enhancement as guides for action and sources of reassurance that they are managing their lives correctly.

Although it is likely that future scientists will synthesize a drug that blocks feelings of guilt without affecting the knowledge that an act is wrong, it is less certain that broad use of this drug would eliminate loyalty to the mutual obligations that make a society habitable. Nonetheless, a posture of vigilance is appropriate, for humans, unlike gorillas, can hold representations of envy, hostility, and anger, even toward those whom they have never met, for a very long time. Therefore, empathy and the anticipation of guilt or shame may restrain rudeness, dishonesty, and aggression when reason fails.

References

Arimitsu, K. (2002). Structure of guilt eliciting situations in Japanese adolescents. *Japanese Journal of Psychology, 77*, 148–156.

Edwards, C. P. (1987). Culture and the construction of moral values. In J. Kagan & S. Lamb (Eds.), *The emergence of morality in young children* (pp. 123–151). Chicago: University of Chicago Press.

Fowles, D. C., & Kochanska, G. (2000). Temperament as a moderator of pathways to conscience in children. *Psychophysiology, 37,* 788–795.
Greene, J. D., Sommerville, R. B., Nystrom, L. E., Darley, J. M., & Cohen, J. D. (2001). An fMRI investigation of emotional engagement in moral judgment. *Science, 293,* 2105–2108.
Kagan, J. (1981). *The second year.* Cambridge: Harvard University Press.
Kagan, J. (1984). *The nature of the child.* New York: Basic.
Kochanska, G. (1997). Multiple pathways to conscience for children with different temperaments. *Developmental Psychology, 33,* 228–240.
Kochanska, G., Coy, K. C., & Murray, K. T. (2001). The development of self-regulation in the first four years of life. *Child Development, 72,* 1091–1111.
Kochanska, G., Gross, J. N., Lin, M., & Nichols, K. E. (2002). Guilt in young children. *Child Development, 73,* 461–482.
Kochanska, G., Tjebkes, T. L., & Forman, D. R. (1998). Children's emerging regulation of conduct. *Child Development, 69,* 1378–1389.
LaGasse, L., Gruber, C., & Lipsitt, L. P. (1989). The infantile expression of avidity in relation to later assessment. In J. S. Reznick (Ed.), *Perspectives on behavioral inhibition* (pp. 159–176). Chicago: University of Chicago Press.
Lamb, S. (1988). *The emergence of moral concern in the second year of life.* Unpublished doctoral dissertation, Harvard Graduate School of Education.
Lewis, M. (1992). *Shame: The exposed self.* New York: Free Press.
Lewis, M., & Brooks-Gunn, J. (1979). *Social cognition and the acquisition of self.* New York: Plenum.
Loken, E., Leichtman, M., & Kagan, J. (2002). *Integrating past and present.* Unpublished manuscript.
Moore, G. E. (1903). *Principia ethica.* Cambridge: Cambridge University Press.
Shweder, R. A., Much, N. A., Mahaptra, M., & Park, L. (1997). The "big three" of morality (autonomy, community, and divinity) and the "big three" examples of suffering. In J. A. Brandt & P. Rozin (Eds.), *Mortality and health* (pp. 119–169). New York: Routledge & Kegan Paul.
Sereny, G. (1998). *Cries unheard.* New York: Holt.
Zahn-Waxler, C., Radke-Yarrow, M., & King, R. A. (1979). Child rearing and children's prosocial intentions toward victims of distress. *Child Development, 50,* 309–330.

The Roots of Goodness: The Fulfillment of Basic Human Needs and the Development of Caring, Helping and Non-aggression, Inclusive Caring, Moral Courage, Active Bystandership, and Altruism Born of Suffering

Ervin Staub

University of Massachusetts, Amherst

Caring that develops can be limited to a particular group of people, to some "in-group." When the basic needs of whole groups of people are frustrated by difficult social conditions, such as economic problems, political upheaval, and great societal change, psychological and social processes can lead those group to turn against and victimize others (Staub, 1989a). If enough people in a group have developed inclusive caring (caring for the welfare of people who are not members of their group, ideally for all human beings) and moral courage (the courage to speak out and act according to one's values and beliefs in the face of potential or actual opposition, i.e., even if these beliefs and values are contrary to prevailing views in one's immediate environment or larger group), their active bystandership, their speaking out in behalf of their values and in behalf of the people who are harmed, can inhibit the evolution of increasing harmdoing and violence. I will note the importance of inclusive caring, moral courage, and positive bystandership both on the societal level and on the level of smaller groups groups—for example, children's peer groups, where they can inhibit bullying. I will also discuss the developmental roots of such processes and how they can be fostered.

I will then discuss an essentially unexplored but seemingly highly important avenue to helpful, altruistic behavior, which I call *altruism born of suffering*. Following victimization and other types of trauma, which greatly frustrate basic needs, many children (and adults) tend to become self-protective and/or aggressive. However, some do become caring and helpful people, even highly committed altruists. I will propose that experiences such as healing, support, and human connection can lead children or adults who have been victims of harsh treatment, abuse, or violence or have suffered in other ways to devote themselves to helping others or prevent others' suffering.

This chapter presents material that is connected to my early work on the determinants and development of caring, helping, and altruism. It makes only limited explicit reference to my work on the origins and prevention of violence between groups, such as genocide and mass killing, healing from victimization and reconciliation between groups (see, e.g., Staub, 1989a, 1998, 1999a, 2003; Staub & Pearlman, 2001; Staub, Pearlman, Gubin, & Hagengimana, in press; Staub, Pearlman, & Miller, 2003). Nonetheless, it draws heavily on that work, both in posing issues and questions (such as inclusive caring, moral courage, and altruism born of suffering) and in addressing them.

Motivations, Psychological Processes, and Personal Characteristics in Helping (and Nonaggression)

Researchers and theorists have identified several psychological processes, and characteristics of individuals out of which such processes arise, that provide motivations for helping. People can help others for *selfish* reasons, motivated by real or hoped-for rewards. They may want to gain approval or to avoid disapproval, punishment, ostracism, or other negative consequences that follow from not doing what social norms prescribe, such as helping people in need (Berkowitz, 1972). They may also try to gain benefits, expecting that those whom they have helped will reciprocate, as a result of powerful and seemingly universal norms of reciprocity (Mauss, 1954). They can also act to maintain their positive mood or help to alleviate their own distress (Carlson & Miller, 1987).

People can also help others for *moral* reasons, guided by values, beliefs, and principles that they have internalized and/or developed and that lead them to promote others' welfare. One such belief is enlightened self-interest. While enlightened self-interest may seem the least moral of moral beliefs since the motivation is to create a world in which one will be helped in turn, it may be a core belief out of which much of morality develops. The motivation here arises from the existence, awareness, or knowledge of and belief in the human proclivity for reciprocity, including "generalized reciprocity" (for a discussion of this, see Staub, 1978). The latter is the notion that, if one helps another person, this person is not only more likely to help oneself in return but also more likely to help some other person in need. Thus, by helping others, one contributes to creating a world in which people in general will be helpful to oneself as well as to important people in one's life. The belief in enlightened self-interest can, and in the course of the evolution of morality in society is likely to, develop into the belief that one should help other people and that people ought to help each other. These, as well as justice and the sanctity of human lives, are among important moral beliefs.

I see motivation as moral when to some substantial degree its focus is to fulfill or live up to a moral belief, value, or principle. One limitation of such motivation is that its focus can become adherence to the norm or principle itself rather than the human welfare that it tries to protect or advance. It can, therefore, lead to distortions, such as justice not mitigated by mercy. Children may be punished to serve justice in ways that make them into less caring people. In the end, the purpose of the moral value or principle, to serve human welfare, is subverted, possibly both at the moment and in the long run. Another possible distortion is a primary focus on living up to one's view of oneself as a moral person rather than on the welfare of the people whom the moral principles aim to serve (Karylowski, 1976).

Altruistic motivation, the desire to benefit someone in need, to reduce a person's distress or enhance his or her well-being, is more directly focused on the person rather than on a belief or principle. It can arise from affective connections to a person or people that make empathy or sympathy possible and more likely. It can also arise from certain types of moral beliefs or values, such as a belief in one's responsibility for others' welfare. It probably often arises from some combination of the two.

Altruistic motivation is likely to have at least two related but not identical roots. One is affective: *empathy*, or the vicarious experience of others' feelings. The kind of empathy that generates *sympathy* has been found especially important in motivating helpful action. Sympathy includes both feeling with and concern about a person (Batson, 1990; Eisenberg, 2002; Eisenberg & Fabes, 1998; Hoffman, 1975a, 1975b; a feeling of sorrow or concern for the distressed or needy other [Eisenberg, 2002, p. 135]). In contrast *personal distress*—when someone's distress generates distress that is seemingly empathic but that is focused on the self (Batson, 1990; Eisenberg, 2002; Eisenberg et al., 1989)—gives rise to motivation to reduce one's own distress. It leads to helping when that is the best way to reduce one's own distress, but not when some other action, like leaving the situation, is a relatively easy way to reduce one's distress (see Eisenberg, in this volume).

Another form of altruistic motivation is what I have called *prosocial value orientation*. This orientation is related to helping people in either physical distress (Erkut, Jaquette, & Staub, 1981; Staub, 1974) or psychological distress (Feinberg, 1978; Grodman, 1979; Staub, 1978, 1980; see also Carlo, Eisenberg, Troyer, Switzer, & Speer, 1991; Shroeder, Penner, Dovidio, & Piliavin, 1995). In these studies prosocial orientation was measured by a combination of existing measures that were factor analyzed, with the scores on a first, dominant factor used as indicators of prosocial orientation. For subsequent studies a measure of prosocial orientation that I developed was used (Staub, 1989b, 2003). Scores on this measure were related to self-reports of varied forms of helping (Staub, 1995, 2003). Prosocial orientation was also positively related to constructive patriotism, which combines love of country with the willingness to oppose policies that are contrary to humane values, and negatively related to blind patriotism, a tendency to be uncritical of one's country, to not consider whether its policies or practices are "right or wrong" (Schatz, Staub, & Lavine, 1999; Schatz & Staub, 1997; Staub, 1997).

As we measured it, the three primary aspects of a prosocial value orientation appear to be a positive view (i.e., a positive evaluation and, hence, valuing) of human beings, a concern for people's welfare, and a feeling of personal responsibility for others' welfare (see Feinberg, 1978; Grodman, 1979; Schatz et al., 1999; Staub, 1974, 1989b, 1995, 2003). Although a prosocial value orientation has been measured "cognitively," in a questionnaire, it appears to be an affective, sympathetic orientation to people combined with a conscious concern about people's welfare and a belief in one's own responsibility for others' welfare. Empathy, and especially sympathy, embody concern for others, which presumably requires a positive evaluation of or orientation to human beings. A feeling of personal responsibility may, however, be an important additional motivational component, making action in behalf of people in need more likely.

When such personal characteristics as the holding of moral values or a prosocial orientation or a tendency to respond with empathy and sympathy are activated by circumstances such as others' need for help or distress, it is likely that they will give rise to motivation to help. As research with a prosocial value orientation indicates, and as one would expect, people inclined to respond with such altruistic motivation to others' needs are helpful under a wide range of conditions.

The literature on aggression also differentiates among motivations for harming others. The most prominent distinction has been between *hostile* aggression, motivated by the desire to harm, and *instrumental* aggression, which aims to gain benefits for oneself and uses aggression as a means to that end (Berkowitz, 1993). *Defensive aggression*, which aims to protect the self (from real or imagined harm)—a common form of aggression (Dodge, 1993; Toch, 1969)—may be differentiated from other forms of instrumental aggression. But, in this as well as in other kinds of aggression, hostile and instrumental motives frequently join (Staub, 1996b). Recently a distinction has been made between physical aggression, on the one hand, and relational aggression (such as excluding others, or spreading rumors about them, or harming their reputation in other ways), on the other. The former has been described as more characteristic of boys, the latter of girls (Crick, 1997).

One would expect that values and emotional orientations that give rise to moral or altruistic motivation for helping would also reduce aggression. This has been explored to a somewhat limited extent. Feshbach and Feshbach (1969), for example, found that very young children who were more empathic were not less aggressive but that somewhat older children who were more empathic were less aggressive. In a number of studies Eisenberg has found that children who respond to others' need with sympathy tend to be less aggressive (see Eisenberg, in this volume). Kohlberg and Candee (1984) found that adults who had higher responsibility subscores at various stages of moral development were less likely to continue to obey the experimenter and administer electric shocks in a Milgram obedience study. Spielman and Staub (2000) found that seventh- and eighth-grade boys who were less aggressive, as measured by teacher ratings and in-school detentions, had higher prosocial value orientation scores (on an adolescent version of the measure).

In addition to characteristics directly relevant to the motivation to help, other characteristics are required to give rise to the motivation and lead to its expression in action. I have called these *supporting characteristics* (Staub, 1980). One of these is a feeling of efficacy (Midlarsky, 1971; Staub, 1980, 1995, 2003), which makes it likely that the motivation for helping is transformed into action and probably even that the motivation arises. Another is the capacity for role taking, for understanding how others' circumstances would affect them or how others actually feel (Eisenberg & Fabes, 1998; Staub, 1979). This is especially important when the need for help is not obvious.

Basic Human Needs, Altruism, and Aggression

Varied psychological theories include assumptions about central psychological needs. Some theorists (Erikson, 1959; Maslow, 1968, 1987; Murray, 1938; and, more recently, Burton, 1990; Kelman, 1990; Pearlman & Saakvitne, 1995; Staub, 1989a, 2003) have proposed the existence of universal human needs. If there are universal, basic, psychological needs, they must play a substantial role in human life. I have been suggesting that the frustration of basic needs is central in the development of hostility and aggression and that their fulfillment is central in the development of caring about other people's welfare and altruism (see Staub, 1989a, 1996b, 1999b, 2003).

The needs on which I have focused, which overlap with needs that others have proposed, are those for security, for a positive identity, for effectiveness and control, for a positive connection to other human beings, for autonomy, for a comprehension of reality, for life satisfaction, and for transcendence of the self (for definitions and detailed discussion, see esp. Staub, 2003). These needs are not seen as hierarchical. Possibly the need for security is more basic than the others, and the needs for life satisfaction and for transcendence (the need to go beyond the self, which can be satisfied by helping others or by connecting to nature or to spiritual entities) are more advanced, deriving from and following the satisfaction of the other needs. However, apart from transcendence, all these needs are present at birth. And even at a very early age children are often in transcendent states, in which there is absorption in something beyond the self—seemingly an element or component of later transcendence (Staub, 2003).

Basic needs are powerful. They press for satisfaction. When they are not fulfilled in constructive ways in the course of normal experience, people will develop destructive modes of need satisfaction. *Destructive need satisfaction* means that a person fulfills one need in a way that frustrates his or her other needs (if not immediately, then in the long run) or that he or she fulfills needs in a way that frustrates other people's fulfillment of their basic needs.

For example, the need for effectiveness and control is the need to feel that one can influence events and, especially important, that one can protect oneself from harmful events and fulfill important goals. When this need is greatly frustrated, and especially when the frustration is the result of traumatic experience, the hallmark of which is lack of control over extremely stressful events that feel life threatening (Herman, 1992; Pearlman & Saakvitne, 1995; Staub, 2003, n.d.-b), then a child (or an adult) may attempt to exercise control over all events, including the behavior of other people. This leads to constant vigilance, or hypervigilance, which is stressful.

The excessive need for control limits the range of the individual's behavior and interferes with the development of his or her own self and, thereby, the satisfaction of his or her need for a positive identity. It will also frustrate the needs of other people whom the individual seeks to control (e.g., their need for effectiveness and autonomy) and evoke reactions that will frustrate the individual's need for positive connection to others. For example, a child may try to constantly direct the activities of friends, including the extent and nature of their relationships to other children. This makes the child less attentive to and less engaged with other things. It also negatively affects the friends, possibly even leading them to terminate the friendship.

Difficult, stressful conditions of life may frustrate the basic needs of whole groups of people, leading to destructive modes of need fulfillment. A group may scapegoat some other group, for example, a subgroup of society, blaming it for the difficulties of life. It may create an ideology (a vision of social arrangements) that is destructive, in that it identifies some people as enemies who must be destroyed to fulfill the "positive" vision of the ideology. These psychological/social practices may help fulfill basic needs by making members of the group feel that they are not at fault for life problems, by giving them a feeling of effectiveness in working to fulfill the ideology, by creating connection among those who scapegoat or are part of an ideological movement. But they fulfill basic needs destructively, in that the group's psychological and social processes do not address the real problems and, over time, tend to lead to violent actions against others (Staub, 1989a). They also usually lead to the defeat, humiliation, and psychological traumatization of the group that has engaged in violence. Creating hopeful visions of the future that are inclusive, that bring everyone together to address life problems, can help fulfill basic needs constructively (Staub, 1989a, 2003).

Socialization Practices and Experiences That Promote Caring, Helping, Altruism, and Nonaggression

Affection and Nurturance Versus Neglect and Harsh Treatment Temperamental characteristics of children enter into the development of altruism and aggression (Coie & Dodge, 1998; Eisenberg & Fabes, 1998). However, impulsiveness, which has been linked to boys' aggression, and other temperamental characteristics that may predispose a child to aggression are both shaped by experience and exert influence in interaction with social experience. Their expressions are shaped by harsh treatment or lack of support from and appropriate guidance by parents and other people. Similarly, temperamental dispositions appear to play a role in the development of empathy in conjunction with early socializing experiences (Zahn-Waxler & Radke-Yarrow, 1990). Surrounding social conditions, like poverty, also play an important role, but they again appear to exert influence primarily by affecting how parents relate to and guide children (McLoyd, 1990). Here I will focus on childrearing practices.

Becoming a caring, helpful, altruistic person, or a hostile, aggressive one, is the result of combinations or patterns of childrearing (Staub, 1979, 1996a, 2003, n.d.-b). Parents responding to their infants' needs and their continuing nurturance, warmth, affection, and sensitivity to their children are the core socializing practices and experiences for the development of helpful tendencies in children (Eisenberg, 1992; Eisenberg & Fabes, 1998; Hoffman, 1970a, 1970b, 1975a;

Shaffer, 1995; Staub, 1971, 1979, 1996a, 1996b, 2003, n.d.-b; Yarrow & Scott, 1972). In contrast, parents neglecting or harshly treating their children—rejection, hostility, the extensive use of physical punishment, and physical or verbal abuse—are the core socializing practices and experiences that contribute to the development of aggression (Coie & Dodge, 1998; Eron, Walder, & Lefkowitz, 1971; Huessman, Eron, Lefkowitz, & Walder, 1984; Huesmann, Lagerspetz, & Eron, 1984; Lykken, 2001; Staub, 1996a, 1996b, 2003, n.d.-b; Weiss, Dodge, Bates, & Pettit, 1992; Widom, 1989a, 1989b).

Warmth, affection and nurturance mean that adults are responsive to the needs of the child. Responsiveness to the infant's and young child's physical and social needs fulfills the basic needs for security and connection. Parents' sensitive responding to the infant's signals also satisfies the child's need for efficacy and control. Responding to signals and satisfying needs also affirm the child and begin to develop the rudiments of a positive identity. Such sensitive parental responding is associated with the development of secure attachment (Ainsworth, Bell, & Stayton, 1974; Bretherton, 1992; Shaffer, 1995; Thompson, 1998; Waters, Wippman, & Sroufe, 1979). In turn, secure attachment is associated with helping peers when children are 3½ years old (Waters et al., 1979) and with empathy and prosocial behavior in preschool (Kestenbaum, Farber, & Sroufe, 1989).

As children get older, love, affection, and caring about a child's welfare can take varied forms. For example, an essential characteristic of the parents of boys who have high self-esteem appears to be that they care about their children's welfare, which makes the children feel cared about. But this caring is expressed by them in many ways and not necessarily through physical affection (Coopersmith, 1967). Sensitivity in caring about and responding to the child's feelings and needs, to who the child is, will fulfill all basic needs. It will develop connection to important adults, which in turn is a source of positive orientation toward people in general. That this is the case is suggested by research findings that show that securely attached children are also capable of *creating* positive connections. Such children have positive relationship to peers in the early school years (Waters et al., 1979). They are able to create nonaggressive interactions in preschool with children who were found avoidantly attached at a younger age and whose interactions with anxiously attached and other avoidantly attached children are aggressive (Troy & Sroufe, 1987). Furthermore, unpublished research that I conducted with Don Operario suggests that college students who rate their parents as affectionate and caring also have a positive view of human beings and express concern about and feelings of responsibility for others' welfare. As noted earlier, such a prosocial value orientation is related to varied forms of helping. Warm parenting is also linked to children's empathy.

In contrast, severe negative effects result from neglect and the ineffectiveness of the child's signals (such as crying) to bring about the satisfaction of essential biological (and social) needs. Research has shown that infants in institutions characterized by poor caretaking become depressed and die in significant numbers. Those who survive later show deficiency in their capacity for human connection and in other domains (Shaffer, 1995; Thompson & Grusec, 1970). The conditions in such institutions frustrate infants' basic needs for security, connection, and effectiveness/control. Because of inadequate staffing, infants are fed and cared for on a rigid schedule and when it is their turn, not when they are in need. Their crying brings no response, and they have no significant connection to their caregivers.

Neglect beyond infancy also has extreme negative consequences. Emotional neglect and inattention to the child as a person and to his or her efforts to gain connection and affirmation appear to have at least as severe consequences as harsh treatment (Erickson & Egeland, 1996). Harsh treatment also frustrates basic needs, increasingly so as it becomes more severe and abusive. When it is unpredictable, it creates insecurity. When it is inescapable, it creates a feeling of ineffectiveness. It diminishes the child and breaks connection with important people. It creates a view of people and the world as hostile and dangerous, which interferes with the ability to develop connections to people. Aggressive boys, as well as men, may come to use their aggression as a destructive mode of fulfilling needs for security, efficacy, positive identity, and even connection. They come to interpret others' behavior toward themselves as hostile (Dodge, 1980, 1993) and see aggression as normal, appropriate, and even inevitable (Huessman & Eron, 1984). When boys are victimized and also have aggressive models and people who coach them in aggression—a situation that has been referred to as *violentization*—they may become intensely aggressive (Rhodes, 1999).

Guidance and Discipline Warmth and affection fulfill basic needs and provide the basis for caring about others' welfare, but they do not develop caring in the child unless accompanied by parental guidance. Parental permissiveness, which is the absence of guidance, has been associated with aggression by adolescents independent of the warmth-hostility dimension (DiLalla, Mitchell, Arthur, & Pagliococca, 1988). Warmth and affection are *not* associated with at least one form of prosocial behavior, generosity, when parents are permissive (Eisenberg, 1992; Eisenberg & Fabes, 1998; Staub, 1979).

Positive guidance itself fulfills basic needs. Guidance provides structure and order in children's lives and makes it easier to gain understanding of the world and develop self-guidance, control, and regulation. By teaching children how to act in order to be successful in their efforts, guidance contributes to the development of a sense of efficacy and positive identity. Parents of high-self-esteem children set high but achievable standards for them (Coopersmith, 1967). Guidance can help children set standards for themselves that make self-reinforcement possible.

Positive guidance uses and further develops the potentials/inclinations developed by the fulfillment of basic needs. In contrast, inherent in harsh treatment is negative guidance—the tendency to use force rather than verbal communication and the modeling of aggression. In such parenting, guidance is not separate from discipline and represents a harsh rather than a moderate form of discipline. The frequent use by parents of their power, in denying or withdrawing privileges, makes the development of caring and helping less likely and of aggression more likely (Coie & Dodge, 1998; Eisenberg & Fabes, 1998; Hoffman, 1970b; Staub, 1996a, 2003, n.d.-b).

Positive guidance consists of adults setting rules for children, but doing so in a democratic manner. Parents can exercise firm control—so that children will act according to important rules—while still being responsive to their children's explaining or reasoning about what they think and want (Baumrind, 1971, 1975). Adults who practice positive guidance also explain reasons for rules. Induction—pointing out to children the consequences of their behavior for others—has been found useful in promoting empathy and prosocial behavior (Eisenberg & Fabes, 1998; Hoffman, 2000; Zahn-Waxler & Radke-Yarrow, 1990). Reasons and explanations, when combined with a positive orientation to other people provided by the fulfillment of basic needs, help children understand others' internal worlds, develop empathy, and feel responsibility to help, and not to harm, others (Staub, 1979). Providing examples of positive behavior toward other people is another important form of guidance, accomplishing similar goals. Through such guidance children learn both the values of caring, empathy, and sympathy and the actions that benefit other people.

When explicit guidance is limited, when rules and explanations that structure and help children understand reality are lacking, then personal experiences, such as interactions that fulfill or frustrate basic needs, and the examples of models become even more powerful. However, explanations that conflict with or are contrary to powerful negative experiences with people—like abuse—will have little positive effect. Verbally guiding children to think about others' needs while they are the objects of abuse or other harmful behaviors is unlikely to be effective. Children who feel uncared for cannot be instructed to care about others. Guidance by the same person that aims to promote caring values, but that is combined with significant levels of harsh treatment, is likely to have limited success in developing caring (see, however, the discussion below of altruism born of suffering). Such behavior represents hypocrisy. Even milder forms of hypocrisy—for example, when an adult tells a child that he should donate a certain number of the rewards that he has won but then herself donates fewer—lead children to ignore the adult's guidance, to not do what the adult said. The children themselves learn hypocrisy. They act as the adult did but give younger children the instructions that the adult gave them (Mischel & Liebert, 1966).

Guidance itself is frequently not explicit, verbal, or even intentional. The reactions of adults to events, which provide information and have affective consequences, can function as guidance. Eisenberg's research shows that parents' facial expressions in response to emotionally arousing film sequences are related to children's regulation of emotion and their sympathetic responsiveness (see Eisenberg, in this volume). Facial expressions and other bodily reactions to members of devalued groups, a parent's grip tightening on the child's hand when they pass by a seedy looking homeless person, an adult's joy or distress, all provide information to and create affective reactions in the child. They tell the child the meaning and affective value of events.

Natural Socialization and Learning by Doing Helping others increases children's later helping behavior (Staub, 1975, 1979, 2003). There is also evidence from research with adults that harming others increases later harmful and aggressive actions (Buss, 1966; Goldstein, Davis, & Herman, 1975). Children and adults, as well as whole groups of people (Staub, 1989a, 2003), learn by doing. Adults can engage in "natural socialization" (Staub, 1979), giving children meaningful responsibilities to help at home or at school (Grusec, Kuczynski, Rushton, & Simutis, 1978; Whiting & Whiting, 1975), or guiding them to engage in helpful actions in relation to peers, adults, or the community. In contrast, parents who allow violent behavior by children or encourage aggression against peers are likely to promote the development of aggressive tendencies.

Children or adults who harm others and have no negative reactions to or other constraints on their actions are likely to justify what they do by both increasingly devaluing those whom they have harmed and finding good reasons for their actions. This makes new and greater harmdoing possible and probable. At the group level as well, lesser harmdoing against members of another group changes individuals, group norms, and even institutions and furthers the motivation for and allows the development of increasingly harmful actions. Intense violence like genocide evolves in this manner. The actions of witnesses, of "bystanders," in exerting positive influence to halt this evolution, whether in individuals or groups, is crucial (Staub, 1989a, 2003).

The constraints on the development of aggressiveness can sometimes be internal, coming from already developed characteristics of a person. One of my students described in a paper his anger at a "friend" who stole a significant amount of money from him. He beat up this friend, giving him a bad nosebleed. But he was so horrified by his action that he became very nonaggressive. However, when values and emotional orientations like sympathy, which can function as internal controls, have not yet developed, the constraints need to be external.

Children learn to be helpful "by doing" for two reasons. First, their actions fulfill basic needs, and, second, they develop values, beliefs, and skills or extend inclinations already developed through the fulfillment of their basic needs, verbal guidance, and other ways. If the experience of engaging in helpful action has positive cultural meaning (as is often the case, except in certain subcultures) and leads to others' improved welfare, it fulfills basic needs for positive identity, effectiveness, and positive connection, both to the people helped and to the larger community the values of which the person fulfills. It also expresses and intrinsically affirms the value of helping and, thereby, is especially effective in leading children both to value others' welfare and to see themselves as helpful persons (Eisenberg & Cialdini, 1984; Grusec et al., 1978; Staub, 1979, 2003).

In a series of studies with fifth- and sixth-grade children, my students and I have found (reviewed in Staub, 1979, 2003) that engaging children in helping others tends to increase their later helping. Children who were led to make toys, either for hospitalized children (especially, in the case of girls, when the benefits of their actions were pointed out to them) or in order to help an art teacher prepare materials, tended later to be more helpful. So were children who had opportunities to teach younger children to make puzzles or to use first-aid techniques.

The benefits of these helping experiences vary depending on particular procedures, on the gender of the children, and on the way they are assessed. For example, fifth- and sixth-grade boys writing letters to hospitalized children as a way of helping them show a base rate that is near zero and does not change. But they show the effects of learning by doing on an envelopes test, in which they are asked to gather pictures, poems, and other interesting materials for hospitalized children. When boys made puzzles to help poor hospitalized children, they did not show the effects of puzzle making on an immediate posttest. I interpreted this as the result of "psychological reactance" (Brehm, 1966), a negative reaction by boys to the perception that their freedom was limited by the influence exerted on them to do something "good," to be helpful. However, they did show positive effects on a delayed posttest, 2–3 weeks later, when presumably the reactance had diminished. The effects of teaching younger children were greater when the interaction between the older child, the subject, and the younger child being taught was more positive.

When aggressive actions are not halted by negative consequences, they lead to more aggression because they fulfill basic needs and, as an aspect of that, affirm the actor's strength and power. However, aggression fulfills basic needs destructively. It may create a feeling of effectiveness and control and affirm identity. But it creates disconnection from the people harmed and, except in violent subcultures, also from the community. It tends to create rejection by others.

Many aggressive youths are unpopular among their peers. However, they are unaware of their unpopularity. This is probably in part because they usually have a few friends similar to themselves, in part because others are afraid to show their dislike, and in part because, owing to their personality, they do not process the cues available to them. But as a result they become increasingly aggressive over time (Zakriski, Jacobs, & Coie 1997).

Peer Socialization of Caring and Altruism versus Aggression

Positive relations between peers have tremendous value in fulfilling basic needs, developing caring values, and helping develop prosocial skills and modes of relating to people. As Piaget has suggested, children learn reciprocity in peer relations. As both Piaget and Kohlberg have emphasized, they learn to take each others' roles. As in their interaction with adults, if they are well treated and also treat others well, they learn to see other people as benevolent and themselves as worthy individuals and effective in positive ways (Staub, 1979). All these are important preconditions for and rudiments of caring about other people and their well-being.

Cross-cultural research has shown that, in all cultures, girls are less aggressive than boys and that girls do substantially more caretaking of younger children than do boys. There is also evidence that boys who do more such caretaking are more prosocial (Whiting & Edwards, 1988), perhaps an example of learning by doing. Caring for younger children requires attention to their needs and is a form of helping—both of the younger child and of the parents.

In contrast, being the recipients of negative behavior from peers is likely to have the opposite effect, leading children to feel insecure and less worthy and to see other people and the world as hostile and dangerous. This may lead to aggression and is likely, at least without healing (see below), to reduce caring for and helping others. Children who are bullied are often deeply affected, in their self-confidence, trust in other people, willingness to initiate relationships, and well-being (Olweus, 1993; Ross & Ross, 1988; Staub, 2003).

Harassment, intimidation, and bullying in schools have negative effects, not just on the victims, but on everyone. Peers as well as adults in schools are often passive bystanders in the face of such actions, with passivity by peers *increasing* with age (Staub, 2003). Across grade levels, active response by peers to protect a target of bullying is less common than peers joining in the bullying (Staub, 2003). As a result, not only victims, but passive bystanders as well, learn that others are dangerous and that one must be careful in one's relationships with people. To reduce empathic distress, created by witnessing the distress of a victimized peer while remaining passive, children and adolescent are likely to distance themselves psychologically from victims—that is, from people in need (Staub, 1989a). Victims suffer, aggressors are likely to become more aggressive, and passive bystanders are likely to become less empathic. The system in which bullying is frequent contributes to the development of a negative view by children probably not only of other people but also of themselves. All this makes the development of caring and helping less likely.

These conditions indicate that, for the development of caring and helping rather than aggression, it is important to guide children to behave in positive ways toward each other. Adults helping develop positive modes of interaction between siblings in the home and peers in the neighborhood or in school is an essential aspect of positive socialization. Children are much more likely, however, to live by rules that promote positive peer interaction if they have had the positive socialization experiences with adults described earlier.

Children are also much more likely to act positively toward peers if they feel included in the peer group or classroom as a community. Children are harmed, not only by bullying, but also by exclusion—as indicated by other children not interacting with them. Excluded children have even fewer positive feelings about their lives at school than do children who are victimized by peers (Staub, 2003). It is essential, therefore, to find ways to include all children in the community, even those who are academically less skilled or for other reasons tend to be excluded and made marginal either in the classroom community or in other peer-group settings. (On caring schools, and on ways to create positive peer relations in schools, see Staub, 2003.)

Basic Needs and the Evolution of the Self

A number of socialization practices that fulfill basic human needs, and then build on the tendencies thus created to foster affective orientation and values, join together to develop helpful, altruistic tendencies in children. Warmth, affection, and adults sensitively responding to their needs, to their temperament and personality, are crucial. Nurturance must be sensitive to be experienced as such. A parent offering what the child does not need may not be perceived as loving. Positive guidance is also crucial, particularly forms of guidance that promote caring values, sympathy, and the effectiveness/competence that leads to their expression in action. Such guidance includes setting rules, with a dominance of prescriptive rather than proscriptive rules, and the explanation of rules in terms of values, induction, modeling, and natural socialization, which leads to learning by doing. Such modes of relating to the child and guidance will promote self-regulation in affective and other realms. The fulfillment of basic needs is a foundation that, when combined with other elements, promotes caring and helping.

Evolution in the psychological and social sense, both of children's personality and of the environment that surrounds them (the social world), is a core process in the development of caring, helping, and altruism. A different evolution leads to aggression. In part, these forms of evolution are simply outcomes of the processes already noted, such as the fulfillment or frustration of basic needs and guiding children by words and examples, combined with opportunities and encouragement to help others. The psychological changes in the course of the evolution involve increasing concern about those helped and the extension of that concern to people beyond one's group (or increasing devaluation of those harmed and the extension of that devaluation to more people) and a view of oneself as helpful (or as willing to use aggression).

An important aspect of this evolution may be the construction of people's basic needs. With experience, needs are likely to be shaped and formed, to become cognitive/emotional constructions, which then limit or expand in varied ways how needs can be fulfilled. Since aggressive men (Toch, 1969) come to see toughness and strength as masculine ideals, they have to be tough and strong to fulfill their need for a positive identity. The tendency to feel empathy and concern for people (except perhaps some intimates) will not fulfill their need for a positive identity. An increase in empathy will not be a desirable "expansion of the self," which I see as an aspect of the fulfillment of the need for a positive identity.

When a child devalues another child, when a group of peers or an ethnic or religious group devalues another group, it becomes unlikely that individuals can and will fulfill their need for connection by friendship with the devalued person or with members of the devalued group. Perpetrators learn to deal with consequences of their actions by closing themselves off to the feelings of their victims, by learning to become less empathic (Staub, 1989a; Staub & Pearlman, 2001; Staub, Pearlman, & Miller, 2003). Over time, their capacity to form connections to people in general may diminish. In the course of the evolution of helping and aggression, the cognitive/emotional construction of basic needs is likely to evolve in ways that contribute to further evolution in the same direction. Individuals—both children and adults—progressively engage in self-socialization, which can take the form of actions that bring forth reactions or of the selection of associates, peers, and environments, both of which further shape the direction in which they have been developing.

The Development of Inclusive Caring

Even among people who have learned to care about others' welfare, caring can be limited to people in their own group. There is a human tendency to differentiate between "us" and "them" and to devalue "them," a tendency rooted in, among other things, the cognitive process of categorization (Fiske & Taylor, 1991) and differences in reactions to the familiar and the unfamiliar (Staub, 1989a). Some groups, especially when they are the victims of discrimination and violence, can be devalued to such an extent that they are excluded from the moral realm (Opotaw, 1990; Staub, 1989a). People do not see them as deserving moral consideration and do not feel empathy and caring for them. To create a nonviolent, caring world, to create goodness, extending the boundaries of "us" is essential. Inclusive caring, the extension of caring to the "other," ideally to all human beings, develops through words and images that humanize all people, through the example of models who show caring for people regardless of their group membership, and through one's own experience of connection to varied people (Staub, 2002a, 2002b).

Many "rescuers"—Christians in Nazi Europe who endangered themselves and often their families as well by attempting to save the lives of Jews—had been raised in families that promoted inclusive caring. They were socialized in a way that was highly consistent with the socialization process described above as important in developing altruism. They received more love and affection and positive guidance than did others who were in similar situations but did not help. They had parents who, in cultures where physical punishment was common, used explanation instead. They were exposed to helpful models, often parents who embodied moral values in their actions. They had parents who engaged more in interaction with, and maintained positive social relations with, people outside their own group, including Jews. They heard their parents make fewer negative statements, if any, about Jews—a group devalued in Germany and in other European countries occupied by or under the influence of Nazi Germany where the Holocaust was perpetrated—than did comparison subjects who were in a position to help out but did not do so (Oliner & Oliner, 1988). It seems from this retrospective research that the socialization that the rescuers had experienced was then elaborated and further developed by their later experience in ways that promoted inclusive caring in relation to people who were devalued and later endangered.

Experiences of significant connection to people who are outside one's group and who are devalued are important in developing inclusive caring. Social psychologists have long hypothesized that contact between members of different groups helps overcome devaluation, prejudice, and hostility (see, among many others, Allport, 1954; Deutsch, 1973; Pettigrew, 1997, 1998; and Staub, 1989a). A recent meta-analysis of a very large number of studies confirms that this is so (Pettigrew & Tropp, 2000). Even though the experience of interaction and engagement was limited in many of the studies, it reduced negative attitudes toward members of another group.

The deeper the contact, and the more it involves shared goals that people work for, the greater the likely benefit. One method of creating such contact in schools has been through cooperative-learning methods. Specifically, in one procedure, six children who are members of different groups—white and minority children—work together. To accomplish their task each must learn some material and teach it to the others (Aronson, Stephan, Sikes, Blaney, & Snapp, 1978). In the course of being both teachers and learners, children are drawn into significant engagement with each other. Such cooperative-learning procedures have led to more positive interaction between white and minority children and improved the academic performance of minority children (see Staub, 2002a, 2002b, 2003).

Learning by doing can also be an avenue to inclusive caring. In the case of aggression by groups toward other groups, the range of victims usually expands. In the case of helping others, the commitment to those who are helped usually deepens, and the range of those who are helped may expand. Rescuers who have initially agreed to help a particular person in a limited way become more engaged and help more. They may have initially agreed to hide some people for a few days but ended up hiding them for years. Or, if they had succeeded in moving some people to a safer place, they then initiated helping others (Oliner & Oliner, 1988; Staub, 1989a). Rescuers who agreed to help a Jew who was a former friend or associate often decided to help others who were strangers.

Concern can also expand from one group to other groups and to all humanity. At the time of the disappearances in Argentina, the Mothers of the Plaza del Mayo demonstrated, marching every day in the centrally located Plaza del Mayo in Buenos Aires. In spite of intimidation, harassment, and even abduction, they continued to protest the disappearance of their children. But over time their concern expanded, to include other disappeared people as well as people who were persecuted and victimized outside Argentina (Ehlstein, 1986).

Culture and education can promote inclusive caring for all human beings, regardless of group membership. This can be done by humanizing—describing in not devaluative but respectful, caring ways—every group (Staub et al., in press; Staub et al., 2003). It can also be done by eliminating discrimination, which expresses and promotes devaluation. It can be done by creating social systems in which people belonging to different groups have equal rights, whether in the classroom or in other settings in society, thereby fostering positive relations characterized by mutual respect (Staub, 2003).

The Development of Moral Courage

Moral courage is of great importance for a nonviolent, caring world. The term *moral courage* refers to the courage to express important values in words and actions, even in the face of opposition, potential disapproval, and ostracism or a violent response. Moral courage may require physical courage, but often it requires only what may be called *psychological courage.*

Is courage in behalf of any kind of belief or value a moral courage? In the perspective that I am proposing, the courage required to act in the face of opposition is moral only if the beliefs or values (including affective reactions like empathy) that motivate it involve protecting or promoting human welfare. For example, young men who joined and persisted in supporting the Nazi movement or joined the SA, the stormtroopers of the Nazi movement, during the 1920s, well before Hitler came to power, often faced opposition from and disapproval by members of the community (Merkl, 1980). So might members of violent gangs and violent ideological movements, including terrorists. Their actions in opposition to these constraining forces do not constitute moral courage.

Identifying courage as moral only if the values and beliefs involved are moral makes it a more difficult matter to judge when people express moral courage. When harmful actions are ideologically motivated, the perpetrators often claim, and probably often believe, that their beliefs and values are moral and that their actions are for the good of their group or of all human beings. Often they believe that they are acting for a higher morality (Staub, 1989a, 2003). To determine whether their actions, the actions of actors in general, are moral requires an "external" judgment. This judgment may be based on the combination of information available about the actors' beliefs and intentions, the form of the actions themselves (do they appear to be actions that would create benefit, harm, or neither?), the potential or actual consequences of the actions, and the preceding conditions that gave rise to them.

It is more difficult to be morally courageous when acting alone than when acting in a group, for example, a child acting to stop the bullying of another child. Members of movements—whether acting in a moral or in an immoral cause—get support and encouragement from other members, who have become their primary reference group. Speaking out within a group or movement against harmful action by the group requires special moral courage.

The importance of support from like-minded others can be found in many instances. For example, even when abolitionists in the United States were acting alone, facing hostile groups while advocating the abolition of slavery, they were supported by their feelings of connection to other abolitionists (Tompkins, 1965). People may also find support from internalized, imagined others—and the ideals that those others set for them.

The Socialization of Moral Courage What might be the roots of moral courage in children's experience? Some of the socialization experiences described above as involved in the development of moral and caring emotions and values also play an important role in the development of moral courage. For example, the parents of many young civil rights activists in the United States who went to the South in the 1960s to advance desegregation by participating in marches and sit-ins modeled moral concern, engagement, and courage. They demonstrated against injustice and for justice. Some of the fathers fought in the Spanish Civil War. The combined influence of varied experiences is shown in that young activists who had both such moral parental models and unconflicted positive relations with their parents were more committed to, more persistent in their civil rights activities than were those who had moral parents toward whom they felt ambivalence (Rosenhan, 1970).

Providing children with opportunities and encouraging them to express their thoughts, beliefs, and values can be important. Baumrind (1971, 1975) has reported that authoritative parents tended to listen to their children's arguments about what they wanted to do, even if what the children wanted was contrary to some rule or to what they had originally been asked to do, and that they sometimes yielded. (However, they would not yield to whining or demanding.) This is likely to encourage children to express themselves.

Teachers in schools may have students participate in making rules for the classroom. This can provide a context in which students learn to engage in discussion, to speak out, and to become comfortable with expressing views that are not necessarily accepted by others (see Staub, 2003, chaps. 15, 20; Staub, n.d.-b). Parents can do the same in the home. This way children can learn to trust their voice and its potential influence. This is especially difficult to bring about, but especially important, in societies where children are taught not to question or challenge authority and where they do not normally develop their own perspective and voice. When parents, teachers, and other adults encourage students to be "active bystanders" when they witness harmful actions toward individuals, when they affirm their speaking out against cruelty or injustice or simply their expressing beliefs or points of view that are contrary to those of others (not necessarily agreeing with the content, but simply affirming the expression of their views), they can help develop moral courage.

The Relationship Between the Self and the Group Teaching children to think not in terms of abstractions and absolutes but in terms of concrete human welfare is also important. An example of this might be the distinction between *blind* and *constructive* patriotism. Blind patriots support their country and its actions unconditionally. Constructive patriots express about the same degree of love for their country as blind patriots. However, they believe that their love of their country requires them to speak out against policies and practices that are contrary to important human values as well as against policies and practices that they see as contrary to the essential values of their country (Staub, 1997). Constructive patriots score higher on prosocial value orientation, are more willing to criticize their country, and report that they spend more time gathering political information and are more politically active (Schatz et al., 1999).

The types of selves that children develop may be important for moral courage. Psychologists have long been interested in the differences between collectivist and individualist cultures (Triandis, 1994). A number of psychologists, inspired by differences found between those two types of cultures in the construction of identity, have proposed that there are differences within Western, individualist cultures in the identities that women and men develop. While terminologies have differed, some have proposed that women have more relational selves, men more autonomous selves (Sampson, 1988; Surrey, 1985).

I have suggested a further differentiation among relational selves. While the connections to others and the orientation to community that collectivist cultures generate have great benefits, they can also pose problems. Individuals may have difficulty separating themselves from their group and, when important from the moral/caring standpoint discussed here, opposing their group. Individuals with what I have called *embedded selves*, which embody both feelings of connection and strong dependence, will have difficulty separating themselves from and opposing others, whether individuals or the group as a whole. In contrast, individuals with *connected selves*, which embody feelings of connection to other individuals and/or the group but also sufficient independence to stand alone if necessary, will be more likely to take morally courageous actions (Staub, 1993). What seems important for the development of the latter kind of self, in addition to what I have already discussed in the context of the development of "goodness" and moral courage, is granting children appropriate autonomy. That is, while guidance and what Baumrind (1971, 1975) has called *firm control* have great value, it is also important to allow children, in the context of adherence to essential rules, values, and principles, the maximum autonomy that is appropriate for their age (Staub, n.d.-b).

Not being embedded in a group makes an independent perspective possible. A fair percentage of rescuers of Jews during the Holocaust were in some way marginal to their communities (Tec, 1986). Marginality was often a function of their social situation, for example, having a foreign-born parent or having a different religion—a Catholic in a Protestant community. But it could also be a function of their personality, the nature of their identity, a history of being "different." Their marginality may have enabled them to separate themselves from their communities, which often supported the persecution of Jews, and thereby maintain an independent perspective. Constructive patriots in contrast to blind patriots also seem to have a separate-enough perspective to question the problematic policies and practices of their group.

A "critical consciousness" seems crucial (Staub, 1989a). In order to act on one's values, it is necessary to realize the relevance of those values to particular events or policies and practices in a group. This often entails using one's own judgment about the meaning of events, rather than accepting the meaning that others explicitly or implicitly communicate about them. For example, there was much public discussion in the United States preceding the beginning of the war against Iraq in 2003 about the connection between Iraq and the September 11 attacks. The Bush administration asserted that such a connection existed. However, CIA reports and all other sources, including discussion in the media, have indicated the absence of evidence for it. Still, polls showed that over 50% of the American public believed that Iraq was involved in the attacks, a seeming lack of a critical consciousness. (The woundedness and insecurity that resulted from the attacks may have created both a strong need to know where the violence originated and an increased reliance on the words of leaders.) Some of the practices already discussed as important for the development of moral courage are also likely to help in the development of critical consciousness.

We must learn more about the origins of moral courage and create conditions that help such courage develop. Morally courageous people who are active bystanders can make a crucial difference, in many settings, at important moments, as individuals or as members of groups opposing harmful or violent social policies and practices or promoting helpful ones. Morally courageous actions can be important at particular times, in response to specific events. But, beyond that, morally committed and courageous people can join to overcome the inertia of social systems, activate other bystanders, and work on creating societies and an international community that promote harmony and caring in human relations (Staub, 2003).

Trauma and Healing, Resilience, Need Fulfillment, and Altruism Born of Suffering

Research on the development of caring, helping, and altruism in children has focused on positive roots, as described so far in this chapter. However, observation and many self-reports and case studies indicate that people who have suffered from victimization and other trauma often come to devote themselves to helping others. My attention first focused on this when I prepared a questionnaire assessing prosocial value orientation and helping for *Psychology Today* (Staub, 1989b; see also Staub 2003) that over 7,000 readers filled out and returned. Many of them, in response to my request, also wrote letters with additional information about themselves. Several of those who wrote reported that their own suffering, early in their lives, led them to help others, especially to try to prevent such suffering by other people.

Research and clinical observation has focused on the traumatic effects of victimization and suffering (Herman, 1992; McCann & Pearlman, 1990). It has also been shown that bad treatment, neglect, and abuse, both physical and verbal, contribute to aggression in children. Some of this research was described earlier. Other research has shown that people who were abused as children are more likely to abuse their own children (Kaufman & Zigler, 1987) and that, among violent criminals, the great majority had experiences of victimization at home or in their community (Gilligan, 1996; Rhodes, 1999; Widom, 1989a, 1989b). According to newspaper reports, at least, many of the school shooters were victimized by peers.

People who have been the object of violence at the hands of others, whether those others acted as individuals or as members of a group, are likely to feel diminished. They will tend to feel that something must be wrong with them, that they must somehow have deserved to be treated that way. They will tend to see the world as dangerous and feel vulnerable. They will be more likely to see, therefore, threat, danger, and potential attack and feel the need to defend themselves, even when there is no real threat (Staub, 1998, 2003; Staub & Pearlman, 2001).

However, not everyone who is victimized becomes aggressive. Many children who come from difficult backgrounds show resilience—effective functioning in spite of their background (Butler, 1997; Masten, 2001; Rutter, 1987; Staub, n.d.-b; Werner, 1987; Werner & Smith, 1992). And some people who have greatly suffered as children become caring and helpful people who devote themselves to the welfare of others. O'Connell Higgins (1994) described adults severely abused as children, some mercilessly beaten by parents, who have become deeply caring people, devoting their lives to helping people in need or to protecting people from suffering the way they themselves have suffered. Valent (1998) noted that many child survivors of the Holocaust are in service professions or work for positive social change.

Some people who have experienced great suffering and the frustration of basic needs that this entails—the need for security, for effectiveness and control, for a positive identity, for a positive connection, and for comprehension of reality—may lack corrective, transformative experiences. They may even have developed such an intensely defensive stance against a hostile world, or an intensely hostile stance, that they cannot use opportunities to ameliorate their hostile orientations. They may not be able to perceive or use opportunities for significant, caring human connections or other healing experiences. However, other people who have been victimized may both have opportunity for and make use of corrective experiences.

I assume that, if they are to become caring, altruistic people, victimized children require that their basic needs be fulfilled, to some degree at least, either before or after their victimization, or both, and that the psychological wounds created by their victimization heal to some degree. Prior need fulfillment may protect them to some extent from the effects of victimization. For example, one of the protective elements for children who come from difficult environments and are resilient seems to be early secure attachment to a caretaker (Werner & Smith, 1992). Subsequent need fulfillment may enable them to see hopeful possibilities in life, the possibility of security, of dignity, and of positive, loving connections between people.

Healing from past trauma requires gaining renewed trust in people. Connection to caring people, adults as well as children, is especially important in this. Resilience in children is usually facilitated by interest and support from and positive connection to one or more persons—teachers, counselors, relatives, neighbors (Butler, 1997; Werner & Smith, 1992). Temperament also contributes to resilience (Rutter, 1987). It may be the case, in part at least, that children who are more outgoing make active efforts to connect with potentially supporting others.

Healing, in part through positive connections to people and the fulfillment of basic needs, enables people who have suffered to become open to the pain of others. This openness to others, combined with a more caring world that they may now be able to envision, may, given their own experiences, lead them to strong feelings of empathy and sympathy and even to a feeling of responsibility to help those in need. Identification with those who suffer may lead to increasing engagement and the development of the intense motivation to help others that some of these altruists describe.

Connection to other children can also help wounded children heal. Freud and Dann (1951) described a group of young children who survived Auschwitz together. Taken to England afterward, they were extremely resistant to adults but fiercely loyal to and supportive of each other. According to Freud and Dann, their deep connections to each other enabled them to begin, over time, to develop connections to adults. Suomi and Harlow (1972) found that monkeys isolated in the first 6 months of their lives were highly inappropriate in their social and sexual interactions with their peers. The only treatment that was reasonably effective was pairing them with normal infant monkeys, who would cling to them. The former isolates would carry these infant monkeys around. Presumably, this helped them change both in the kind of emotions that they experienced and in emotional self-regulation. As the growing infants began to develop social skills, the isolates would learn along with them. Research with children has shown that socially ineffective children's social interactions improved after they spent time supervising/interacting with younger children (Furman, Rahe, & Hartup, 1979).

In the case of survivors of genocide, many of them had their basic needs fulfilled through close, loving connections to their families and their group before the genocide and to other survivors afterward. In addition, many survivors were helped by other people. Many also engaged in courageous action to help themselves. This was true of survivors of the Holocaust: even young children often engaged in amazing acts of initiative to help themselves or their families (Staub, n.d.-a). Such experiences fulfill, in the midst of horrible circumstances, needs for connection, effectiveness, and identity and a comprehension of reality that provides hope and makes caring for others possible.

Some of these considerations about the roots of altruism born of suffering are supported by case histories provided by my students. In the course of teaching, I have over the past 10–15 years come to guide students to write papers in which they apply psychological research and theory to their own experiences, to an exploration of the connection between their life experiences and the people they have become.

One of my students, a bright, attractive young woman, had a terrible year in the eighth grade. There was a boys' clique that dictated the rules by which the girls were to behave. In addition to sexual teasing, they would touch the girls—their breasts, their buttocks. They engaged in many degrading actions, which most of the girls endured, and which some even acted as if they welcomed. Because she did not go along with this, my student was viciously teased and ostracized, not only by the boys, but by the girls as well. The teachers witnessed all this but did nothing, even making comments to her like, "Boys will be boys." She suffered all this without yielding, but suffered greatly.

In her home life, however, she had received a great deal of love and affection before this and much love and support while this was happening. She also saw her parents as moral, spiritual people, instilling in her both an understanding of others (she came to interpret the behavior of the boy who was the main gang leader as a child of busy socialites who paid little attention to him) and a sense of independence. She believes that it was the combination of her suffering that year and her background and the support that she received that led her to engage in her many and varied activities to help others: volunteering with mentally and physically disabled children; spending time helping rebuild a town in a poor area of the country after a disaster; serving as a peer mention, as a tutor, and as a counselor for emotionally disturbed girls; volunteering at many charities and organizations; being the kind of person to whom others turn for consolation; and more. An interesting aspect of this situation, perhaps having to do with moral courage, perhaps with concern for their daughter, is that, while the parents were highly supportive of her, they were passive in relation to the school, not taking action to stop the bullying.

Another student described a great deal of criticism by her parents, which made her feel diminished and helpless. Perhaps because of this she dropped out of and reentered college several times. One of these times a teacher in a community college showed special interest and caring, not just for my student, but for all her students. My student was able to experience and was deeply affected by her caring and benevolence and by her trust in her ability. Later she worked as an intern in a school with mentally less developed children. Being distressed by the way the teachers treated the children, she was both strongly motivated and able to engage in what she felt were supportive and helpful interactions with the children. She felt that both these experiences, the benevolence of her teacher and her own helpful actions, gave her hope and strength and led her to go on to a four-year college and do well there.

Positive connections to and support by other people are important to the healing of victimized children and adults and to the fulfillment of previously deeply frustrated basic needs. They affirm the self, fulfill the need for connection, and offer a more hopeful view of the world. However, other processes of healing are also important. One of these is engagement with painful experiences, in combination with empathy and support from other people. This helps a person realize that the past is not the present and see the present as safe and more hopeful. With children this may be facilitated by reading and discussing literature that is relevant to their difficult and painful experiences (Staub, 2003). Such indirect engagement may be safer but still helpful nonetheless. Writing about personal experiences may also be helpful, as it has been found to be in research with college students (Pennebacker & Beall, 1986). If done under the right supportive conditions, talking about personal experiences can be highly beneficial for children. Parents who have divorced have reported to me, for example, that their children gained self-confidence and reassurance from participating in school in group discussions with other children whose parents have divorced.

Another avenue to healing from victimization is understanding how the perpetrators came to do what they did. In Rwanda, discussing with people how genocide comes about (Staub & Pearlman, 2001; Staub et al., in press; Staub et al., 2003; on the origins of genocide, see also Staub, 1989a), with examples of other instances of genocide, seemed to have highly beneficial effects. Coming to see genocide as an understandable even if a tragic and horrible human process, rather than incomprehensible evil, seemed to help both survivors and bystanders feel more "human," rather than outcasts from the human fold. (While members of both groups, Tutsis and Hutus, participated, perpetrators were not included.) In addition, during the course of the discussion people realized that, if they understood how it happened, they could take action to prevent it from happening again (Staub & Pearlman, 2001; Staub et al., in press; Staub et al., 2003). A formal evaluation of an intervention in which the exploration of the roots of genocide was one of several components showed reduction in trauma symptoms and a more positive orientation by members of the groups involved toward each other (Staub, 2003; Staub et al., in press).

In her case histories of resilient adults, O'Connell Higgins (1994) also reports that understanding can be useful. In one of the chapters we learn about Dan, who was an object of his father's rage and frequently and severely beaten by him. He was also given enemas by his mother to make him a better child. Later he found that understanding the source of his parents' behavior—for example, seeing in his mind's eye his father, who was severely neglected by his parents, stand in his crib screaming and shaking it, with nobody responding, this giving rise to his rage—helped him to some degree accept who his father was. Dan himself has become a successful person whose work involves helping others, in efficient and effective ways.

There is substantial evidence that altruism born of suffering is a real and important phenomenon. While I have suggested here some of the experiences that are likely to contribute to its evolution, both the extent to which people who have suffered victimization and other traumas become altruists and the conditions required for this to happen ought to be a focus of concentrated study.

Conclusions: Optimal Human Functioning and the Good Society

In conclusion, I want to stress two important matters. First, the fulfillment of basic human needs is not just an individual matter, that is, a matter of the circumstances of a particular person, but to a great extent a cultural/societal matter. Second, the fulfillment of these needs contributes, not only to goodness, but also to individuals' continued development or growth, to their fulfillment of their human and personal potentials—to what may be called *optimal human functioning* (Staub, 2003).

Starting with the second issue, I have suggested that an important avenue to goodness is through the constructive fulfillment of basic needs, in combination with guidance that develops sympathetic emotions and caring values. However, as basic needs are fulfilled, they also provide the base for continued personal growth. They undergo transformation, become less pressing, and evolve into personal goals (Staub, 1980), the desire to bring about particular valued outcomes. The outcomes that people value will differ, depending on their life experiences. Realms of effectiveness, sources of positive identity, the importance of connections to individuals or a larger community, may all vary.

While people whose needs have been fulfilled will differ, they are likely to have in common an openness to experience (since they perceive other people and the world as reasonably benevolent), a capacity for processing their experience and self-awareness (since, given their positive identity and feelings of effectiveness and control, they do not need to protect themselves because of who they are or what they think and feel), as well as other important characteristics that contribute to continued personal growth (Maslow, 1987). Given a sense of effectiveness in the work realm, they will be open to new knowledge and creative endeavors. They are, thus, likely to continue to develop both in the personal and in the work realms. According to the conception of personal goals with which I have been working (Staub, 1989a, 1996b, 1999b, 2003), when other needs are fulfilled, the need for transcendence, to go beyond the self, emerges or becomes more dominant. Thus, people whose basic needs have been constructively fulfilled are able to focus less on themselves and more on other people, the world, and spiritual matters.

What might be the relation between altruism born of suffering and optimal human functioning? It is possible that, even though people who have suffered and whose basic needs have been frustrated can become true altruists under certain conditions, their continued personal growth and evolution will be hindered and made more difficult by the painful experiences that they have had. It is also possible, however, that their caring and altruistic orientation becomes for them an avenue to continued personal growth (Colby & Damon, 1992; O'Connell Higgins, 1994).

With regard to the first issue, the actions of members of families, adults in schools, and peers fulfill or frustrate basic needs. However, families, schools, and peers are located in a society. How they act is affected by the characteristics of that society: beliefs about how children are to be treated; the devaluation of and discrimination against members of particular groups; and so on. Poverty, which varies by society and subgroups in it, creates stress and negatively affects parenting (McLoyd, 1990), frustrating children's needs. Teenage single mothers, especially if they are poor, are likely to have their own needs frustrated by their circumstances and to have difficulty fulfilling the needs of their children. Unless they receive support from others, they are much more likely to abuse their children than are other mothers (Garcia-Coll, Hoffman, & Oh, 1987). When a society helps its members fulfill basic needs constructively, there is likely to be more belief in enlightened self-interest and more generalized reciprocity in people helping each other. It would make great sense to evaluate the goodness of societies in terms of the ease or difficulty of fulfilling basic human needs and to identify desirable social changes in terms of their probable contribution to the fulfillment of basic needs (Staub, 2003).

References

Ainsworth, M. D. S., Bell, S. M., & Stayton, D. J. (1974). Infant-mother attachment and social development: Socialization as a product of reciprocal responsiveness to signals. In M. P. M. Richards (Ed.), *The integration of the child into a social world*. London: Cambridge University Press.

Allport, G. W. (1954). *The nature of prejudice*. Reading MA: Addison-Wesley.

Aronson, E., Stephan, C., Sikes, J., Blaney, N., & Snapp, M. (1978). *The jigsaw classroom*. Beverly Hills CA: Sage.

Batson, C. D. (1990). How social an animal? The human capacity for caring. *American Psychologist, 45*, 336–347.

Baumrind, D. (1971). Current patterns of parental authority. *Developmental Psychology, 4*, 1–101.

Baumrind, D. (1975). *Early socialization and the discipline controversy*. Morristown NJ: General Learning.

Berkowitz, L. (1972). Social norms, feelings, and other factors affecting helping behavior and altruism. In L. Berkowitz (Ed.), *Advances in experimental social psychology* (Vol. 6, pp. 63–108). New York: Academic.

Berkowitz, L. (1993). *Aggression: Its causes, consequences, and control*. New York: McGraw-Hill.

Brehm, J. W. (1966). *A theory of psychological reactance*. New York: Academic.

Bretherton, I. (1992). The origins of attachment theory: John Bowlby and Mary Ainsworth. *Developmental Psychology, 28*, 759–775.

Burton, J. W. (1990). *Conflict: Human needs theory*. New York: St. Martin's.

Buss, A. H. (1966). The effect of harm on subsequent aggression. *Journal of Experimental Research in Personality, 1*, 249–255.

Butler, K. (1997, March/April). The anatomy of resilience. *Family Therapy Networker*, 22–31.

Carlo, G., Eisenberg, N., Troyer, D., Switzer, G., & Speer, A. K. (1991). The altruistic personality: In what contexts is it apparent? *Journal of Personality and Social Psychology, 61*, 450–458.

Carlson, M., & Miller, N. (1987). Explanation of the relation between negative mood and helping. *Psychological Bulletin, 102*, 91–108.

Coie, J. D., & Dodge, K. A. (1998). Aggression and antisocial behavior. In W. Damon (Series Ed.), N. Eisenberg (Vol. Ed.), *Handbook of child psychology: Vol. 3. Social, emotional, and personality development* (5th ed., pp. 779–862). New York: Wiley.

Colby, A., & Damon, W. (1992). *Some do care*. New York: Free Press.

Coopersmith, S. (1967). *Antecedents of self-esteem*. San Francisco: Fremont.

Crick, N. R. (1997). Engagement in gender normative versus non-normative forms of aggression: Links to social-psychological adjustment. *Developmental Psychology, 33,* 610–617.

Deutsch, M. (1973). *The resolution of conflict: Constructive and destructive processes.* New Haven: Yale University Press.

DiLalla, L. F., Mitchell, C. M., Arthur, M. W., & Pagliococca, P. M. (1988). Aggression and delinquency: Family and environmental factors. *Journal of Youth and Adolescence, 73,* 233–246.

Dodge, K. A. (1980). Social cognition and children's aggressive behavior. *Child Development, 51,* 162–170.

Dodge, K. A. (1993). Social cognitive mechanisms in the development of conduct disorder and depression. *Annual Review of Psychology, 44,* 559–584.

Ehlstein, J. (1986, December). *Reflections on political torture and murder: Visits with the mothers of the Plaza del Mayo.* Invited talk, Department of Psychology, University of Massachusetts, Amherst.

Eisenberg, N. (1992). *The caring child.* Cambridge: Harvard University Press.

Eisenberg, N. (2002). Empathy-related emotional responses, altruism, and their socialization. In R. J. Davidson & A. Harrington (Eds.), *Visions of compassion.* New York: Oxford University Press.

Eisenberg, N., & Cialdini, R. B. (1984). The role of consistency pressures in behavior: A developmental perspective. *Academic Psychology Bulletin, 6,* 115–126.

Eisenberg, N., & Fabes, R. A. (1998). Prosocial development. In W. Damon (Series Ed.), N. Eisenberg (Vol. Ed.), *Handbook of child psychology: Vol. 3. Social, emotional, and personality development* (5th ed., pp. 701–778). New York: Wiley.

Eisenberg, N., Fabes, R. A., Miller, P. A., Fultz, J., Mathy, R. M., Shell, R., & Reno, R. R. (1989). The relations of sympathy and personal distress to prosocial behavior: A multimethod study. *Journal of Personality and Social Psychology, 57,* 55–66.

Erickson, M., & Egeland, B. (1996). The quiet assault: A portrait of child neglect. In J. Briere, L. Berliner, S. Bulkley, C. Jenny, & T. Reid (Eds.), *The handbook of child maltreatment* (pp. 4–20). Newbury Park CA: Sage.

Erikson, E. H. (1959). *Identity and the life cycle: Selected papers* (Psychological Issues, Vol. 1, No. 1, Monograph 1). New York: International Universities Press.

Erkut, S., Jaquette, D., & Staub, E. (1981). Moral judgment–situation interaction as a basis for predicting social behavior. *Journal of Personality, 49,* 1–44.

Eron, L. D., Gentry, J. H., & Schlegel, P. (1994). *Reason to hope: A psychosocial perspective on violence and youth.* Washington DC: American Psychological Association.

Eron, L. D., Walder, L. O., & Lefkowitz, M. N. (1971). *Learning of aggression in children.* Boston: Little, Brown.

Feinberg, J. K. (1978). *Anatomy of a helping situation: Some personality and sit-*

uational determinants of helping in a conflict situation involving another's psychological distress. Unpublished doctoral dissertation, University of Massachusetts.

Feshbach, N. D., & Feshbach, S. (1969). The relationship between empathy and aggression in two age groups. *Development Psychology, 1,* 102–107.

Fiske, S. T., & Taylor, S. E. (1991). *Social cognition* (2d ed.). New York: McGraw-Hill.

Freud, A., & Dann, S. (1951). An experiment in group upbringing. In R. Eissler et al. (Eds.), *The psychoanalytic study of the child* (Vol. 6, pp. 127–163). New York: International Universities Press.

Furman, W., Rahe, D. F., & Hartup, W. W. (1979). Rehabilitation of socially withdrawn children though mixed age and same age socialization. *Child Development, 50,* 915–922.

Garcia-Coll, C. T., Hoffman, J., & Oh, W. (1987). The social ecology and early parenting of Caucasian adolescent mothers. *Child Development, 58,* 955–963.

Gilligan, J. (1996). *Violence: Our deadly epidemic and its causes.* New York: Putnam.

Goldstein, J. H., Davis, R. W., & Herman, D. (1975). Escalation of aggression: Experimental studies. *Journal of Personality and Social Psychology, 31,* 162–170.

Grodman, S. M. (1979). *The role of personality and situational variables in responding to and helping an individual in psychological distress.* Unpublished doctoral dissertation, University of Massachusetts, Amherst.

Grusec, J. E., Kuczynski, L., Rushton, J. P., & Simutis, Z. M. (1978). Modeling, direct instruction, and attributions: Effects on altruism. *Developmental Psychology, 14,* 51–57.

Herman, J. (1992). *Trauma and recovery.* New York: Basic.

Heusmann, L. R., & Eron, L. D. (1984). Cognitive processes and the persistence of aggressive behavior. *Aggressive Behavior, 10,* 243–251.

Heusmann, L. R., Eron, L. D., Lefkowitz, M. M., & Walder, L. O. (1984). Stability of aggression over time and generations. *Developmental Psychology, 20,* 1120–1134.

Heusmann, L. R., Lagerspetz, K., & Eron, L. D. (1984). Intervening variables in the television violence–aggression relation: Evidence from two countries. *Developmental Psychology, 20,* 746–775.

Hoffman, M. L. (1970a). Conscience, personality, and socialization technique. *Human Development, 13,* 90–126.

Hoffman, M. L. (1970b). Moral development. In P. H. Mussen (Ed.), *Carmichael's manual of child psychology* (3d ed., Vol. 2, pp. 261–359). New York: Wiley.

Hoffman, M. L. (1975a). Altruistic behavior and the parent-child relationship. *Journal of Personality and Social Psychology, 31,* 937–943.

Hoffman, M. L. (1975b). Developmental synthesis of affect and cognition and its implications for altruistic motivation. *Developmental Psychology, 11,* 607–622.

Hoffman, M. L. (2000). *Empathy and moral development.* New York: Cambridge University Press.

Karylowski, J. (1976). Self-esteem, similarity, liking, and helping. *Personality and Social Psychology Bulletin, 2,* 71–74.

Kaufman, J., & Zigler, E. (1987). Do abused children become abusive parents? *American Journal of Orthopsychiatry, 57,* 186–192.

Kelman, H. C. (1990). Applying a human needs perspective to the practice of conflict resolution: The Israeli-Palestinian case. In J. Burton (Ed.), *Conflict: Human needs theory* (pp. 283–297). New York: St. Martin's.

Kestenbaum, R., Farber, E. A., & Sroufe, L. A. (1989). Individual differences in empathy among preschoolers: Relation to attachment history. *New Directions in Child Development, 44,* 51–64.

Kohlberg, L., & Candee, L. (1984). The relationship of moral judgment to moral action. In W. M. Kurtines & J. L. Gewirtz (Eds.), *Morality, moral behavior, and moral development* (pp. 52–73). Mahwah NJ: Wiley.

Lykken, D. T. (2001). Parental licensure. *American Psychologist, 56,* 885–894.

Maslow, A. H. (1968). *Toward a psychology of being* (2d ed.). New York: Van Nostrand.

Maslow, A. H. (1987). *Motivation and personality* (3d ed.). New York: Harper & Row. (Original work published 1954)

Masten, A. S. (2001). Ordinary magic: Resilience processes in development. *American Psychologist, 59,* 227–238.

Mauss, M. (1954). *The gift: Forms and functions of exchange in archaic societies.* Glencoe IL: Free Press.

McCann, I. L., & Pearlman, L. A. (1990). *Psychological trauma and the adult survivor: Theory, therapy, and transformation.* New York: Brunner Mazel.

McLoyd, V. C. (1990). The impact of economic hardship on black families and children: Psychological distress, parenting, and socioemotional development. *Child Development, 61,* 311–346.

Merkl, P. H. (1980). *The making of a stormtrooper.* Princeton: Princeton University Press.

Midlarsky, E. (1971). Aiding under stress: The effects of competence, dependence, visibility, and fatalism. *Journal of Personality, 39,* 132–149.

Mischel, W., & Liebert, R. M. (1966). Effects of discrepancies between observed and imposed reward criteria on their acquisition and transmission. *Journal of Personality and Social Psychology, 3,* 45–53.

Murray, H. A. (1938). *Explorations in personality.* New York: Oxford University Press.

O'Connell Higgins, C. (1994). *Resilient adults overcoming a cruel past.* San Francisco: Jossey-Bass.

Oliner, S. B., & Oliner, P. (1988). *The altruistic personality: Rescuers of Jews in Nazi Europe.* New York: Free Press.

Olweus, D. (1993). *Bullying at school: What we know and what we can do*. Oxford: Blackwell.
Opotaw, S. (1990). Moral exclusion and injustice. *Journal of Social Issues, 46*(1), 1–20.
Pearlman, L. A., & Saakvitne, K. W. (1995). *Trauma and the therapist: Countertransference and vicarious traumatization in psychotherapy with incest survivors*. New York: Norton.
Pennebacker, J. W., & Beall, S. K. (1986). Confronting a traumatic event: Toward an understanding of inhibition and disease. *Journal of Abnormal Psychology, 95*, 274–281.
Pettigrew, T. F. (1997). Generalized intergroup contact effects on prejudice. *Personality and Social Psychology Bulletin, 23*, 173–185.
Pettigrew, T. F. (1998). Intergroup contact theory. *Annual Review of Psychology, 49*, 65–85.
Pettigrew, T. F., & Tropp, L. R. (2000). Does intergroup contact reduce prejudice? Recent meta-analytic findings. In S. Oskamp (Ed.), *Reducing prejudice and discrimination* (pp. 93–114). London: Erlbaum.
Rhodes, R. (1999). *Why they kill*. New York: Knopf.
Rosenhan, D. (1970). The natural socialization of altruistic autonomy. In J. Macauley & L. Berkowitz (Eds.), *Altruism and helping behavior* (pp. 251–268). New York: Academic.
Ross, D., & Ross, S. (1988). *Childhood pain: Current issues, research, and management*. Baltimore and Munich: Urban & Schwarzenberg.
Rutter, M. (1987). Psychosocial resilience and protective mechanisms. *American Journal of Orthopsychiatry, 57*, 316–331.
Sampson, E. E. (1988). The debate on individualism. *American Psychologist, 47*, 15–22.
Schatz, R. T., & Staub, E. (1997). Manifestations of blind and constructive patriotism. In D. Bar-Tal & E. Staub (Eds.), *Patriotism in the lives of individuals and groups* (pp. 229–245). Chicago: Nelson-Hall.
Schatz, R. T., Staub, E., & Lavine, H. (1999). On the varieties of national attachment: Blind versus constructive patriotism. *Political Psychology, 20*, 151–175.
Shroeder, D. A., Penner, L. A., Dovidio, J. F., & Piliavin, J. A. (1995). *Psychology of helping and altruism: Problems and puzzles*. New York: McGraw-Hill.
Shaffer, D. R. (1995). *Social and personality development*. Monterey CA: Brooks-Cole.
Spielman, D., & Staub, E. (2000). Reducing boys' aggression: Learning to fulfill basic needs constructively. *Journal of Applied Developmental Psychology, 21*, 165–181.
Staub, E. (1971). The learning and unlearning of aggression: The role of anxiety, empathy, efficacy, and prosocial values. In J. Singer (Ed.), *The control of aggression and violence: Cognitive and physiological factors* (pp. 93–125). New York: Academic.
Staub, E. (1974). Helping a distressed person: Social, personality, and stim-

ulus determinants. In L. Berkowitz (Ed.), *Advances in experimental social psychology* (Vol. 7, pp. 203–242). New York: Academic.

Staub, E. (1975). To rear a prosocial child: Reasoning, learning by doing, and learning by teaching others. In D. J. DePalma & J. M. Foley (Eds.), *Moral development: Current theory and research* (pp. 113–135). Hillsdale NJ: Erlbaum.

Staub, E. (1978). *Positive social behavior and morality: Vol. 1. Social and personal influences*. New York: Academic.

Staub, E. (1979). *Positive social behavior and morality: Vol. 2. Socialization and development*. New York: Academic.

Staub, E. (1980). Social and prosocial behavior: Personal and situational influences and their interactions. In E. Staub (Ed.), *Personality: Basic aspects and current research* (pp. 237–294). Englewood Cliffs NJ: Prentice-Hall.

Staub, E. (1989a). *The roots of evil: The origins of genocide and other group violence*. New York: Cambridge University Press.

Staub, E. (1989b, May). What are your values and goals? *Psychology Today*, 46- 49.

Staub, E. (1993). The psychology of bystanders, perpetrators, and heroic helpers. *International Journal of Intercultural Relations, 17*, 315–341.

Staub, E. (1995). How people learn to care. In P. G. Schervish, V. A. Hodgkinson, M. Gates, et al. (Eds.), *Care and community in modern society: Passing on the tradition of service to future generations* (pp. 51–67). San Francisco: Jossey-Bass.

Staub, E. (1996a). Altruism and aggression in children and youth: Origins and cures. In R. Feldman (Ed.), *The psychology of adversity* (pp. 115–147). Amherst: University of Massachusetts Press.

Staub, E. (1996b). The cultural-societal roots of violence: The examples of genocidal violence and of contemporary youth violence in the United States. *American Psychologist, 51*, 17–132.

Staub, E. (1997). Blind versus constructive patriotism: Moving from embeddedness in the group to critical loyalty and action. In E. Staub & D. Bar-Tal (Eds.), *Patriotism in the lives of individuals and nations* (pp. 213–228). Chicago: Nelson-Hall.

Staub, E. (1998). Breaking the cycle of genocidal violence: Healing and reconciliation. In J. Harvey (Ed.), *Perspectives on loss* (pp. 231–238). Washington DC: Taylor & Francis.

Staub, E. (1999a). The origins and prevention of genocide, mass killing, and other collective violence. *Peace and Conflict: Journal of Peace Psychology, 5*, 303–337. (Lead article, followed by commentaries)

Staub, E. (1999b). The roots of evil: Personality, social conditions, culture, and basic human needs. *Personality and Social Psychology Review, 3*, 179–192.

Staub, E. (2002a). From healing past wounds to the development of inclusive caring: Contents and processes of peace education. In G. Salomon & B. Nevo (Eds.), *Peace education: The concepts, principles, and practices around the world* (pp. 73–89). Mahwah NJ: Erlbaum.

Staub, E. (2002b). Preventing terrorism: Raising "inclusively" caring children in the complex world of the 21st century. In C. E. Stout (Ed.), *The psychology of terrorism* (pp. 119–131). New York: Praeger.

Staub, E. (2003). *The psychology of good and evil: Why children, adults, and groups help and harm others*. New York: Cambridge University Press.

Staub, E. (n.d.-a). *Another form of heroism: Survivors saving themselves and its impact on their lives*. Manuscript in preparation.

Staub, E. (n.d.-b). *A brighter future: Raising caring, nonviolent, morally courageous children*. Manuscript in preparation.

Staub, E., & Pearlman, L. (2001). Healing, reconciliation, and forgiving after genocide and other collective violence. In S. J. Helmick & R. L. Petersen (Eds.), *Forgiveness and reconciliation: Religion, public policy, and conflict transformation*. Radnor PA: Templeton Foundation Press.

Staub, E., Pearlman, L. A., Gubin, A., & Hagengimana, A. (in press). "Healing, forgiveness, and reconciliation: Intervention and its experimental evaluation in Rwanda." *Journal of Social and Clinical Psychology*.

Staub, E., Pearlman, L. A., & Miller, V. (2003). Healing and roots of genocide in Rwanda. *Peace Review, 15*(3), 287–294.

Suomi, S. J., & Harlow, H. F. (1972). Social rehabilitation of isolate-reared monkeys. *Developmental Psychology, 6*, 487–496.

Surrey, J. (1985). *Self-in-relation: A theory of women's development*. Wellesley MA: Stone Center, Wellesley College.

Tec, N. (1986). *When light pierced the darkness: Christian rescue of Jews in Nazi-occupied Poland*. New York: Oxford University Press.

Thompson, R. A. (1998). Early sociopersonality development. In W. Damon (Series Ed.), N. Eisenberg (Vol. Ed.), *Handbook of child psychology: Vol. 3. Social, emotional, and personality development* (5th ed., pp. 25–104). New York: Wiley.

Thompson, W. R., & Grusec, J. (1970). Studies of early experience. In P. H. Mussen (Ed.), *Carmichael's manual of child psychology* (3d ed., Vol. 2, pp. 565–656). New York: Wiley.

Toch, H. (1969). *Violent men*. Chicago: Aldine.

Tompkins, S. (1965). The constructive role of violence and suffering for the individual and for his society. In S. S. Tomkins & C. E. Izard (Eds.), *Affect, cognition and personality: Empirical studies* (pp. 148–171). New York: Springer.

Triandis, H. C. (1994). *Cultural and social behavior*. New York: McGraw-Hill.

Troy, M., & Sroufe, L. A. (1987). Victimization among preschoolers: Role of attachment relationships. *Child and Adolescent Psychiatry, 26*, 166–172.

Valent, P. (1998). Child survivors: A review. In J. Kestenberg & C. Kahn (Eds.), *Children surviving persecution: An international study of trauma and healing*. New York: Praeger.

Waters, E., Wippman, J., & Sroufe, L. A. (1979). Attachment, positive affect, and competence in the peer group: Two studies in construct validation. *Child Development, 50*, 821–829.

Weiss, B., Dodge, K., Bates, S. E., & Pettit, G. S. (1992). Some consequences of early harsh discipline: Child aggression and a maladaptive social information processing style. *Child Development, 63,* 1325–1333.

Werner, E. E. (1987). Vulnerability and resiliency in children at risk for delinquency: A longitudinal study from birth to young adulthood. In J. D. Burchard & S. N. Burchard (Eds.), *Primary prevention of psychopathology: Vol. 10. Prevention of delinquent behavior* (pp. 16–43). Newbury Park CA: Sage.

Werner, E. E., & Smith, R. S. (1992). *Overcoming the odds: High risk children from birth to adulthood.* Ithaca: Cornell University Press.

Whiting, B. B., & Edwards, C. P. (1988). *Children of different worlds: The formation of social behavior.* Cambridge: Harvard University Press.

Whiting, B. B., & Whiting, J. W. M. (1975). *Children of six cultures: A psycho-cultural analysis.* Cambridge: Harvard University Press.

Widom, C. S. (1989a). The cycle of violence. *Science, 224,* 160–166.

Widom, C. S. (1989b). Does violence beget violence? A critical examination of the literature. *Psychological Bulletin, 106,* 3–28.

Yarrow, M. R., & Scott, P. M. (1972). Limitation of nurturant and nonnurturant models. *Journal of Personality and Social Psychology, 8,* 240–261.

Zahn-Waxler, C., & Radke-Yarrow, M. (1990). The origins of empathic concern. *Motivation and Emotion, 14,* 107–130.

Zakriski, A., Jacobs, M., & Coie, J. (1997). Coping with childhood peer rejection. In S. A. Wolchik & I. N. Sandler (Eds.), *Handbook of children's coping: Linking theory and intervention* (pp. 423–451). New York: Plenum.

The Development of Empathy-Related Responding

Nancy Eisenberg
Arizona State University

Over the centuries a minority of philosophers have argued that benevolence or caring plays a fundamental role in morality—a role even greater than that of rationality (Blum, 1980; Hume, 1777/1966; Noddings, 1984; Slote, 2001). Similarly, in recent decades numerous psychologists have proposed that empathy-related responding, including caring or sympathetic concern, motivates moral behavior, especially prosocial behavior (e.g., Batson, 1991; Hoffman, 1982; Mussen & Eisenberg-Berg, 1977; Staub, 1979), inhibits aggression and other antisocial behaviors (Feshbach & Feshbach, 1982), and contributes to the broader domain of social competence (e.g., Eisenberg & Miller, 1987). Thus, psychologists have increasingly recognized the potential importance of empathy in moral and socioemotional development.

The purpose of this chapter is to present research, primarily from our laboratory, pertaining to the role of empathy-related responding in moral and social development and to the origins of individual differences in empathy-related responding. Although the primary focus of my program of research in graduate school was moral reasoning, over time I became convinced by my own findings (as well as by

Work on this chapter was supported by a grant from the National Institute of Mental Health (R01 MH 60838).

those of others) that emotional factors were at least as important as purely rational ones in explaining moral motivation and behavior. Thus, I have become increasingly interested in the nature, effects, and origins of empathy-related responding.

In this chapter, I begin by defining critical constructs. Then I examine the relation of empathy-related responding to prosocial behavior, both in specific helping situations and in regard to dispositional differences (i.e., general, relatively enduring individual differences) in prosocial tendencies over time. In this body of research, there are findings that are consistent with the view that empathy/sympathy contributes to the continuity of prosocial behavior over time. I also briefly review findings from our laboratory on the relations of empathy-related responding to prosocial moral reasoning, aggression, and the quality of social functioning more generally. In the two final sections of this chapter, I briefly discuss two bodies of work related to the origins of empathy/sympathy: (1) research on the association of empathy-related responding with individual differences in emotionality and emotion-related regulation and (2) selected findings concerning the socialization of empathy-related responding.

Conceptual and Methodological Issues

As previously mentioned, many theorists and researchers have argued, and even assumed, that empathy motivates some prosocial behavior, especially prosocial acts based on other-oriented motives. However, in a meta-analytic review in 1982, Underwood and Moore found no empirical relation between empathy and an array of prosocial measures (e.g., helping, sharing). This unexpected pattern of findings probably was due to at least two factors (Eisenberg & Miller, 1987). First, prior to 1982, some important conceptual distinctions were not reflected in the empirical literature on empathy. Moreover, most of the early work reviewed by Underwood and Moore had been conducted with relatively young children using measures that had methodological problems.

In regard to conceptual issues, most investigators before 1982 had not differentiated between different types of empathy-related responding that might involve different affective motivations. By the early 1980s, Batson (1991; Batson, Duncan, Ackerman, Buckley, &

Birch, 1981), a social psychologist studying adults' empathy-related responding, had begun to differentiate empirically between empathy (i.e., what I will label *sympathy* below) and personal distress. In addition, Hoffman (1975) talked about sympathy emerging from empathic distress, although he did not clearly differentiate between these two responses.

Building on the work of Batson and Hoffman, my colleagues and I (Eisenberg & Fabes, 1998; Eisenberg, Shea, Carlo, & Knight, 1991) have attempted to differentiate among empathy, sympathy, and personal distress. We define *empathy* as an affective response that stems from the apprehension or comprehension of another's emotional state or condition and is similar to what the other person is feeling or would be expected to feel in the given situation. Thus, if a person views someone else who is sad and, consequently, feels sad himself or herself, that person is experiencing empathy. Sometimes this vicariously induced response is the outcome of direct exposure to another's emotion. In addition, if a person views another individual in a situation likely to elicit sadness (e.g., at a funeral of a loved one), the viewer might experience empathic sadness even if the other person does not overtly exhibit sadness. In this case, it is assumed that stored information about the effects of being in the given situation (e.g., experiencing the death of a loved one) or the process of mentally putting oneself in the other's situation has elicited empathy (given the lack of overt cues of emotion). Thus, empathic responding may be fairly automatic (although it must involve at least some self-other differentiation) or based on the cognitive process of accessing information relevant to another's emotional state (see Eisenberg, Shea, et al., 1991; Preston & de Waal, 2002).

We have argued that, in most situations, especially after infancy, empathy is likely to lead to sympathy, personal distress, or perhaps both of these emotional reactions (probably experienced sequentially). *Sympathy* is an emotional response stemming from the apprehension of another's emotional state or condition that is not the same as the other's state or condition but consists of feelings of sorrow or concern for the other. Thus, if a boy sees a sad girl and feels concern for her, he is experiencing sympathy. Such a sympathetic reaction often is based on empathic sadness (or a related empathic emotion), although it is probable that sympathy also can be based on cognitive perspective taking or accessing information from memory that is relevant to the other's experience (in addition to, or instead of, empathy). Further, we have suggested that empathy also can lead to personal distress rather than sympathy. *Personal distress* is a self-focused, aversive affective reaction to the apprehension of another's emotion (e.g., discomfort, anxiety; Batson, 1991). As I discuss later, we believe that personal distress often may stem from empathic over-arousal or a kind of distortion of highly arousing empathic emotion. However, it is possible that personal distress sometimes stems from other emotion-related processes (e.g., shame) or from retrieving relevant information from mental storage or through perspective taking (which then creates an aversive emotional state). Thus, empathy, sympathy, and personal distress are expected to involve different emotional experiences, although all three involve emotion and at least some minimum of cognitive processing (Eisenberg, Shea, et al., 1991).

The distinctions among empathy-related responses are critical if the goal is to predict social and moral functioning. For example, empathy-related responding frequently has been viewed as a motivator of prosocial behavior or the lack thereof. *Prosocial behavior* generally is defined as voluntary behavior intended to benefit another (Mussen & Eisenberg-Berg, 1977; Staub, 1979). It is a superordinate category that includes different kinds of prosocial behaviors, for example, helping, sharing, and comforting. More relevant to the issue at hand, prosocial behaviors often differ in regard to their motive. They can be motivated by a host of diverse factors, including egoistic concerns (e.g., the desire for reciprocity, a concrete reward, or social approval or the desire to alleviate one's own aversive emotional arousal), practical concerns (e.g., the desire to prevent unnecessary damage to an object), other-oriented concern (e.g., sympathy), and moral values (e.g., the desire to uphold internalized moral values such as those related to the worth or equality of all people or responsibilities for others). *Altruistic behaviors* often are defined as those prosocial behaviors motivated by other-oriented or moral concerns/emotions rather than egoistic or pragmatic concerns (Eisenberg, 1986) (although Batson (1991) seems to believe that internalized moral values do not motivate altruism).

Regardless of the precise definition of *altruism*, Batson (1991) argued that sympathy is associated with the desire to reduce another person's distress or need and, therefore, is likely to result in altruistic behavior. If this is true, sympathy would not be expected to relate to those prosocial behaviors motivated by factors such as personal gain, social approval, or the desire to alleviate one's own feelings of guilt, shame, or distress. In contrast, Batson proposed that, because personal distress is experienced as aversive, it is associated with the motivation to reduce one's own distress. Often this is achieved by avoiding contact with the needy or distressed other if it is possible to do so without too much cost (e.g., social disapproval). Individuals experiencing personal distress would be expected to assist others only when that is the easiest way to reduce helpers' own distress.

Given the differences in the hypothesized motivational bases and behaviors stemming from sympathy and personal distress, failure to differentiate between them (as well as among prosocial behaviors with different motivations) probably prevented early investigators from obtaining consistent findings concerning the relation between empathy-related responding and prosocial behavior. In addition, another factor that probably contributed to Underwood and Moore's (1982) failure to find this association was the type of measures used to study empathy in the 1970s, especially empathy in children. Most of the early studies of children's empathy involved the use of picture-story measures of empathy in which children were told a number of very short stories about evocative events (e.g., a child who lost his or her dog or at a birthday party), often accompanied by a small number of static pictures of the events. After hearing each story, children were asked how they themselves felt (and often how the story character felt). The brief scenarios used probably were too short to elicit much of an emotional response, and the children were expected to change emotions every couple of minutes in response to a new story. Moreover, with this method, children were pushed to report how they felt even if they may not have experienced any empathic emotion. Thus, these picture-story measures probably tapped children's desire to provide the desired or socially appropriate response more than children's actual empathic emotion (Eisenberg & Lennon, 1983; Eisenberg-Berg & Lennon, 1980; Lennon, Eisenberg, & Carroll, 1983; Miller, 1979). In fact, in a meta-analysis in which picture-story measures were examined separately from other indexes of empathy, they were unrelated to children's prosocial behavior (Eisenberg & Miller, 1987). Moreover, younger children's self-reported empathic reactions to others in experimental settings (usually involving videotapes of distressed or needy others) often (but not always) have been weakly related or unrelated to their prosocial behavior (Eisenberg & Fabes, 1990), probably because younger children have difficulty assessing or reporting their own emotional reactions. In contrast, most other types of measures (e.g., facial indices used with children, physiological indices, self-report questionnaires used with older children and adults, experimental manipulations) tend to be significantly associated with prosocial responding (Eisenberg & Fabes, 1990, 1991; Eisenberg & Miller, 1987). Thus, the heavy reliance on picture-story measures in early studies of empathy probably accounted, in part, for the lack of an association between empathy-related responding and prosocial behavior in many studies conducted in the 1970s and 1980s.

The Relation of Empathy-Related Responding to Prosocial Behavior: Empirical Findings

In the last two decades, researchers have obtained considerable evidence that children and adults who experience sympathy in response to empathy-evoking stimuli (e.g., audio- or videotapes) in the laboratory are more likely to assist others than are people who experience personal distress. For example, Batson (1991) conducted a series of primarily experimental studies in which he attempted to induce either sympathy or personal distress (e.g., through instructions to participants regarding perspective taking or distancing oneself while being exposed to empathy-inducing information). He found that adults in sympathy-eliciting situations (who generally tended to report more sympathy) were more likely to help the target of their sympathy than were adults who were in situations likely to induce less sympathy or more personal distress (or who reported more personal distress). In this research, Batson tried to minimize both social rewards for helping (i.e., the possibility of approval) and pressure to interact with the person in need.

Using measures that were more appropriate for children, Eisenberg, Fabes, and their colleagues and students obtained similar results with children. In this research, they used self-report, facial, and physiological measures of empathy-related responding. First they conducted a series of studies to validate that children and adults report different reactions and exhibit different physiological and facial reactions in sympathy-inducing and distressing contexts involving vicariously induced affect; then they examined the relations of these measures of sympathy and personal distress to prosocial behavior. In the first set of studies, Eisenberg, Fabes, and their colleagues found that children and adults tended to exhibit facial concerned attention and/or empathic sadness in sympathy-inducing contexts and, to a lesser degree, facial distress in situations believed to elicit personal distress. Moreover, older children's and adults' self-reports of their sympathy and personal distress were somewhat consistent with the emotional context (especially for sympathy; Eisenberg, Fabes, et al., 1988; Eisenberg, Fabes, Schaller, Miller, et al., 1991; Eisenberg, Schaller, et al., 1988; for reviews, see Eisenberg & Fabes, 1990; and Eisenberg, Losoya, & Spinrad, 2003). Young school-aged children's self-reports of sympathy and personal distress were less differentiated and contextually appropriate than those of older children and adults, although their reports of emotion in the evocative situations generally were somewhat consistent with the evocative stimulus (i.e., sympathy or distress inducing). Moreover, as predicted, study participants exhibited higher heart rate (HR) and skin conductance (SC) in the distressing situations. Both HR and SC arousal, especially the latter, have been viewed as measures of emotional arousal (Lazarus, 1974; MacDowell & Mandler, 1989; Winton, Putnam, & Krauss, 1984); thus, if the evocative stimuli are likely to elicit relatively high levels of empathy-related responding, relatively large increases in HR or SC may reflect personal distress (or empathic overarousal). In contrast, HR deceleration appears to coincide with interest in, and processing of information coming from, external stimuli—in this case the sympathy-inducing stimulus person (Cacioppo & Sandman, 1978). Thus, when HR deceleration co-occurs with the processing of important information about another's emotional state or situation, it may tap a process that contributes to the experience of sympathy.

Once we had at least partially validated our self-report, facial, and physiological measures of sympathy and personal distress, we used them to examine the relation between markers of empathy-related responding and adults' and children's prosocial behavior. In a series of studies we exposed individuals to empathy-inducing film clips, assessed their self-reported, facial, and physiological reactions to these clips, and then related individual differences in these reactions to children's and adults' helping or sharing with needy/distressed individuals (or others in a similar distressing situation) when it was easy to avoid contact with the needy other. For example, in some studies children and/or adults viewed a film of injured children who were talking about their experiences in the hospital. We measured HR and/or SC while the children watched the film, taped and coded their facial expressions during the film, and asked them to rate how they felt during the film (using a list of adjectives) soon after it was over. A short time later, they had the opportunity to assist the children in the film or others like them by helping in some way (e.g., giving up recess time to assist with compiling schoolwork or doing a boring task that would help the needy or distressed children rather than playing with attractive toys) or by donating part of their payment for participating in the study.

Across a number of studies we have found, as predicted by many theorists, links between empathy-related responding and prosocial behavior. In general findings with self-reports have been more mixed than those with facial and physiological measures. Nonetheless, by mid–elementary school or later, children's reports of positive mood to an empathy-inducing film tend to be negatively related with prosocial behavior, whereas reports of negative mood and distress often have been positively related (helping or donating; e.g., Eisenberg & Fabes, 1990; Eisenberg et al., 1989; Fabes, Eisenberg, & Eisenbud, 1993; Fabes, Eisenberg, & Miller, 1990). Even among preschoolers, reports of sad reactions (e.g., by pointing to pictures of facial expressions) to an empathy-inducing film have been positively related to helping of distressed children in a film, whereas reports of happiness have been negatively related (Miller, Eisenberg, Fabes, & Shell, 1996). Children's reports of feeling sorry for others generally have not predicted prosocial behavior in the same context (Fabes, Eisenberg, Karbon, Bernzweig, et al., 1994; Fabes, et al., 1993; Miller et al., 1996), although sometimes such reports have related to prosocial behavior in another context or toward other people (Eisenberg et al., 1990; Miller et al., 1996). Among adults, reports of experiencing sympathy often predict high levels of helping (Carlo, Eisenberg, Troyer, Switzer, & Speer, 1991; Eisenberg et al., 1989; see also Batson, 1991). Unexpectedly, adults' reports of relatively high distress sometimes also predict higher levels of prosocial behavior, perhaps because many adults have difficulty differentiating between distress for another and distress for themselves in their self-reports (especially when the empathy-inducing context is not highly distressing; Batson, Bolen,

Cross, & Neuringer-Benefiel, 1986; Eisenberg et al., 1989). Positive correlations between adults' reports of sympathy or personal distress and indices of social desirability suggest that their self-reports sometimes may not reflect their true emotional reactions (Eisenberg et al., 1989), although social desirability does not seem to be substantially related to younger children's reports of situational empathy-related responding (e.g., Eisenberg, Fabes, Schaller, Carlo, & Miller, 1991).

Findings for physiological markers of sympathy and personal distress are somewhat more consistent than are findings for self-reported empathy-related responding. Thus, despite some variability in the findings, HR deceleration (vs. acceleration) during the critical, evocative portion of an empathy-inducing film generally has been associated with higher levels of prosocial behavior (Eisenberg & Fabes, 1990; Eisenberg et al., 1989; Eisenberg et al., 1990; see also Zahn-Waxler, Cole, Welsh, & Fox, 1995). Similarly, using a more life-like paradigm, Fabes, Eisenberg, Karbon, Troyer, and Switzer (1994) also found that HR responding in response to a crying baby (acceleration vs. deceleration) was negatively related to young elementary school children's quality (but not quantity) of comforting behavior (cf. Eisenberg, Fabes, Carlo, et al., 1993). In contrast, HR taken while children view an entire empathy-inducing film (rather than an evocative short segment) has been positively related to prosocial behavior (Hastings, Zahn-Waxler, Robinson, Usher, & Bridges, 2000), perhaps because the aforementioned HR deceleration in response to viewing an especially evocative event lasts only a brief period of time. Moreover, as is discussed further shortly, when the empathy-evoking stimuli are not highly evocative, higher levels of physiological responding may reflect empathy rather than personal distress.

Although there is less research on the relation between SC and prosocial behavior, SC during exposure to empathy stimuli also has been associated with lower levels of prosocial behavior. For example, in a study with elementary school children, SC reactivity accounted for a significant amount of the variance in helping behavior, above and beyond all other predictors (i.e., facial indexes; Fabes, Eisenberg, Karbon, Bernzweig, et al., 1994). In other studies, SC responsivity has been negatively related to teachers' reports of children's prosocial behavior (Holmgren, Eisenberg, & Fabes, 1998) and mothers' ratings of girls' (but not boys') helpfulness (Fabes et al., 1993). Thus, SC—believed to be an indicator of personal distress—has been linked not only to low prosocial responding in an empathy-inducing context but also to low levels of dispositional prosocial behavior.

Finally, facial concerned attention (or sadness) in children when viewing empathy-inducing films tends to be positively related to prosocial behavior, whereas facial distress or happiness tends to be negatively related, although in general this pattern of findings is more consistent for boys than for girls (e.g., Eisenberg & Fabes, 1990; Eisenberg et al., 1990; Fabes et al., 1990; Fabes, Eisenberg, Karbon, Bernzweig, et al., 1994). Similarly, facial distress in response to hearing a crying infant was negatively related to children's attempts to calm the infant in one study (Eisenberg, Fabes, Carlo, et al., 1993) albeit not in another (Fabes, Eisenberg, Karbon, Troyer, and Switzer, 1994). In another paradigm in which adults (mothers and an experimenter) simulated injuries, preschoolers' facial concern/worry in response to these simulations was associated with attempts to help the adults, whereas their distressed reactions were negatively related (Miller et al., 1996). Thus, facial reactions in a specific situation (e.g., in reaction to a film or a crying infant) tend to predict helping in the near future of the same or a similar victim.

In summary, findings from our laboratory, as well as from others' research programs (for reviews, see Batson, 1991; Eisenberg & Fabes, 1998; Eisenberg & Miller, 1987), are consistent with the notion that sympathy elicited by a specific situation is associated with enhanced prosocial responding toward the needy or distressed individual(s) (or others similar to them) whereas personal distress reactions sometimes are negatively related to helping/sharing. As might be expected, empathy-related reactions elicited in one specific setting do not always predict prosocial behavior in other settings, although they sometimes predict prosocial dispositions as rated by others or prosocial behavior directed toward people in another context (e.g., Fabes et al., 1993; Holmgren et al., 1998; Miller et al., 1996). Moreover, measures of dispositional sympathy (often questionnaires) sometimes predict adults' reports of children's prosocial behavior or children's actual prosocial behavior that is not specifically linked to the measure of sympathy (e.g., Eisenberg, Carlo, Murphy, & Van Court, 1995; Eisenberg, Miller, Shell, McNalley, & Shea, 1991; Knight, Johnson, Carlo, & Eisenberg, 1994).

In considering the association between empathy-related responding and prosocial behavior, it is important to keep in mind that sympathy would be expected to be associated primarily with altruistic prosocial behaviors, whereas distress reactions might predict relatively high levels of nonaltruistic prosocial behavior, such as helping others when it is difficult to escape from another's distress or requests for assistance. Although there is relatively little research in which sympathy and personal distress have been examined in relation to various types of prosocial actions, initial findings with preschoolers illustrate the importance of such distinctions. For example, Eisenberg and colleagues found that children's spontaneously offered prosocial behaviors, especially costly sharing (rather than less costly minor helping behaviors), tend to be correlated with children's sympathy/empathy (Eisenberg et al., 1999; Eisenberg, McCreath, & Ahn, 1988). In contrast, young children's prosocial behaviors that occur in response to peers' requests tend to be related to high levels of personal distress (e.g., Eisenberg et al., 1990; Eisenberg, McCreath, & Ahn, 1988). It appears that preschoolers who engage in relatively high frequencies of such compliant behavior may not comply to a higher proportion of requests (Eisenberg, McCreath, & Ahn, 1988); rather, they assist more often because they frequently are the target of peers' requests for sharing or helping (Eisenberg, Cameron, Tryon, & Dodez, 1981) and are not very assertive in their interactions with peers (Eisenberg et al., 1981; Eisenberg et al., 1990). Thus, these children frequently seem to help because they are not assertive enough to resist attempts by peers to secure their toys or assistance, not because of concern for others. As is discussed shortly, preschoolers' spontaneously emitted and compliant prosocial behaviors also relate differently to their moral reasoning and to the prediction of prosocial tendencies over time. Therefore, it is possible that some of the inconsistencies in the research on the relation between empathy-related responding and prosocial behavior are due to lack of attention to, or information regarding, the motivational significance of the given prosocial behavior.

The Relation of Empathy-Related Responding to the Prediction of Prosocial Dispositions Across Development

As when predicting concurrent relations between empathy-related responding and prosocial behavior, it also is important to consider the motivation underlying prosocial behaviors when predicting their consistency over time. For individuals who assist others primarily for egoistic gain, one would not expect much consistency in measures of prosocial functioning over time. This is because such individuals would be expected to assist only in situations in which gain is likely, not in the many situations in which another person is needy or distressed but helping is not especially likely to result in benefits for the benefactor. In contrast, people prone to sympathy would be expected to assist others in a variety of situations in which others are experiencing, or might be expected to experience, distress, sadness, or some other negative emotion or need. Of course, sympathetic people may not be prone to assist others who are not in need or experiencing negative emotions, but in many helping situations the other person is in distress or need or is at risk for some negative outcome in the future. Thus, individuals prone to sympathy, in comparison to those who are not (or who are prone primarily to egoistic personal distress), would be expected to exhibit prosocial behavior across a wider variety of settings and with greater frequency.

Consistent with this reasoning, in a longitudinal study of prosocial responding, we have found that children who appear to experience concern for others' needs are those who are most likely to exhibit prosocial dispositions, not only concurrently, but also across childhood into early adulthood. When the participants in this longitudinal study were 4 or 5 years old, we observed their naturally occurring prosocial behaviors at school. These behaviors were coded as occurring spontaneously (without a peer's verbal or nonverbal request) or in response to a request (i.e., compliant prosocial behavior) and also as helping or sharing (little comforting was observed). Helping behaviors usually were low in cost, such as reaching for paint for someone or tying a peer's apron. Sharing generally was higher in cost because it required giving up an object or space in the child's possession. At age 4–5 (i.e., the first assessment), we found that spontaneous sharing, but not the other types of prosocial behavior (e.g., compliant helping or sharing), was related to preschoolers' references to others' needs in their moral reasoning about prosocial moral dilemmas (i.e., dilemmas in which one person's needs conflict with those of another in a situation in which the role of rules, laws, authorities' dictates, or formal obligations was minimal; Eisenberg-Berg & Hand, 1979). Thus, consistent with findings in another study in which preschoolers' spontaneous sharing was negatively related to hedonistic prosocial moral reasoning (Eisenberg, Pasternack, Cameron, & Tryon, 1984), preschoolers' spontaneous sharing seemed to be related to rudimentary other-oriented, rather than self-oriented, concerns (Eisenberg-Berg & Hand, 1979).

This sample of children has been studied approximately every 1½ or 2 years for over 20 years since preschool. Starting when they reached late childhood, and continuing in their adolescence, we obtained measures of low-cost (e.g., helping pick up dropped paper clips) and/or high-cost (e.g., donating money) prosocial behaviors, mothers' reports of prosocial behaviors (at ages 13–14, 15–16, and 17–18), and self-reports of helping, empathy, sympathy, personal distress, and/or perspective taking (fewer measures were obtained at younger ages). In early adulthood, we obtained self-reports of prosocial tendencies and values, sympathy, perspective taking, and personal distress as well as friends' reports of the participants' helping behavior, sympathy, and perspective taking.

In general, we have found remarkable relations between children's early prosocial behavior and their later prosocial tendencies, sympathy, and perspective taking, but primarily for the type of prosocial behavior (spontaneous sharing) that seemed to involve self-initiation and a cost to the self—that is, prosocial behaviors most likely to involve sympathy. Eisenberg et al. (2002) and Eisenberg et al. (1999) found that spontaneous sharing was at least marginally significantly correlated with costly donating of money at ages 9–10 and 11–12; costly helping (doing extra work for the experimenter for no additional pay) at age 17–18; self-reported helping at age 15–16; self-reported consideration for others at age 19–20; a self-report prosocial aggregate measure at ages 21–22, 23–24, and 25–26 (which included helping, care orientation, social responsibility, consideration for others, suppression of aggression, sympathy, and perspective taking combined); mothers' reports of helpfulness at ages 15–16 and 17–18; self-reported sympathy at ages 13–14, 15–16, 17–18, 19–20, and 21–22; perspective taking at ages 17–18, 19–20, and 21–22; and friends' reports of sympathy at ages 19–20, 21–22, 23–24, and 25–26. In contrast, spontaneous sharing generally was unrelated to self-reported empathy in childhood (a measure likely to reflect a combination of empathy, sympathy, personal distress, perspective taking, and other variables), self-reported personal distress, and adult friends' reports of perspective taking or prosocial behavior (although, as already noted, it was related to friends' reports of sympathy). It is quite possible that adult friends had few opportunities to observe many of the specific prosocial actions that they were asked to rate for their friend in the helping questionnaire measure (e.g., helping someone across the street) and may have had difficulty assessing whether the study participants cognitively took the perspective of others (because this is a mental process, not an overt behavior). In any case, spontaneous sharing in preschool was fairly consistently related to self-reports of prosocial responding and sympathy in late childhood, adolescence, and early adulthood and sometimes predicted actual prosocial behavior and mothers' reports thereof. This relation between early spontaneous sharing and both self-reported prosocial tendencies (e.g., helping, sympathy, perspective taking, care orientation, social responsibility) and friend-reported prosocial tendencies was evident even at age 25–26 (although the latter relation was marginally significant; Eisenberg et al., 2002). Of particular interest, individual differences in sympathy appeared to mediate the relation between early levels of spontaneous sharing and prosocial tendencies in late adolescence and early adulthood (Eisenberg et al., 1999).

In contrast to the findings for spontaneous sharing, there were relatively few relations between the other types of prosocial behavior (especially spontaneous or compliant helping) and measures of prosocial responding in childhood, adolescence, or adulthood. Preschoolers higher in compliant sharing reported being relatively helpful at three ages during adolescence and again at age 25–26; however, compliant sharing was not correlated with actual prosocial behavior, mothers' reports of prosocial behavior, or friends' reports of prosocial tendencies or sympathy in adulthood (Eisenberg, Miller, et al., 1991; Eisenberg et al., 2002), although it was marginally positively related to friends' reports of sympathy at age 25–26 (unreported data in Eisenberg et al., 2002). Thus, early compliant sharing was related to self-perceptions of helping in adolescence and the mid-20s but was not related to other, non-self-report measures of prosocial tendencies (or to measures of sympathy; Eisenberg et al., 2002; Eisenberg et al., 1999).

It is also of interest that there was considerable consistency in the various indices of prosociality over time from early adolescence into adulthood. Indeed, measures of self-reported prosociality were nearly always substantially related to the same or similar measures assessed up to 16 years earlier. For example, self-reported helping at ages 21–22, 23–24, and 25–26 on a short version of Rushton, Chrisjohn, and Fekken's (1981) self-report prosocial behavior scale were significantly related to reports on the longer version of the scale at ages 13–14, 15–16, and 17–18 (average $r = .52$). Similarly, self-reports of sympathy on Davis's (1994) measure of empathy-related responding at ages 21–22, 23–24, and 25–26 were positively related to empathy on Bryant's (1982) empathy scale at ages 11–12 (average $r = .54$) and 13–14 (average $r = .66$). Self-reported sympathy at 23–24 (but not at other ages in early adulthood) also was related to self-reported empathy at 9–10 years of age ($r = .49$). In addition, self-reported prosocial dispositions at age 21–22 or older (i.e., the composite measures discussed previously) generally were at least marginally positively correlated with mothers' reports of participants' prosocial behavior in adolescence. Moreover, all correlations between self-reported sympathy at the three assessments when the participants were in their 20s and those at ages 15–16, 17–18, or 19–20 were significant (average $r = .62$). Thus, it appeared that individual differences in prosocial dispositions were quite stable in adolescence into early adulthood. Notably these correlations changed little when controlling for social desirability. Moreover, the findings were not due to highly skewed variables or outliers (we checked especially carefully because the sample size in this study was small).

In summary, it appears that other-oriented, costly prosocial behaviors in early childhood are predictive of prosocial tendencies in adolescence and adulthood and that there is considerable consistency in sympathetic and prosocial tendencies in adolescence into adulthood. It is likely that this consistency in prosocial tendencies is partly due to consistency in the empathic/sympathetic tendencies that were reflected in young children's spontaneous sharing behaviors (recall that this type of prosocial behavior was related to preschoolers' other-oriented moral reasoning) and continued to be associated with prosocial behavior (and concurrent moral reasoning, as is discussed next) in adolescence and early adulthood. The finding that sympathy statistically mediated the relation between early spontaneous sharing behaviors and later measures of prosocial functioning is consistent with this view (Eisenberg et al., 1999), as is the finding that spontaneously emitted prosocial behaviors tend to be correlated with empathy/sympathy (Eisenberg, McCreath, & Ahn, 1988). In future research it would be interesting to more clearly delineate the degree to which sympathy (or the lack thereof) and personal distress differentially motivate prosocial behaviors in different contexts and across development.

Empathy-Related Responding and Moral Reasoning

If empathy-related responding, especially sympathy, frequently is the motive for other-oriented (altruistic) prosocial behavior, we would expect it to relate to moral reasoning as well as to prosocial behavior. This is because the beliefs and motives that guide moral decisions are believed to be reflected in the level of moral reasoning that a person expresses, at least within the range of levels that the individual is capable of understanding (Eisenberg, 1986). Thus, even if children are not capable of understanding or expressing higher levels of moral judgment, we would expect children prone to empathy and sympathy (especially the latter) to verbalize higher levels of rudimentary other-oriented concerns and fewer hedonistic, egoistic concerns than their less sympathetic peers (Eisenberg, 1986). Because moral judgment has been associated with individual differences in moral behavior (Blasi, 1980; Underwood & Moore, 1982), including prosocial behavior (e.g., Carlo, Koller, Eisenberg, DaSilva, & Frohlich, 1996; for reviews, see Eisenberg, 1986; and Eisenberg & Fabes, 1998), associations of empathy-related responding to moral judgment suggest another pathway through which empathy-related responding may affect moral behavior.

An association between empathy-related vicarious responding and moral reasoning is likely to be particularly evident in regard to individuals' prosocial (in contrast to justice-oriented; Colby, Kohlberg, Gibbs, & Lieberman, 1983) moral reasoning. Recall that prosocial moral reasoning is reasoning about moral dilemmas in which one person's needs or desires conflict with those of others in a context in which the role of formal prohibitions, authorities' dictates, and formal obligations is minimal (Eisenberg, 1986; Eisenberg-Berg, 1979). Given the content of the moral dilemmas used to assess prosocial moral reasoning, it is not surprising that the empathy-related reasons are quite common in prosocial moral judgment—probably more so than in moral reasoning related to justice (Kohlberg, 1984)—even in the moral judgments of younger children (Eisenberg-Berg,

1979; Eisenberg-Berg & Hand, 1979). Research and theory on prosocial moral reasoning are outgrowths of the larger body of work on moral judgment, which is based on Kohlberg's (1981) pioneering theory and research.

The relative roles of cognition and affect in morality—including in moral reasoning—have been a topic of debate for many years, especially in philosophy (e.g., Hume, 1777/1966; Kant, 1797/1964; Rawls, 1971). Influenced by philosophers such as Kant, cognitive-developmental theorists have asserted that cognition and rationality are central to morality (Kohlberg, 1969). For example, Kohlberg (1976; see also Colby et al., 1983) argued that the capabilities for complex perspective taking (cognitively taking the perspective of another) and for understanding abstract, morally relevant conceptions underlie advances in moral reasoning and in the quality of prosocial behavior. Children are expected to develop higher-level moral reasoning as they become capable of the cognitive skills required for understanding such reasoning and are viewed as most often reasoning at the highest levels of their understanding (although individuals are believed to express some reasoning slightly below or above the level they best comprehend).

Kohlberg's view differs from that of other investigators (e.g., Eisenberg, 1986; Rest, 1979), who have suggested that individuals use a variety of levels of moral judgment among those within their competence, depending on the situation and on individual differences in their beliefs, values, needs, goals, and empathy-related capacities. From this perspective, affect, especially empathy-related responding or guilt, not only functions as a motive for other-oriented moral behavior, but also can influence individuals' moral reasoning (Eisenberg, 1986; Haidt, 2001; Hoffman, 2000). As already discussed, people who experience sympathy are expected to be motivated to consider and respond to others' needs, even if there is a moderate cost of doing so (Batson, 1991; Hoffman, 2000). Hoffman (1987) further argued that sympathy/empathy stimulates the development of internalized moral reasoning reflecting concern for others' welfare; thus, he posited that empathy-related responding contributes to the development of moral reasoning. In addition, Eisenberg (1986) suggested that sympathy primes the use of preexisting other-oriented moral cognitions in given situations; thus, sympathy (and perhaps empathy) is viewed as affecting the construction of moral judgments in specific situations (as well as its development). On the basis of such theoretical assertions, Eisenberg, Zhou, and Koller (2001) hypothesized, not only that empathy-related responding and prosocial moral reasoning are related, but also that prosocial moral reasoning also partly mediates the relation of sympathy to prosocial behavior.

In a number of studies, we have obtained support for the view that empathy-related responding is related to prosocial or care-oriented moral reasoning (for a discussion of the role of affect in moral reasoning, see also Haidt, 2001). Skoe, Eisenberg, and Cumberland (2002) examined adults' care-related reasoning, a type of moral judgment based on Gilligan's (1982) differentiation of care-related and justice-related reasoning. They found an association between adults' reports of experiencing sympathy when resolving moral conflicts and their care-related moral reasoning, especially when discussing a real-life moral dilemma. In addition, the adults' reports of feelings of sympathy in regard to a particular moral conflict were positively correlated with their ratings of the importance of the given real-life or hypothetical moral dilemma.

Moreover, in the longitudinal study of prosocial moral reasoning discussed previously, we have repeatedly found concurrent correlations between reported sympathy (or empathy at younger ages) and higher-level prosocial moral reasoning, the greater use of empathy-related types of moral reasoning, and/or reduced use of hedonistic reasoning (Eisenberg, Carlo, et al., 1995; Eisenberg, Miller, et al., 1991; Eisenberg et al., 1987). For example, at age 9–10, self-reported empathy on Bryant's (1982) scale was negatively related to hedonistic reasoning and positively related to the overall level of children's prosocial moral reasoning. At age 11–12, empathy also was related to higher levels of simple reasoning pertaining to the needs of another (Eisenberg, Miller, et al., 1991). In adolescence, self-reported sympathy often was negatively related to hedonistic moral reasoning and positively related to overall moral reasoning; occasionally it also was positively related to needs-oriented reasoning or to higher-level internalized moral reasoning (Eisenberg, Carlo, et al., 1995; Eisenberg, Miller, et al., 1991). In addition to these concurrent correlations, there were numerous relations between measures of prosocial moral judgment in early adulthood (ages 21–22, 23–24, or 25–26) and measures of sympathy or empathy at younger ages, including some with empathy reported at age 9–10 or 11–12. Indeed, the majority of the correlations between measures of prosocial moral reasoning in adulthood and self-reported empathy at ages 9–10, 11–12, and 13–14 were significant, as were most of the correlations with 15–16- and 17–18-year-olds' reports of sympathy. This finding of a correlation between moral reasoning in the mid-20s and empathy/sympathy in childhood and adolescence is especially notable because prosocial moral reasoning as assessed with interviews in early adulthood seldom was significantly related to similar moral reasoning assessed more than 6 years prior. In contrast to sympathy, personal distress infrequently was related to measures of prosocial moral judgment (Eisenberg et al., 2002).

A similar pattern of relations between sympathy and moral reasoning has been obtained in other samples of adolescents in the United States (e.g., Carlo, Eisenberg, & Knight, 1992; Eisenberg-Berg & Mussen, 1978) and in Brazil (e.g., Eisenberg, Zhou, & Koller, 2001). For example, Carlo et al. (1992) found that U.S. adolescents' self-reported sympathy was negatively related to their hedonistic and approval-oriented moral reasoning (i.e., relatively low-level types of prosocial moral reasoning) and positively related to their higher-level, internalized moral reasoning. In contrast, personal distress was positively related to approval-oriented reasoning and negatively related to internalized (and stereotypical) moral reasoning (relatively advanced modes of moral judgment). Furthermore, the association between prosocial moral reasoning and sympathy/empathy has been found in the preschool years. In one study, preschoolers who exhibited facial concern (for boys) or sadness (for girls) and/or who reported feeling sad while viewing two empathy-inducing films used relatively high prosocial moral reasoning for their age (i.e., social-normative reasoning). In contrast, the children's self-reported happiness when viewing the films was negatively related to their need-oriented moral reasoning and positively related to lower-level (authority-oriented or hedonistic) moral reasoning (Miller et al., 1996). Findings such as these, albeit correlational, are consistent with the view that empathy-related responding contributes to moral reasoning (and perhaps vice versa).

In a study of adolescents in Brazil, we (Eisenberg, Zhou, & Koller, 2001) explicitly examined the possibility that prosocial moral reasoning mediates the relation of sympathy to prosocial behavior. In a structural equation model, sympathy (as well as cognitive perspective taking) predicted adolescents' level of prosocial moral reasoning, which in turn predicted their self-reported prosocial behavior (this measure correlated substantially with peer-reported prosocial behavior in another sample). In this model, perspective taking had a direct path to sympathy, and sympathy had a direct path, as well as a mediated path (through moral reasoning), to prosocial behavior (see Figure 1). Thus, although the model was based on concurrent, correlational data and cannot prove causality, the results are consistent with the view that sympathy contributes to prosocial behavior directly as well as through its effects on prosocial moral reasoning. Of further interest, a model with a direct path added from perspective taking to prosocial behavior (in addition to the mediated relation of perspective taking to prosocial behavior through prosocial moral reasoning) did not fit the data as well as the model without that path, and the added path was not significant. Thus, the findings were consistent with the view that any effects of perspective taking on prosocial behavior were through its effects on sympathy and prosocial moral reasoning. This supports the view that perspective taking does not always promote prosocial behavior and that the degree to which it does is based on how much it stimulates sympathy and/or contributes to higher-level moral reasoning.

The Relations of Empathy-Related Responding to Antisocial Behavior and Social Competence

Although theorists and researchers have been particularly interested in the relation of empathy-related responding to prosocial behavior, they have also suggested that empathy/sympathy contributes to individual differences in adjustment (especially aggression) and social competence (Cohen & Strayer, 1996; Miller & Eisenberg, 1988). Feshbach (e.g., Feshbach & Feshbach, 1982) and others (e.g., Mehrabian & Epstein, 1972) have suggested that empathy plays an important function in the reduction or inhibition of aggressive actions toward others. According to this view, people who tend to experience vicariously the negative emotions of others when they perceive cues of others' negative emotions are inclined to inhibit behaviors that have hurtful effects for others and to reduce their aggression in subsequent interactions. This argument is consistent with the recognition that deficits in empathy and remorse are common in individuals with

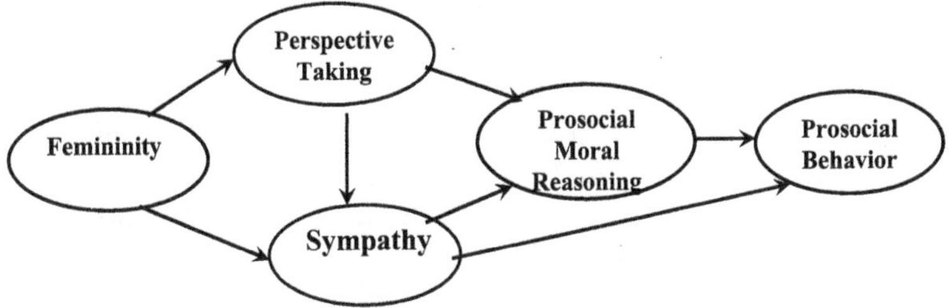

Figure 1. Adapted from Eisenberg, Zhou, and Koller (2001). All paths are significant and positive.

antisocial personality disorders (American Psychiatric Association, 1994; Frick, 1998; Lynam, 1997).

There is some empirical support for the proposed link between empathy/sympathy and antisocial tendencies. In a meta-analytic review (Miller & Eisenberg, 1988), empathic/sympathetic responding was negatively related to aggression and externalizing behaviors when the aggression/externalizing problems were assessed with questionnaires (that probably tap dispositional or trait empathy/sympathy across a range of settings). In contrast, the relation between empathy and aggression/externalizing problems was not significant when empathy/sympathy was assessed with facial/gestural reactions or self-reports in reaction to experimental stimuli designed to evoke empathy/sympathy (i.e., measures of situational empathy/sympathy).

Thus, according to this 1988 review, the association between empathy and antisocial or externalizing behavior is weakest when empathy/sympathy is assessed in a specific situation. However, in some of the studies in this review involving situational measures of empathy, empathy was assessed using the picture-story measures that have been found to be problematic (e.g., that probably are not very evocative and may assess social desirability more than empathy; Eisenberg & Lennon, 1983; Lennon, Eisenberg, & Carroll, 1983). In addition, in some studies in that review, facial or self-reported reactions to viewing others' emotions tapped empathic responding to others' positive as well as negative emotions (see Miller & Eisenberg, 1988). As suggested by a number of theorists (e.g., Hoffman, 1982; Feshbach, 1982), empathy with positive emotions (e.g., happiness) may not be equivalent to empathy with negative emotions (e.g., sadness, fear). In fact, empathy with positive emotions has been positively related to boys' aggression, whereas empathy with negative emotions has been negatively related (Feshbach, 1982). Moreover, men's empathy with positive emotions has been related to their cognitive role-taking skills, whereas their empathy with negative emotions has been associated with sympathy (called *empathic concern*; Davis, Hull, Young, & Warren, 1987). Thus, it is possible that Miller and Eisenberg found weak, generally nonsignificant relations between empathy-related responding and situational measures of empathy/sympathy because empathy with others' positive emotions relates differently to aggression than does empathy with negative emotions and these two types of empathic reactions sometimes were not differentiated. In addition, in most of the early studies included in the Miller and Eisenberg meta-analysis, sympathy and personal distress generally were not differentiated, which could have reduced the strength of obtained relations. Consistent with this notion, Cole, Zahn-Waxler, Fox, Usher, and Welsh (1996) found that children's moderate level of expressiveness in response to empathy-inducing films (probably indicative of sympathy) was positively related to adjustment, whereas high levels of expressivity (probably indicative of personal distress) were related to high levels of externalizing problems.

If empathy or sympathy inhibits aggression and promotes prosocial behavior, it also would be expected to foster social competence. Consistent with this view, Eisenberg and Miller (1987) conducted a meta-analysis and found a positive, albeit weak, association between measures of empathy-related responding and diverse measures of social competence. However, at that time, relevant data were limited, and many studies included the same problematic picture-story measures of empathy used in the Eisenberg and Miller (1987) and Underwood and Moore (1982) reviews.

More recent findings often have been consistent with the view that dispositional empathy-related responding is linked with individual differences in social competence and aggression/antisocial. For example, in a longitudinal study, we found that teachers' reports of 6- to 8-year-olds' dispositional sympathy were significantly correlated with relatively high teacher-rated social skills 2 years earlier (in preschool/kindergarten), concurrent teacher ratings of nonaggressive/socially appropriate behavior and prosocial/social competence (e.g., popularity), mothers' ratings of low levels of concurrent externalizing problems (including aggression and antisocial behavior), and children's socially competent enacted and verbal responses in a puppet game in which they indicated what they would do in various hypothetical social conflicts with peers (concurrently and 2 years before). Children's self-reported dispositional sympathy was positively related to teachers' ratings of their social skills 2 years prior, peer sociometric status 2 years earlier, and children's socially constructive responses on the puppet task (concurrently and 2 years prior). Four years later, when the children were 10–12 years old, teachers' reports of students' dispositional sympathy were at least marginally positively related to teachers' reports of social competence concurrently and 2, 4, and 6 years earlier (more so for girls for the early assessments) as well as to same-sex peers' reports of social status 8 years earlier. Similarly, mothers' reports of children's dispositional sympathy were negatively related to mothers' and/or fathers' reports of externalizing problems (e.g., aggression, stealing) 2, 4, and 6 years before, especially for boys (Murphy, Shepard, Eisenberg, Fabes, & Guthrie, 1999).

We also have found links between sympathy and social functioning/adjustment in a study of third graders in Indonesia. In this study, teachers' or parents' reports of children's dispositional sympathy tended to be associated with adults' own reports of children's adjustment (i.e., low levels of externalizing problems) and popularity. In addition, teachers' reports of children's sympathy were positively related to parents' and peers' reports of popularity/social status and negatively related to parents' reports of externalizing problems and peers' reports of fighting (parents' reports of children's sympathy were correlated only with their own reports of low externalizing behavior and high popularity; Eisenberg, Liew, & Pidada, 2001).

Children's aggressive tendencies also have been correlated with situational measures of empathy-related responding. In a study of kindergartners and third graders, Fabes, Eisenberg, Karbon, Troyer, & Switzer, (1994) found that mothers' reports of children's aggressive coping were positively associated with markers of boys' (but not girls') personal distress (i.e., HR acceleration and facial stress) when the children heard a crying infant. In a more recent study, Zhou et al. (2002) found that children's situational empathy with slides depicting negative facial expressions or people in negative situations was correlated with both relatively high social competence and low levels of externalizing problems. In this study, children's facial and self-reported reactions to viewing mildly evocative slides of other people in positive or negative situations were assessed at two times, 2 years apart, in elementary school. In addition, parents and teachers reported on the children's externalizing problem behaviors and social skills (i.e., socially appropriate behavior and peer social status). In early elementary school, children's facial empathy (negative facial affect) in response to the slides depicting negative (but not positive) situations or others' facial expressions was negatively related to parents' and teachers' reports of children's externalizing problem behaviors; children's self-reported reactions were not related to their externalizing problems or social skills. Two years later, children's facial empathy to negative slides and their self-reported empathy to both positive and negative slides (i.e., matching of the emotion in the slides) tended to be associated with higher levels of adult-reported social skills and lower levels of adult-reported externalizing problems. In a structural equation model, empathy with the negative slides at the second assessment had stronger unique relations with children's concurrent social skills and low levels of externalizing problems than did empathy with positive slides, and this relation with problem behaviors held even when controlling for level of empathy 2 years before. Thus, children's empathy was related to their social functioning, especially for empathy in response to others' negative emotions. Findings such as these suggest that there is an association between empathy-related responding and aggression but that it is important to consider whether empathy with positive or negative emotions is assessed.

Consistent with Zhou et al.'s (2002) findings, low levels of empathy may be especially important in the development of psychopathic tendencies and externalizing problems. Psychopaths or people with psychopathic traits appear to be less physiologically responsive to emotion-inducing stimuli (often mildly evocative slides) and to cues of others' distress than are nonpsychopaths (Blair, 1999; Blair, Jones, Clark, & Smith, 1997; Levenston, Patrick, Bradley, & Lang, 2000; see also Hastings et al., 2000). Thus, children who are not reactive to mild empathy-inducing stimuli may be at risk for externalizing problems. In a recent study, we (e.g., Liew et al., 2003) found that boys (but not girls) who exhibited more HR or SC responsivity when viewing slides depicting mild negative events or facial expressions were better regulated and had fewer externalizing problem behaviors than their less responsive peers. Because the stimuli were so mild, physiological arousal in this sample would not be expected to indicate personal distress (as it would in studies involving more evocative stimuli). It is important to keep in mind that a lack of either empathy or empathic overarousal (i.e., personal distress) may contribute to problems in moral and socioemotional development.

Regulation, Emotion, and Empathy-Related Responding

As discussed previously, investigators generally have found that markers of sympathy and personal distress relate differently to prosocial behavior and moral reasoning. Thus, we started to speculate about the nature and origins of the experience of these vicarious emotions. Hoffman (1982) suggested that overarousal due to empathy results in a self-focus. Consistent with this view, we hypothesized that empathic overarousal in situations involving negative emotion results in an aversive emotional state, which leads to a self-focus—that is, to personal distress. Individuals who are unable to maintain their emotional reactions within a tolerable range (and become overaroused) would be expected to focus on their own emotional needs and to behave in a manner that does not foster positive social interactions in situations involving negative emotion (one's own or others'). Evidence for the notion that empathic overarousal results in self-focused personal distress includes the following: (*a*) negative emotional arousal is associated with a focus on the self (Wood, Saltzberg, & Goldsamt, 1990; Wood, Saltzberg, Neale, Stone, & Rachmiel, 1990); (*b*) people exhibit higher SC and HR, and sometimes report more distress, in situations likely to elicit personal distress (in contrast to sympathy; Eisenberg, Fabes, Schaller, Carlo, & Miller, 1991; Eisenberg, Fabes, Schaller, Miller, et al., 1991); and (*c*) for boys, personal distress has been associated with lower HR variability, whereas sympathy sometimes has been linked to high vagal tone; these HR measures (especially vagal tone) are viewed as rough markers of physiological regulation (Eisenberg, Fabes, et al., 1995; Fabes et al., 1993).

Conceptualizing personal distress and sympathy in this manner led to the next logical question: What factors might account for individual differences in the tendencies to experience personal distress and sympathy? One possible set of factors is environmental, including socialization. I briefly consider this issue later in this chapter. Another approach is to consider person variables such as temperament (which likely reflect both environmental and constitutional factors) that influence whether individuals become emotionally overaroused in social contexts involving emotion.

We have focused on two categories of person variables that we believe influence whether individuals become emotionally overaroused in social contexts: (1) the individual's temperamentally based level of emotional responsivity, particularly the intensity and/or quantity of responding, and (2) individuals' abilities to regulate (modulate) their emotional reactions and to cope behaviorally with the emotion and with the evocative situation. We have been especially concerned with *effortful emotion related regulation*, defined as the process of effortfully initiating, avoiding, inhibiting, maintaining, or modulating the occurrence, form, intensity, or duration of internal feeling states, emotion-related physiological processes, emotion-related goals, and/or behavioral concomitants of emotion, generally in the service of accomplishing one's goals (Eisenberg & Morris, 2002).

Emotion-related regulation is believed to include (*a*) effortful attentional regulation (the abilities to voluntarily focus or shift attention as needed in a given situation; e.g., to focus on some things rather than others as required to control one's experience or expression of emotion and to behave in an adaptive manner) and (*b*) inhibitory and activation control (i.e., the abilities to effortfully inhibit behavior or activate behavior as appropriate, even if the person does not really want to do so). An example of inhibitory control is a person controlling his or her expression of anger; an example of activation control is getting oneself to do a task that induces anxiety. These abilities reflect what Rothbart (Rothbart & Bates, 1998) has labeled *effortful control* and are believed to involve executive functioning in the anterior cingulate gyrus and related parts of the brain.

Our view is that individual differences in emotionality and regulation jointly contribute to the prediction of numerous aspects of social functioning. In some cases the contributions of emotionality and regulation are additive; in others we predict interactive or moderating effects (Eisenberg & Fabes, 1992; Eisenberg & Morris, 2002). We have argued that, if sympathy involves optimal regulation, in general regulation would be expected to be positively, linearly related to sympathy. Conversely, low regulation, particularly low attentional control, is expected to be associated with personal distress because personal distress reflects, in our view, high levels of insufficiently modulated negative emotion. Further, emotional intensity, in general (i.e., for positive and negative emotions) or for emotions such as sadness, is predicted to be moderately associated with sympathy (in that somewhat higher sympathy is expected for higher-intensity people), although optimally regulated people are expected to be relatively sympathetic regardless of level of emotional intensity (Eisenberg et al., 1994; Eisenberg et al., 1996). Anger, however, might be expected to be negatively related to sympathy because it probably interferes with concern for others. People high in emotional intensity and frequency of negative emotion were expected to be high in personal distress, *particularly* if they were low in the ability to regulate negative emotion.

In general, we have obtained empirical support for the hypothesis that individual differences in emotionality and regulation predict differences among people in dispositional sympathy and personal distress. In an initial study with college students (Eisenberg et al., 1994), we found that personal distress was related to low levels of both self-reported regulation and friends' reports of students' coping. Although sympathy was unrelated to regulation in zero-order correlations, it was significantly positively related to regulation once the effects of negative emotional intensity (as well as social desirability) were controlled. This finding was replicated in a later study with elders (Okun, Shepard, & Eisenberg, 2000). In addition, in the college study both personal distress and sympathy were positively related with intensity of negative emotion and with dispositional proneness to experience sadness, and frequency (rather than intensity) of negative emotionality was especially related to personal distress. Friends' reports of negative emotionality also related to students' personal distress. Intensity of positive emotion was related with self-reported dispositional sympathy but not with personal distress, whereas frequency of positive emotion was negatively related with dispositional, self-reported personal distress. The effects generally held even when scores on social desirability were controlled. In regression analyses regulation and emotionality contributed unique variance to the prediction of empathy-related responding.

In a similar study with elders (Eisenberg & Okun, 1996), the pattern of findings was even more consistent with expectations. Self-reported regulation, especially emotion regulation, was positively related to sympathy and negatively related to personal distress. Negative emotional intensity was positively related to both personal distress and sympathy, although the relation was somewhat stronger for the former. In general, the predicted moderating effects have not been obtained in studies conducted with adults. In this study, for example, there was an interaction between dispositional negative emotional intensity and regulation (a composite of emotional and behavioral regulation) when predicting personal distress (but not sympathy). Personal distress decreased as the level of regulation increased for women at all levels of negative emotional intensity but particularly for women who were low or average in negative emotional intensity. Thus, the relation between regulation and personal distress was stronger for women who were not prone to intense negative emotions. Perhaps older women who were high in negative emotional intensity were somewhat more likely than their peers to be overwhelmed by vicariously induced negative emotion, even if they were well regulated. Nonetheless, even this group of women showed a significant decline in personal distress as a function of increasing regulation.

In similar research conducted with elementary school children, we obtained teachers' and self-reports of children's sympathy and parents' and teachers' reports of children's emotionality and regulation (Eisenberg et al., 1996; Eisenberg, Fabes, et al., 1998; Murphy et al., 1999). At three points in time, 2 years apart, adults' reports of regulation generally were positively related to dispositional sympathy. In addition there was evidence that, for boys, physiological arousal when exposed to a relatively distressing film clip was related to low dispositional sympathy. Thus, boys prone to physiological overarousal appeared to be low in dispositional sympathy.

In this longitudinal study, adults' reports of children's negative emotionality predicted low sympathy 2, 4, and 6 years later, and reports of regulation predicted over shorter periods of time (e.g., 2–4 years, depending on the measure and age of assessment; Eisenberg, Fabes, et al., 1998; Murphy et al., 1999). Unlike what had been found for adults, children's negative emotional intensity was negatively related to sympathy, probably because adults (especially teachers) tend to focus on children's frustration/anger when reporting on children's negative emotional intensity (Eisenberg, Fabes, Bernzweig, et al., 1993). Of interest, however, there was some evidence of an interaction between general emotional intensity and regulation when predicting teacher-reported child sympathy. General emotional intensity is the general tendency to feel emotions strongly, without specific reference to valence of the emotion (positive or negative). Children low in regulation were low in sympathy regardless of their general emotional intensity. However, for children who were moderate or relatively high in regulation, sympathy increased with the level of general emotional intensity. Thus, children who were likely to be emotionally intense were sympathetic if they were at least moderately well regulated (Eisenberg et al., 1994). A similar interaction was found between general emotional intensity and behavioral regulation 2 years later, but only for boys (Eisenberg, Fabes et al., 1998).

The relation between children's dispositional sympathy and regulation also has been found in a study of third graders in Indonesia. In this study (Eisenberg, Liew, & Pidada, 2001) parents' and teachers' reports of children's dispositional sympathy were positively related to their reports of children's regulation, even across reporters.

Thus, in general we have found that temperamental regulation and emotionality are related to dispositional sympathy and dispositional personal distress, albeit sometimes in complicated ways (and often for some, but not all, measures). Findings for measures of situational sympathy and personal distress are less consistent than those for dispositional measures of empathy-related responding (e.g., Eisenberg et al., 1994). However, there is some evidence that children's reports of experiencing sympathy (e.g., Eisenberg, Fabes, et al., 1998; Guthrie et al., 1997), as well as their facial concern or sadness and HR deceleration versus acceleration while viewing empathy-inducing films (Guthrie et al., 1997), are positively related to adults' reports of children's regulation. However, these relations generally are relatively weak and inconsistent.

In summary, individuals who are well regulated appear to be relatively high in sympathy, especially dispositional sympathy. Relations of emotionality with empathy-related responding vary with the measure of emotionality (negative, positive, or general) and with the age of the study participant and reporter (i.e., self- or other-reported emotion). Yet overall the findings suggest that empathy-related responding is related to temperamentally based individual differences in regulation and emotionality, which suggests that constitutional factors contribute to individual differences in empathic capabilities.

Socialization Correlates of Empathy-Related Responses

As was just noted, the relation of empathy-related responding to individual differences in regulation and emotionality supports the assumption that empathy-related responding has a biological basis. This notion is further strengthened by evidence in adult twin studies indicating that self-reported empathy has a hereditary basis (e.g., Matthews, Batson, Horn, & Rosenman, 1981; Rushton, Fulker, Neale, Nias, & Eysenck, 1986). Even more relevant, in a longitudinal study with young children, Zahn-Waxler and her colleagues (Zahn-Waxler, Robinson, & Emde, 1992; Zahn-Waxler, Schiro, Robinson, Emde, & Schmitz, 2001) found evidence of a hereditary basis of sympathetic concern and prosocial behavior (but not self-distress). Nonetheless, it is highly plausible that environmental factors, including socialization in the home, also contribute to the development of, and individual differences in, empathy-related responding.

In the final section of this chapter, a few examples of research linking parental characteristics or behavior to empathy-related responding are presented. These examples pertain solely to parental warmth and expression of emotion. These examples are illustrative; more extensive reviews of the larger literature on the socialization of empathy-related responding can be found elsewhere (e.g., Eisenberg & Fabes, 1998; Eisenberg, Valiente, & Champion, 2004). However, these examples provide some evidence of associations between parent variables and children's empathy-related responding, even if the empirical links are merely correlational.

PARENTAL WARMTH AND SUPPORT

Investigators have argued that parents' warmth during parent-child interactions promotes children's sense of security, attachment, and self-regulation (e.g., Davies & Cummings, 1994; Eisenberg, Cumberland, & Spinrad, 1998), all of which probably contribute to children's abilities to process, consider, and respond to others' feelings (Hoffman, 2000; Kestenbaum, Farber, & Sroufe, 1989; Staub, 1979; Waters, Wippman, & Sroufe, 1979). In addition, children are likely to model warm, concerned parental behavior and probably are more disposed to adopt parental values related to caring if their parents are warm (Zahn-Waxler, Radke-Yarrow, & King, 1979).

Although empirical relations between parental warmth and children's empathy-related responses are mixed, they are somewhat more consistent when one examines studies in which sympathy was differentiated from empathy (see Eisenberg & Fabes, 1998). In our laboratory, for example, we found that parents' observed warmth/positive affect, encouragement, and low levels of negative affect while doing a puzzle task with their child were positively related to their children's self-reported sympathy (Spinrad et al., 1999).

In another study in which empathy with negative or positive slides was examined, parental warmth was positively related to children's facial and self-reported empathic reactions to slides. However, this relation held more consistently when parental warmth was assessed earlier in elementary school (Zhou et al., 2002).

It is probable that the relations of parental warmth to children's sympathy are mediated by other variables. For example, parental warmth may promote high levels of children's regulatory abilities (Eisenberg, Gershoff, et al., 2001), which generally have been positively related to sympathy and negatively related to personal distress (Eisenberg, Liew, & Pidada, 2001; Eisenberg, Wentzel, & Harris, 1998). Moreover, the relation of parental warmth to children's sympathy/empathy may be mediated by (or indirect through) other aspects of parents' behavior. In a longitudinal study Zhou et al. (2002) used structural equation modeling to examine whether parental expressivity in response to empathy-inducing slides (in view of the child) mediated the relations of parental warmth to children's empathy. At the initial assessment, there was an indirect relation of mothers' warmth to children's empathy with positive (but not negative) emotions through mothers' positive expressivity, whereas 2 years later mediation was significant only for children's empathy with negative emotions (see Figures 2 and 3). The latter finding was significant even when controlling for the stability of the variables over time (see Figure 4). Nonetheless, a model predicting parenting from indices of child functioning also fit the data nearly as well as the parent-driven socialization model. The fact that the causal relations could go in either direction probably is because there is a bidirectional process

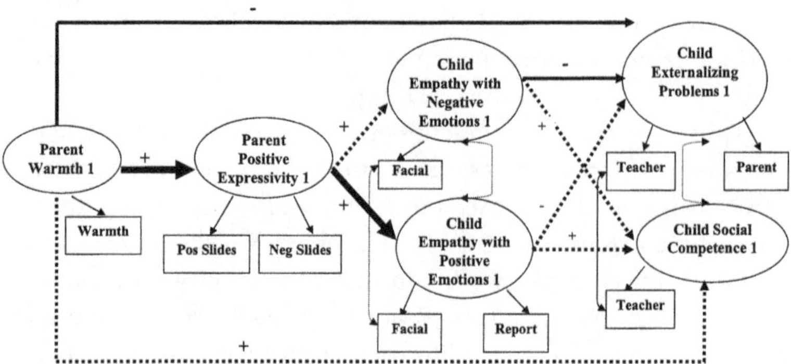

Figure 2. Pattern of relations in Zhou et al. (2002) at the second assessment. Solid lines indicate significant paths; dotted lines are not significant. Larger solid lines indicate a mediated path. Adapted from Zhou et al. (2002, p. 906).

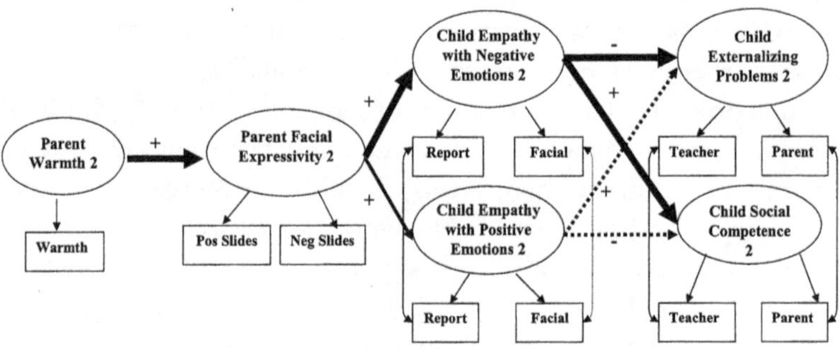

Figure 3. Pattern of relations in Zhou et al. (2002) at the first assessment. Solid lines indicate significant paths; dotted lines are not significant. Larger solid lines indicate a mediated path. Adapted from Zhou et al. (2002, p. 906).

in which parenting and children's functioning influence each other as children develop (Maccoby & Martin, 1983).

PARENTS' EXPRESSIVITY

As was just illustrated, parents' expression of emotion may affect children's empathy-related responding. Halberstadt, Crisp, and Eaton (1999) and others (e.g., Eisenberg et al., 1992) have hypothesized that children's willingness to express, and to some degree experience, emotions—including vicarious emotions—is related to parents' expression of emotion. Children with expressive parents

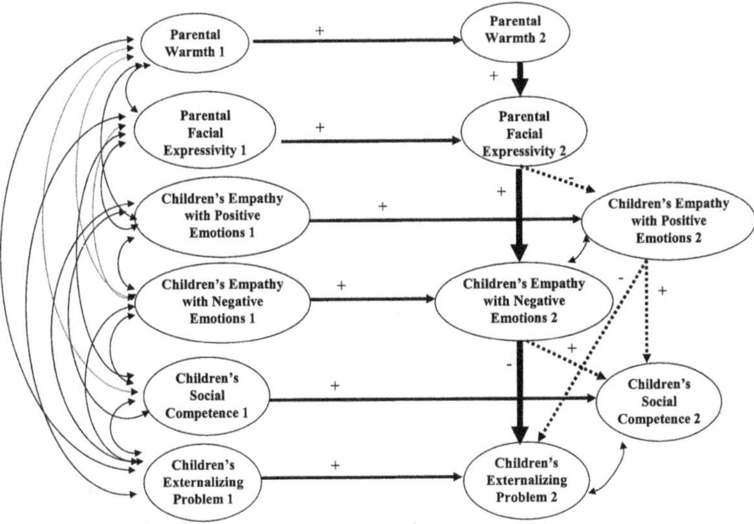

Figure 4. Pattern of relations in Zhou et al. (2002) in the longitudinal model. Solid lines indicate significant paths; dotted lines are not significant. Larger solid lines indicate a mediated path. Adapted from Zhou et al. (2002, p. 908).

may learn that it is acceptable to experience and express emotions, and parental expression of some emotions (e.g., positive ones and perhaps softer negative ones) is correlated with parental warmth, which (as was just discussed) often is related to children's empathy or sympathy (Barnett, 1987; Zhou et al., 2002). Of course, another possible explanation for part of the association between parents' and children's expressivity is that parents and children share genetic predispositions for emotionality.

In fact, parents' expression of positive and negative emotions has been related to children's tendencies to express emotions similar in valence to those of their parents (Halberstadt et al., 1999). Moreover, in several studies we have found links between parental expressivity and offsprings' empathy-related responding. In regard to parental positive expressivity, we found that young women's (but not young men's) reports of their parents' expression of positive emotion were positively related to their sympathy, sadness, and distress in response to a sympathy-inducing film and marginally negatively related to their HR reactions to the film (Eisenberg, Fabes, Schaller,

Miller, et al., 1991). Similarly, Eisenberg and McNally (1993) found that mothers' self-reported positive emotional communication was positively related to adolescent girls' reported sympathy and negatively to boys' reported personal distress. As already discussed, parents' positive facial expressivity also appears to relate positively to children's facial and/or self-reported empathy in response to specific evocative stimuli (Zhou et al., 2002), although parents' reports of positive expressivity have not always been significantly related to situational (Eisenberg et al., 1992) or dispositional (Eisenberg, Liew, & Pidada, 2001) measures of children's sympathy/empathy. Thus, although parents' positive expressivity sometimes has been linked to children's empathy-related responding, this association appears to be relatively weak.

Parents' expression of negative emotions in the family, especially dominant (assertive) negative emotions, more often has been linked to children's empathy-related responses than has parental expression of positive emotion. In a study of adults, Eisenberg, Fabes, Schaller, Miller, et al. (1991) found that parents' negative submissive expressivity (softer, less assertive negative emotions such as loss) was positively correlated with female undergraduates' reported sympathy, sadness, and distress; negative dominant expressivity (e.g., anger, hostility) was marginally correlated with low levels of SC during a distressing film (perhaps indicating less empathic responsivity or personal distress). In a study of young elementary school children, mothers' repeated expression of negative submissive emotion in the home was positively related to girls' facial concerned attention (an index of sympathy), whereas mothers' reports of the expression of negative dominant emotion were associated with girls' facial distress, facial sadness (but only for young girls), and low levels of boys' facial concern (Eisenberg et al., 1992). Similar positive relations between negative dominant expressivity and children's facial distress were found for another sample of children who viewed a distressing film (Valiente et al., 2003). Moreover, in an Indonesian sample, parents' (mostly mothers') reports of the expression of both submissive and dominant emotion in the family were negatively related to third graders' dispositional sympathy (Eisenberg, Liew, & Pidada, 2001). Finally, in the Zhou et al. (2002) study assessing children's empathy, parents' expression of negative emotion while viewing empathy-inducing positive and negative slides in the child's presence was not significantly correlated with children's empathy, perhaps because sensitive parents tended to try to buffer their children from empathic overarousal in this context (see also Fabes, Eisenberg, Karbon, Bernzweig, et al., 1994).

Thus, although not all findings are consistent, the overall pattern of findings suggests that parental warmth and positive expressivity relate weakly to high levels of children's sympathy (and perhaps empathy), whereas negative expressivity, especially negative dominant expressivity, is negatively related to sympathetic responses (and perhaps positively related to personal distress). Parental negative submissive emotion sometimes has been positively related to empathy/sympathy in the United States (although the findings are not highly consistent), but it was negatively related in Indonesia; thus, the relation of parental expression of less dominant negative emotions to sympathy may vary depending on context and the emotions' cultural significance. For example, the expression of any negative emotion is viewed more negatively in Indonesia than in the United States, which may explain why Indonesian parents' reported expression of submissive negative emotion was negatively related to children's dispositional sympathy (Eisenberg, Liew, & Pidada, 2001).

It is likely that the relations of parental expressivity to empathy-related responding are moderated by other variables, such as children's regulation. Consistent with this notion, we recently found that children's regulation and parental expressivity interacted when predicting children's dispositional and situational sympathy. For example, the positive relation of situational sympathy with parental negative expressivity was negative primarily for children who were low in regulation. Regulation may be especially important for the emergence of children's sympathy if children must cope with high levels of negative emotion in the home (Valiente et al., 2004).

Conclusions

Empathy-related responding clearly is related to a host of morally and socially important outcomes for children and adults. Although it is difficult to prove causal relations, it also is probable that empathy and/or sympathy actually contribute, perhaps in complex ways, to these domains of development. Prediction of important moral and social developmental outcomes from empathy-related responding appears to be enhanced by consideration of a number of factors, including the differentiation of various modes of empathy-related responding, consideration of the motivational significance of predicted behaviors (e.g., whether the target prosocial behavior is altruistically motivated), and the nature of the stimulus used to elicit empathy-related responding (e.g., whether it assesses empathy with positive or negative emotions and whether it is mild or likely to induce overarousal in some individuals). Different aspects of empathy-related responding may differentially predict various developmental outcomes; for example, high levels of prosocial behavior probably are best predicted by high sympathy and low levels of personal distress (and perhaps least predicted by measures of pure empathy), whereas aggression and hurtful types of antisocial behavior may be best predicted by low levels of empathy, sympathy, or personal distress (empathy is likely to inhibit aggression but perhaps less likely to foster prosocial behavior). Further, the relations of empathy-related responding to moral behaviors undoubtedly are moderated by other variables, such as perspective taking and moral reasoning (e.g., Knight et al., 1994; Miller et al., 1996), although we currently know little about such moderation.

Our findings also suggest that individual differences in spontaneously emitted, costly prosocial behaviors—a type of prosocial behavior that is linked with other-oriented concern and sympathy relatively early in life—predict prosocial and sympathetic tendencies (as well as perspective taking) throughout childhood and into early adulthood. Therefore, early individual differences in empathy-related responding may have implications for moral and social development across the life span. Individual differences in empathy-related responding probably have a temperamental basis (e.g., being based on individual differences in regulation and emotional reactivity), which may partly account for their apparent effects over time. In addition, early empathy or sympathetic tendencies likely provide children with opportunities to learn about the effects of their behavior on others (e.g., because they attend more to these issues), with the result that empathic/sympathetic children's development of moral and social capacities is accelerated beyond, or may even differ in quality from, that of their peers.

I am not arguing that empathy-related responding is fixed and cannot be changed; the research on socialization and emotion-related prevention programs (Greenberg, 1996; Greenberg & Kusche, 1997) suggests that it can be. Indeed, the existing evidence is consistent with the view that the home environment plays an important role in the development of empathy-related responding. However, as with most complex social and emotional characteristics, both biological and environmental factors probably contribute to both the normative development of empathy-related responding and individual differences in such responding. An important task for the future is to better delineate the range of influences on empathy-related development and how the relations of individual differences in empathy-related characteristics to important developmental outcomes are mediated or moderated by various constitutionally based and environmental factors.

References

American Psychiatric Association. (1994). *Diagnostic and statistical manual of mental disorders* (4th ed.). Washington DC: American Psychiatric Association.

Barnett, M. A. (1987). Empathy and related responses in children. In N. Eisenberg & J. Strayer (Eds.), *Empathy and its development* (pp. 46–162). Cambridge: Cambridge University Press.

Batson, C. D. (1991). *The altruism question: Toward a social-psychological answer.* Hillsdale NJ: Erlbaum.

Batson, C. D., Bolen, M. H., Cross, J. A., & Neuringer-Benefiel, H. E. (1986). Where is the altruism in the altruistic personality? *Journal of Personality and Social Psychology, 50,* 212–220.

Batson, C. D., Duncan, B., Ackerman, P., Buckley, T., & Birch, K. (1981). Is empathic emotion a source of altruistic emotion? *Journal of Personality and Social Psychology, 40,* 290–302.

Blair, R. J. R. (1999). Responsiveness to distress cues in the child with psychopathic tendencies. *Personality and Individual Differences, 27,* 135–145.

Blair, R. J. R., Jones, L., Clark, F., & Smith, M. (1997). The psychopathic individual: A lack of responsiveness to distress cues? *Psychophysiology, 34,* 192–198.

Blasi, A. (1980). Bridging moral cognition and moral action: A critical review of the literature. *Psychological Bulletin, 88,* 1–45.

Blum, L. A. (1980). *Friendship, altruism, and morality.* London: Routledge & Kegan Paul.

Bryant, B. K. (1982). An index of empathy for children and adolescents. *Child Development, 53,* 413–425.

Cacioppo, J. T., & Sandman, C. A. (1978). Physiological differentiation of sensory and cognitive tasks as a function of warning processing demands and reported unpleasantness. *Biological Psychology, 6,* 181–192.

Carlo, G., Eisenberg, N., & Knight, G. P. (1992). An objective measure of adolescents' prosocial moral reasoning. *Journal of Research on Adolescence, 2,* 331–349.

Carlo, G., Eisenberg, N., Troyer, D., Switzer, G., & Speer, A. L. (1991). The altruistic personality: In what contexts is it apparent? *Journal of Personality and Social Psychology, 61,* 450–458.

Carlo, G., Koller, S. H., Eisenberg, N., DaSilva, M. S., & Frohlich, C. B. (1996). A cross-national study on the relations among prosocial moral reasoning, gender role orientations, and prosocial behaviors. *Developmental Psychology, 32,* 231–240.

Cohen, D., & Strayer, J. (1996). Empathy in conduct-disordered and comparison youth. *Developmental Psychology, 32,* 988–998.

Colby, A., Kohlberg, L., Gibbs, J., & Lieberman, M. (1983). A longitudinal study of moral judgment. *Monographs of the Society for Research in Child Development, 48*(1–2, Serial No. 200).

Cole, P. M., Zahn-Waxler, C., Fox, N. A., Usher, B. A., & Welsh, J. D. (1996). Individual differences in emotion regulation and behavior problems in preschool children. *Journal of Abnormal Psychology, 105,* 518–529.

Davies, P. T., & Cummings, E. M. (1994). Marital conflict and child adjustment: An emotional security hypothesis. *Psychological Bulletin, 116,* 387–411.

Davis, M. H. (1994). *Empathy: A social psychological approach.* Madison WI: Brown & Benchmark.

Davis, M. H., Hull, J. G., Young, R. D., & Warren, G. G. (1987). Emotional reactions to dramatic film stimuli: The influence of cognitive and emotional empathy. *Journal of Personality Psychology and Social Psychology, 52,* 126–133.

Eisenberg, N. (1986). *Altruistic emotion, cognition, and behavior.* Hillsdale NJ: Erlbaum.

Eisenberg, N., Cameron, E., Tryon, K., & Dodez, R. (1981). Socialization of prosocial behavior in the preschool classroom. *Developmental Psychology, 17,* 773–782.

Eisenberg, N., Carlo, G., Murphy, B., & Van Court, P. (1995). Prosocial development in late adolescence: A longitudinal study. *Child Development, 66,* 1179–1197.

Eisenberg, N., Cumberland, A., & Spinrad, T. L. (1998). Parental socialization of emotion. *Psychological Inquiry, 9,* 241–273.

Eisenberg, N., & Fabes, R. A. (1990). Empathy: Conceptualization, assessment, and relation to prosocial behavior. *Motivation and Emotion, 14,* 131–149.

Eisenberg, N., & Fabes, R. A. (1991). Prosocial behavior and empathy: A multimethod, developmental perspective. In M. Clark (Ed.), *Review of person-*

ality and social psychology: Vol. 12. Prosocial behavior (pp. 34–61). Newbury Park CA: Sage.

Eisenberg, N., & Fabes, R. A. (1992). Emotion, regulation, and the development of social competence. In M. S. Clark (Ed.), *Review of personality and social psychology: Vol. 14. Emotion and social behavior* (pp. 119–150). Newbury Park CA: Sage.

Eisenberg, N., & Fabes, R. A. (1998). Prosocial development. In W. Damon (Series Ed.), N. Eisenberg (Vol. Ed.), *Handbook of child psychology: Vol. 3. Social, emotional, and personality development* (5th ed., pp. 701–778). New York: Wiley.

Eisenberg, N., Fabes, R. A., Bernzweig, J., Karbon, M., Poulin, R., & Hanish, L. (1993). The relations of emotionality and regulation to preschoolers' social skills and sociometric status. *Child Development, 64,* 1418–1438.

Eisenberg, N., Fabes, R. A., Bustamante, D., Mathy, R. M., Miller, P., & Lindholm, E. (1988). Differentiation of vicariously-induced emotional reactions in children. *Developmental Psychology, 24,* 237–246.

Eisenberg, N., Fabes, R. A., Carlo, G., Speer, A. L., Switzer, G., Karbon, M., & Troyer, D. (1993). The relations of empathy-related emotions and maternal practices to children's comforting behavior. *Journal of Experimental Child Psychology, 55,* 131–150.

Eisenberg, N., Fabes, R. A., Carlo, G., Troyer, D., Speer, A. L., Karbon, M., & Switzer, G. (1992). The relations of maternal practices and characteristics to children's vicarious emotional responsiveness. *Child Development, 63,* 583–602.

Eisenberg, N., Fabes, R. A., Miller, P. A., Fultz, J., Mathy, R. M., Shell, R., & Reno, R. R. (1989). The relations of sympathy and personal distress to prosocial behavior: A multimethod study. *Journal of Personality and Social Psychology, 57,* 55–66.

Eisenberg, N., Fabes, R. A., Miller, P. A., Shell, C., Shea, R., & May-Plumlee, T. (1990). Preschoolers' vicarious emotional responding and their situational and dispositional prosocial behavior. *Merrill-Palmer Quarterly, 36,* 507–529.

Eisenberg, N., Fabes, R. A., Murphy, B., Karbon, M., Maszk, P., Smith, M., O'Boyle, C., & Suh, K. (1994). The relations of emotionality and regulation to dispositional and situational empathy-related responding. *Journal of Personality and Social Psychology, 66,* 776–797.

Eisenberg, N., Fabes, R. A., Murphy, B., Karbon, M., Smith, M., & Maszk, P. (1996). The relations of children's dispositional empathy-related responding to their emotionality, regulation, and social functioning. *Developmental Psychology, 32,* 195–209.

Eisenberg, N., Fabes, R. A., Murphy, M., Maszk, P., Smith, M., & Karbon, M. (1995). The role of emotionality and regulation in children's social functioning: A longitudinal study. *Child Development, 66,* 1360–1384.

Eisenberg, N., Fabes, R. A., Schaller, M., Carlo, G., & Miller, P. A. (1991). The relations of parental characteristics and practices to children's vicarious emotional responding. *Child Development, 62,* 1393–1408.

Eisenberg, N., Fabes, R. A., Schaller, M., Miller, P., Carlo, G., Poulin, R., Shea, C., & Shell, R. (1991). Personality and socialization correlates of vicarious emotional responding. *Journal of Personality and Social Psychology, 61,* 459–470.

Eisenberg, N., Fabes, R. A., Shepard, S. A., Murphy, B. C., Jones, J., & Guthrie, I. K. (1998). Contemporaneous and longitudinal prediction of children's sympathy from dispositional regulation and emotionality. *Developmental Psychology, 34,* 910–924.

Eisenberg, N., Gershoff, E. T., Fabes, R. A., Shepard, S. A., Cumberland, A. J., Losoya, S. H., Guthrie, I. K., & Murphy, B. C. (2001). Mothers' emotional expressivity and children's behavior problems and social competence: Mediation through children's regulation. *Developmental Psychology, 37,* 475–490.

Eisenberg, N., Guthrie, I., Cumberland, A., Murphy, B. C., Shepard, S. A., Zhou, Q., & Carlo, G. (2002). Prosocial development in early adulthood: A longitudinal study. *Journal of Personality and Social Psychology, 82,* 993–1006.

Eisenberg, N., Guthrie, I. K., Murphy, B. C., Shepard, S. A., Cumberland, A., & Carlo, G. (1999). Consistency and development of prosocial dispositions: A longitudinal study. *Child Development, 70,* 1360–1372.

Eisenberg, N., Zhou, Q., & Koller, S. (2001). Brazilian adolescents' prosocial moral judgment and behavior: Relations to sympathy, perspective taking, gender-role orientation, and demographic characteristics. *Child Development, 72*(2), 518–534.

Eisenberg, N., & Lennon, R. (1983). Gender differences in empathy and related capacities. *Psychological Bulletin, 94,* 100–131.

Eisenberg, N., Liew, J., & Pidada, S. U. (2001). The relations of parental emotional expressivity with quality of Indonesian children's social functioning. *Emotion, 1,* 116–136.

Eisenberg, N., Losoya, S., & Spinrad, T. L. (2003). Affect and prosocial responding. In R. J. Davidson, K. Scherer, & H. H. Goldsmith (Eds.), *Handbook of affective science* (pp. 787–803). Oxford: Oxford University Press.

Eisenberg, N., McCreath, H., & Ahn, R. (1988). Vicarious emotional responsiveness and prosocial behavior: Their interrelations in young children. *Personality and Social Psychology Bulletin, 14,* 298–311.

Eisenberg, N., & McNally, S. (1993). Socialization and mothers' and adolescents' empathy-related characteristics. *Journal of Research on Adolescence, 3,* 171–191.

Eisenberg, N., & Miller, P. (1987). The relation of empathy to prosocial and related behaviors. *Psychological Bulletin, 101,* 91–119.

Eisenberg, N., Miller, P. A., Shell, R., McNalley, S., & Shea, C. (1991). Prosocial development in adolescence: A longitudinal study. *Developmental Psychology, 27,* 849–857.

Eisenberg, N., & Morris, A. S. (2002). Children's emotion-related regulation. In R. Kail (Ed.), *Advances in child development and behavior* (Vol. 30, pp. 190–229). Amsterdam: Academic.

Eisenberg, N., & Okun, M. A. (1996). The relations of dispositional regulation and emotionality to elders' empathy-related responding and affect while volunteering. *Journal of Personality, 64,* 157–183.

Eisenberg, N., Pasternack, J. F., Cameron, E., & Tryon, K. (1984). The relation of quality and mode of prosocial behavior to moral cognitions and social style. *Child Development, 155,* 1479–1485.

Eisenberg, N., Schaller, M., Fabes, R. A., Bustamante, D., Mathy, R. M., Shell, R., & Rhodes, K. (1988). Differentiation of personal distress and sympathy in children and adults. *Developmental Psychology, 24,* 766–775.

Eisenberg, N., Shea, C. L., Carlo, G., & Knight, G. (1991). Empathy-related responding and cognition: A "chicken and the egg" dilemma. In W. Kurtines & J. Gewirtz (Eds.), *Handbook of moral behavior and development: Vol. 2. Research* (pp. 63–88). Hillsdale NJ: Erlbaum.

Eisenberg, N., Shell, R., Pasternack, J., Lennon, R., Beller, R., & Mathy, R. M. (1987). Prosocial development in middle childhood: A longitudinal study. *Developmental Psychology, 24,* 712–718.

Eisenberg, N., Valiente, C., & Champion, C. (2004). Empathy-related responding: Moral, social, and socialization correlates. In A. G. Miller (Ed.), *The social psychology of good and evil* (pp. 386–415). New York: Guilford.

Eisenberg, N., Wentzel, M., & Harris, J. D. (1998). The role of emotionality and regulation in empathy-related responding. *School Psychology Review, 27,* 506–521.

Eisenberg, N., Zhou, Q., & Koller, S. (2001). Brazilian adolescents' prosocial moral judgment and behavior: Relations to sympathy, perspective taking, gender-role orientation, and demographic characteristics. *Child Development, 72,* 518–534.

Eisenberg-Berg, N. (1979). The development of children's prosocial moral judgment. *Developmental Psychology, 15,* 128–137.

Eisenberg-Berg, N., & Hand, M. (1979). The relationship of preschooler's reasoning about prosocial moral conflicts to prosocial behavior. *Child Development, 50,* 356–363.

Eisenberg-Berg, N., & Lennon, R. (1980). Altruism and the assessment of empathy in the preschool years. *Child Development, 51,* 552–557.

Eisenberg-Berg, N., & Mussen P. (1978). Empathy and moral development in adolescence. *Developmental Psychology, 14,* 185–186.

Fabes, R. A., Eisenberg, N., & Eisenbud, L. (1993). Behavioral and physiological correlates of children's reactions to others in distress. *Developmental Psychology, 29,* 655–663.

Fabes, R. A., Eisenberg, N., Karbon, M., Bernzweig, J., Speer, A. L., & Carlo, G. (1994). Socialization of children's vicarious emotional responding and prosocial behavior: Relations with mothers' perceptions of children's emotional reactivity. *Developmental Psychology, 30,* 44–55.

Fabes, R. A., Eisenberg, N., Karbon, M., Troyer, D., & Switzer, G. (1994). The relations of children's emotion regulation to their vicarious emotional responses and comforting behavior. *Child Development, 65,* 1678–1693.

Fabes, R. A., Eisenberg, N., & Miller, P. A. (1990). Maternal correlates of children's vicarious emotional responsiveness. *Developmental Psychology, 26,* 639–648.

Feshbach, N. D. (1982). Sex differences in empathy and social behavior in children. In N. Eisenberg (Ed.), *The development of prosocial behavior* (pp. 315–338). New York: Academic.

Feshbach, N. D., & Feshbach, S. (1982). Empathy training and the regulation of aggression: Potentialities and limitations. *Academic Psychology Bulletin, 4,* 399–413.

Frick, P. J. (1998). *Conduct disorders and severe antisocial behavior.* New York: Plenum.

Gilligan, C. (1982). *In a different voice: Psychological theory and women's development.* Cambridge: Harvard University Press.

Greenberg, M. T. (1996). Final report to NIMH. *The PATHS Project: Preventive intervention for children* (Grant No. R01MH42131). University of Washington.

Greenberg, M. T., & Kusche, C. A. (1997, April). *Improving children's emotion regulation and social competence: The effects of the PATHS curriculum.* Paper presented at the biennial meeting of the Society for Research in Child Development, Washington DC.

Guthrie, I. K., Eisenberg, N., Fabes, R. A., Murphy, B. C., Holmgren, R., Maszk, P., & Suh, K. (1997). The relations of regulation and emotionality to children's situational empathy-related responding. *Motivation and Emotion, 21,* 87–108.

Haidt, J. (2001). The emotional dog and its rational tail: A social intuitionist approach to moral judgment. *Psychological Review, 108,* 814–834.

Halberstadt, A. G., Crisp, V. W., & Eaton, K. L. (1999). Family expressiveness: A retrospective and new directions for research. In P. Philippot & R. S. Feldman (Eds.), *The social context of nonverbal behavior: Studies in emotion and social interaction* (pp. 109–155). New York: Cambridge University Press.

Hastings, P. D., Zahn-Waxler, C., Robinson, J., Usher, B., & Bridges, D. (2000). The development of concern for others in children with behavior problems. *Developmental Psychology, 36,* 531–546.

Hoffman, M. L. (1975). Developmental synthesis of affect and cognition and its implications for altruistic motivation. *Developmental Psychology, 11,* 607–622.

Hoffman, M. L. (1982). Development of prosocial motivation: Empathy and guilt. In N. Eisenberg (Ed.), *The development of prosocial behavior* (pp. 281–313). New York: Academic.

Hoffman, M. L. (1987). The contribution of empathy to justice and moral judgment. In N. Eisenberg & J. Strayer (Eds.), *Empathy and its development* (pp. 47–80). Cambridge: Cambridge University Press.

Hoffman, M. L. (2000). *Empathy and moral development: Implications for caring and justice*. Cambridge: Cambridge University Press.

Holmgren, R. A., Eisenberg, N., & Fabes, R. A. (1998). The relations of children's situational empathy-related emotional to dispositional prosocial behaviour. *International Journal of Behavioral Development, 22,* 169–193.

Hume, D. (1966). *Enquiries concerning the human understanding and concerning the principles of morals* (2d ed.). Oxford: Clarendon. (Original work published 1777)

Kant, I. (1964). *The doctrine of virtue*. New York: Harper & Row. (Original work published 1797)

Kestenbaum, R., Farber, E. A., & Sroufe, L. A. (1989). Individual differences in empathy among preschoolers: Relations to attachment history. *New Directions in Child Development, 44,* 51–64.

Knight, G. P., Johnson, L. G., Carlo, G., & Eisenberg, N. (1994). A multiplicative model of the dispositional antecedents of a prosocial behavior: Predicting more of the people more of the time. *Journal of Personality and Social Psychology, 66,* 178–183.

Kohlberg, L. (1969). Stage and sequence: The cognitive-developmental approach to socialization. In D. A. Goslin (Ed.), *Handbook of socialization theory and research* (pp. 325–480). New York: Rand McNally.

Kohlberg, L. (1976). Moral stage and moralization: The cognitive-developmental approach. In T. Lickona (Ed.), *Moral development and behavior: Theory, research, and social issues* (pp. 84–107). New York: Holt, Rinehart & Winston.

Kohlberg, L. (1981). *The philosophy of moral development: Moral stages and the idea of justice*. San Francisco: Harper & Row.

Kohlberg, L. (1984). *Essays on moral development: Vol. 2. The psychology of moral development*. San Francisco: Harper & Row.

Lazarus, R. S. (1974). A cognitively oriented psychologist looks at biofeedback. *American Psychologist, 30,* 553–561.

Lennon, R., Eisenberg, N., & Carroll, J. (1983). The assessment of empathy in early childhood. *Journal of Applied Developmental Psychology, 4,* 295–302.

Levenston, G. K., Patrick, C. J., Bradley, M. M., & Lang, P. J. (2000). The psychopath as observer: Emotion and attention in picture processing. *Journal of Abnormal Psychology, 109,* 373–385.

Liew, J., Eisenberg, N., Losoya, S. H., Fabes, R. A., Guthrie, I. K., & Murphy, B. C. (2003). Maternal expressivity as a moderator of the relations of children's vicarious emotional responses to their regulation, emotionality, and social functioning. *Journal of Family Psychology, 17,* 584–597.

Lynam, D. R. (1997). Pursuing the psychopath: Capturing the fledgling psychopath in a nomological net. *Journal of Abnormal Psychology, 106,* 425–438.

Maccoby, E. E., & Martin, J. A. (1983). Socialization in the context of the family: Parent-child interaction. In P. H. Mussen (Series Ed.), E. M. Hetherington (Vol. Ed.), *Handbook of child psychology: Vol. 4. Socialization, personality, and social development* (4th ed., pp. 1–101). New York: Wiley.

MacDowell, K. A., & Mandler, G. (1989). Constructions of emotion: Discrepancy, arousal, and mood. *Motivation and Emotion, 13,* 105–124.

Matthews, K. A., Batson, C. D., Horn, J., & Rosenman, R. H. (1981). Principles in his nature which interest him in the fortune of others: The heritability of empathic concern for others. *Journal of Personality, 49,* 237–247.

Mehrabian, A., & Epstein, N. A. (1972). A measure of emotional empathy. *Journal of Personality, 40,* 523–543.

Miller, P., & Eisenberg, N. (1988). The relation of empathy to aggression and externalizing/antisocial behavior. *Psychological Bulletin, 103,* 324–344.

Miller, P. A., Eisenberg, N., Fabes, R. A., & Shell, R. (1996). Relations of moral reasoning and vicarious emotion to young children's prosocial behavior toward peers and adults. *Developmental Psychology, 32,* 210–219.

Miller, S. M. (1979). Interrelationships among dependency, empathy, and sharing. *Motivation and Emotion, 3,* 183–199.

Murphy, B. C., Shepard, S. A., Eisenberg, N., Fabes, R. A., & Guthrie, I. K. (1999). Contemporaneous and longitudinal relations of young adolescents' dispositional sympathy to their emotionality, regulation, and social functioning. *Journal of Early Adolescence, 19,* 66–97.

Mussen, P., & Eisenberg-Berg, N. (1977). *Roots of caring, sharing, and helping: The development of prosocial behavior in children.* San Francisco: Freeman.

Noddings, N. (1984). *Caring: A feminine approach to ethics and moral education.* Berkeley and Los Angeles: University of California Press.

Okun, M. A., Shepard, S. A., & Eisenberg, N. (2000). The relations of emotionality and regulation to dispositional empathy-related responding among volunteers-in-training. *Personality and Individual Differences, 28,* 367–382.

Preston, S. D., & de Waal, F. B. M. (2002). Empathy: Its ultimate and proximate bases. *Behavioral and Brain Sciences, 26,* 1–20.

Rawls, J. (1971). *A theory of justice.* Cambridge: Harvard University Press.

Rest, J. R. (1979). *Development in judging moral issues.* Minneapolis: University of Minnesota Press.

Rothbart, M. K., & Bates, J. E. (1998). Temperament. In W. Damon (Series Ed.), N. Eisenberg (Vol. Ed.), *Handbook of child psychology: Vol. 3. Social, emotional, and personality development* (5th ed., pp. 105–176). New York: Wiley.

Rushton, J. P., Chrisjohn, R. D., & Fekken, G. C. (1981). The altruistic personality and the self-report altruism scale. *Personality and Individual Differences, 2,* 1–11.

Rushton, J. P., Fulker, D. W., Neale, M. C., Nias, D. K. B., & Eysenck, H. J. (1986). Altruism and aggression: The heritability of individual differences. *Journal of Personality and Social Psychology, 50,* 1192–1198.

Skoe, E., Eisenberg, N., & Cumberland, A. (2002). The role of reported emotion in real-life and hypothetical moral dilemmas. *Personality and Social Psychology Bulletin, 28,* 962–973.

Slote, M. (2001). *Moral from motives.* Oxford: Oxford University Press.

Spinrad, T. L., Losoya, S., Eisenberg, N., Fabes, R. A., Shepard, S. A., Cumberland, A., Guthrie, I. K., & Murphy, B. C. (1999). The relation of parental affect and encouragement to children's moral emotions and behaviour. *Journal of Moral Education, 28,* 323–337.

Staub, E. (1979). *Positive social behavior and morality: Vol. 2. Socialization and development.* New York: Academic.

Underwood, B., & Moore, B. (1982). Perspective-taking and altruism. *Psychological Bulletin, 91,* 143–173.

Valiente, C., Eisenberg, N., Fabes, R. A., Shepard, S. A., Cumberland, A., & Losoya, S. H. (2004). Prediction of children's empathy-related responding from their effortful control and parents' expressivity. *Developmental Psychology, 40,* 911–926.

Valiente, C., Eisenberg, N., Shepard, S. A., Fabes, R. A., Cumberland, A. J., Losoya, S. H., & Spinrad, T. L. (2003). The relations of mothers' negative expressivity to children's experience and expression of negative emotion. *Journal of Applied Developmental Psychology, 25,* 215- 236.

Waters, E., Wippman, J., & Sroufe, L. A. (1979). Attachment, positive affect, and competence in the peer group: Two studies in construct validation. *Child Development, 50,* 821–829.

Winton, W. M., Putnam, L. E., & Krauss, R. M. (1984). Facial and autonomic manifestations of the dimensional structure of emotion. *Journal of Experimental Social Psychology, 20,* 195–216.

Wood, J. V., Saltzberg, J. A., & Goldsamt, L. A. (1990). Does affect induce self-focused attention? *Journal of Personality and Social Psychology, 58,* 899–908.

Wood, J. V., Saltzberg, J. A., Neale, J. N., Stone, A. A., & Rachmiel, T. B. (1990). Self-focused attention, coping responses, and distressed mood in everyday life. *Journal of Personality and Social Psychology, 58,* 1027–1036.

Zahn-Waxler, C., Cole, P. M., Welsh, J. D., & Fox, N. A. (1995). Psychophysiological correlates of empathy and prosocial behaviors in preschool children with problem behaviors. *Development and Psychopathology, 7,* 27–48.

Zahn-Waxler, C., Radke-Yarrow, M., & King, R. A. (1979). Child rearing and children's prosocial initiations toward victims of distress. *Child Development, 50,* 319–330.

Zahn-Waxler, C., Robinson, J. J., & Emde, R. N. (1992). The development of empathy in twins. *Developmental Psychology, 28,* 1038–1047.

Zahn-Waxler, C., Schiro, K., Robinson, J. L., Emde, R. N., & Schmitz, S. (2001). Empathy and prosocial patterns in young MZ and DZ twins. In R. N. Emde & J. K. Hewitt (Eds.), *Infant to early childhood: Genetic and environmental influences on developmental change* (pp. 141–162). Oxford: Oxford University Press.

Zhou, Q., Eisenberg, N., Losoya, S. H., Fabes, R. A., Reiser, M., Guthrie, I. K., Murphy, B. C., Cumberland, A. J., & Shepard, S. A. (2002). The relations of parental warmth and positive expressiveness to children's empathy-related responding and social functioning: A longitudinal study. *Child Development, 73,* 893–915.

The Neo-Kohlbergian Tradition and Beyond: Schemas, Expertise, and Character

Darcia Narvaez
University of Notre Dame

Kohlberg's cognitive-developmental paradigm has been enormously influential, spawning hundreds of research projects in the United States and around the world. From Kohlberg we have much for which to be grateful. For example, he was among the vanguard against the behaviorist majority who helped bring about the cognitive revolution. He helped bring American attention to the work of Piaget. He provided a new way to look at morality beyond that of virtues and traits. He did not shrink from difficult problems, trying to do the impossible in tackling the naturalistic fallacy on philosophers' terms. He encouraged contrary viewpoints and supported alternative research paradigms (e.g., Gilligan, 1982). He developed the just-community approach to education that my colleague Clark Power addresses elsewhere in this volume.

The cognitive revolution, although still evolving, has moved far beyond the stereotyped ages and stages of Piaget and Kohlberg. Critics have pointed out the oversimplified perspectives and the globality of their theories, noting that the view from the ground is much more complicated and messy. Yet there is more empirical support for Kohlberg's general theory than ever before. Thus, it is important to give it a second look, with the caveats and modifications necessary to fit the data. First, I will describe the criticisms of Kohlberg's approach and then describe how neo-Kohlbergian theory addresses them. But then I too will move beyond Kohlberg, describing an approach that seeks to incorporate cognitive science and social-cognitive psychology into a moral psychology theory. Finally I discuss some implications of these moves for deliberative character education in the classroom and in everyday life.

Responding to Critiques of Kohlberg: The Shift to a Neo-Kohlbergian Perspective

Like the theory of his intellectual mentor, Jean Piaget, Kohlberg's theory has fallen on hard times among psychologists for a variety of reasons.[1] Stage theories generally are viewed as too broad-brush, missing much of development, and underestimating early signs of change in younger children and infants.

Recently a neo-Kohlbergian perspective was formulated in Minnesota by four of us: the late Jim Rest, Mickey Bebeau, Steve Thoma, and myself (Rest, Narvaez, Bebeau, & Thoma, 1999a, 1999b, 2000). We sought to address the issues raised by critics and to exploit the massive amount of data collected with the Defining Issues Test (DIT), an objective measure of moral judgment. The DIT consists of several dilemmas and sets of considerations for respondents to rate and rank according to how important they are for making a decision about the dilemma. Data have been collected on tens of thousands of respondents from around the world. Our reconceptualization of Kohlberg's theory is based on DIT data that have been collected for over 25 years. This fact is both a help and a hindrance in building a theory. Whereas using the same instrument for a lengthy period of time enables one to establish extensive validity and relate scores to many variables over time, the instrument itself is only one small tool for examining a vast area that needs to be explored with many tools in many different ways.

Kohlberg's critics from the ranks of psychology have made the following contentions. I mention briefly how neo-Kohlbergian theory approaches these controversies (for a more thorough discussion, see Rest, Narvaez, Bebeau, & Thoma, 1999b).

1. *Kohlberg focuses on one small piece of morality in terms of important psychological processes.* For Kohlberg, moral judgment was the key to moral development. If you could explain a person's moral judgment

stage, you had a window into his or her motivations, sensitivities, and potential for action. Yet the neo-Kohlbergian view agrees with critics that the moral judgment window is not big enough. Blasi (1980), Eisenberg (1982), and others have long considered moral judgment as too narrow a focus for moral psychology. Likewise, neo-Kohlbergian theory has long-standing roots in considering moral judgment as only one of at least four psychological processes that must occur for moral behavior to ensue (Narvaez & Rest, 1995; Rest, 1983). Later I discuss in more detail the importance of four processes in moral behavior: moral sensitivity; moral motivation; moral action; and moral judgment.

2. *Kohlberg focuses on only one piece of morality in terms of justice.* Kohlberg addressed the perfect duties of justice and minimized the imperfect duties of care (Nunner-Winkler, 1984). Although the neo-Kohlbergian perspective also emphasizes the primacy of justice, like Kohlberg it conceives of care as inherent in justice, becoming more fundamentally integrated in the later stages (Kohlberg, Levine, & Hewer, 1983). What is usually called *care* reasoning often falls into what neo-Kohlbergians call *moral sensitivity* (e.g., considering the needs of others) or *motivation* (e.g., feeling responsible). The development of imperfect duties is discussed as part of the ethical expertise model that I propose in this chapter.

3. *Kohlberg overextended Piaget's operations to moral thinking.* Kohlberg's enterprise was to build the logical necessity of moral stage development as Piaget did with logical operations. But Kohlberg's attempt has been criticized as inadequate (e.g., Gibbs, 1979). The neo-Kohlbergian perspective has abandoned any attempt to measure formal operations, such as the INRC group (a single mental structure representing the operations of identity, negation, reciprocity, and commutative properties; see Piaget & Inhelder, 1969), and instead adopts a more cognitive science perspective, looking for changes in schemas, adopting a more fuzzy-trace theory of activation in which structure is not so easily separated from content, as in expert knowledge. Experts have more and better-organized knowledge. Likewise those with higher levels of moral judgment have more and better-organized understandings of social cooperation. In fact my work (Gleason & Narvaez, 2003; Narvaez, 1999, 2001) shows that those with higher levels of moral judgment perform like other experts, for

example, in terms of how they react to domain texts when thinking aloud.

4. *Kohlberg's hard-stage model is too strict.* Some say that Kohlberg was more Piagetian than Piaget, sticking to hard stages when Piaget himself maintained a softer view. The data in moral judgment research have rarely, if ever, supported a hard-stage model in which a person's functioning can be defined by one stage. Parallel to moves in developmental psychology (e.g., Siegler, 1997), neo-Kohlbergian theory adopts a soft-stage model of cognitive development, focusing instead on how types of reasoning change in distribution across development.

5. *Kohlberg's method is overly dependent on verbal expressiveness.* Neo- Kohlbergian theory is in agreement with those who say that individuals know more than they can express in words (Keil & Wilson, 1999). The DIT examines tacit moral judgment as measured by recognition memory, rather than relying on interview methods, which tend to reward verbal articulation with higher scores.

6. *In Kohlberg's interview studies there is little evidence for stages 5–6 (postconventional) thinking.* When using an interview methodology in which the respondent must articulate philosophical argumentation in order to receive a high moral judgment score, it is rare to find a capable respondent. However, when one measures tacit moral judgment with the DIT, one can find evidence of postconventional thinking. One of the characteristics of cognitive development that has been emphasized in a post-Piagetian world is the emergent quality of developmental structures, from less elaborated knowledge (e.g., identification knowledge) to more elaborated knowledge (Marshall, 1995). Later, I discuss the sequential development of schemas.

7. *Kohlberg underestimates children's moral capabilities.* Like Piaget, Kohlberg placed high demand characteristics on subjects for evidence of development. Subtler measures find propensities in very young children. On the basis of the work of Turiel and colleagues (Turiel, 1998), we agree that children have more capacities than are evident in Kohlbergian and neo-Kohlbergian research. However, the moral judgment data that we use (from the DIT) are from adolescents and adults and do not provide us with anything specific to say about children.

8. *According to Turiel, Kohlberg confuses two domains: convention and morality.* Turiel (Turiel, 1983, 1998) separates convention from moral-

ity and argues that each follows a separate track of development. We disagree, aligning neo-Kohlbergian theory with Blasi's (1990) view that Turiel (1983) has made a priori philosophical decisions about what morality entails, defining too narrowly and as an intrinsic characteristic of actions, ignoring what subjects might think about his distinctions, and abandoning the phenomenological perspective that Kohlberg adopted.

As it turns out, the evidence for the development of Turiel's moral domain is close to nonexistent, consisting of one cross-sectional study of 61 subjects of 6, 8, and 10 years of age (Davidson, Turiel, & Black, 1983). Using ANOVA, two of the nine justification categories showed statistical significance for age-group differences (*personal choice*, $p < .0001$; and *appeal to authority*, $p < .05$). However, Tisak and Turiel (1988) failed to replicate age-based differences, demonstrating instead differences at all ages. No subsequent studies showing developmental differences in the moral domain have been published.

Domain theory studies do show that people distinguish one kind of action from another. Yet we agree with Blasi (1990) and Lourenço and Machado (1996) that, although people do make distinctions among types of actions, there is no evidence that they do so on moral grounds: "From the subjects' perspective (though not from Turiel's external perspective), the two classes of action may be differentiated and yet be seen as equally moral, in the same way that adults differentiate altruism and honesty within the domain of morality" (Blasi, 1990, p. 44).

Instead of separating convention from morality, we agree with Kohlberg that moral judgment development is in part a matter of moving into convention (from preconventional) and beyond it (to postconventional). The most important growth in moral judgment occurs in adolescence, when initially convention is seen as moral, and then later, in the college years, convention is distinguished from the moral in the move to postconventional thinking.

9. *Culture overwhelms developmental differences in morality*. Shweder and colleagues have argued that culture is more important than individual development. Yet moral judgment data show that more variability exists within cultures than between them (Jensen, 1996). The data indicate developmental differences worldwide in terms of the preconventional and conventional types of moral thinking, so

culture does not overwhelm justice moral thinking as currently measured (Rest, 1986; Snarey, 1985). Development in tacit postconventional moral thinking, as measured by the DIT, is evident worldwide as well but is dependent on an education system that fosters critical thinking (Gielen & Markoulis, 1994; McNeel, 1994). Explicit postconventional reasoning is exhibited largely only among those who participate in deliberative, focused study (Edelstein & Krettenauer, 2004; Narvaez, 1999).

Shweder (1982, 1991; Shweder, Mahapatra, & Miller, 1987) has attempted to show the priority of culture in moral judgment, but these studies have used Turiel's (1983) narrow definitions of *morality* and *convention*, making their findings noncomparable with Kohlbergian and neo-Kohlbergian research.

Kohlberg's critics came not only from the ranks of psychologists. Kohlberg defined his domain of study in philosophical terms, building on Hare's (1963) neo-Kantian definition of *morality*: a judgment is moral if it is prescriptive or obligatory and if it is universalizable; moral judgment development is the increasing "differentiation of prescriptive and universalizable judgments from prudential and aesthetic judgments" (Kohlberg et al., 1983, p. 17). As he intruded onto the terrain of philosophy, among his critics were philosophers who viewed a deontological perspective as too narrow for a moral psychology. As philosophy moved away from foundational principlism in the late 20th century, Kohlberg was criticized for grounding his theory in principles—à la Rawls (1971), as if principles were guide enough in the particularity of situations (Clouser & Gert, 1990; DeGrazia, 1992; Strike, 1982; Toulmin, 1981). In not revising the philosophical side of his theory, Kohlberg ignored the field's moves toward a more useful "bottom-up" morality—the use of paradigmatic cases (Beauchamp & Childress, 1994) emphasizing communal and historical contexts—and toward a "common morality" approach to solving moral dilemmas in which common sense and the reflective traditions of the community (the "bottom up") interact with moral principles (the "top down") in a type of reflective equilibrium (Beauchamp & Childress, 1994). Neo-Kohlbergian theory has attempted to respond to these criticisms by embracing a wider moral philosophical foundation beyond principlism, by emphasizing the importance of intermediate ethical constructs for situational decision-making, and by supporting a common morality approach to solving ethical problems. (For further discussion, see Rest, Narvaez, Bebeau, & Thoma, 1999b.)

The neo-Kohlbergian theory of moral judgment maintains Kohlberg's emphasis on rationality, on development and the construction of a moral epistemology, and on the critical shift from conventional to postconventional thinking. Furthermore, the neo-Kohlbergian perspective uses Kohlberg's same starting point: assessing responses to a limited set of hypothetical dilemmas and the systematic measure of phenomenological psychological moral development. Moreover, neo-Kohlbergian theory adopts Kohlberg's perspective on moral psychology theory as "a rational reconstruction of the ontogenesis of justice reasoning" (Kohlberg et al., 1983, p. 10).

THE THREE MORAL SCHEMAS MEASURED BY THE DIT

In several factor analyses, the DIT has been found to measure three different types of thinking or schemas (see Table 1). These three schemas do *not* correspond to Kohlberg's three levels. According to neo-Kohlbergian theory, the DIT's three schemas measure the ways in which people answer macromorality questions, how to organize societywide cooperation with unknown others, rather than micromorality questions, those relevant to getting along with family and friends.

The *personal interests schema* develops in childhood, and its use is on the wane at the time individuals take the DIT (one must have a 12-year-old reading capacity). The personal interests schema includes not only the instrumental hedonism of Kohlberg's stage 2 but also the personal relational orientation of his stage 3 (Kohlberg, 1976). Using this type of thinking, a person filters moral stimulus information on the basis of its effects on matters of personal interest. There is no sociocentric perspective. Cooperating with others is viewed as if there were only micromorality relationships to consider. This kind of thinking appeals to the personal stake that a decisionmaker has in the situation; prudence and personal advantage are considered virtues.

One of the most noticeable advances in cognitive development during adolescence is the *discovery of society*, the awareness that people relate to each other through institutions, role systems, and established practices as well as on a personal, face-to-face basis (Adel-

Table 1. *Neo-Kohlbergian Theory Moral Schemas*

Personal Interest Schema
- *Self-focus*:
  - Arbitrary, impulsive cooperation
  - Self-focused
  - Advantage to self is primary
  - Survival orientation
- *Other focus*:
  - Negotiated cooperation
  - Scope includes others who are known
  - In-group reciprocity
  - Responsibility orientation

Maintaining Norms Schema
- Need for norms
- Societywide view
- Uniform categorical application
- Partial societywide reciprocity
- Duty orientation

Postconventional Schema
- Appeal to an ideal
- Shareable ideals
- Primacy of moral ideal
- Full reciprocity
- Rights orientation

son, 1971; Youniss & Yates, 1997). Questions of moral authority become increasingly paramount: How does one organize a fair society? How should wealth, power, and opportunity be distributed? What is the role of government and the use of force? These issues of macromorality are distinctive from those of micromorality (i.e., getting along with people you know) and mark the shift from the personal interest schema to the *maintaining norms schema*. The maintaining norms schema emerges as a more sophisticated form of moral thinking because the individual begins to be able to take into account the welfare of unknown others. The reasoner begins to discern the advantages of role systems and established practices. The reasoner perceives that there is a need for generally accepted norms to govern the social collective and that these norms must apply to everyone in the society. The norms provide a rule of law that is clear, uniform, and categorical. The norms establish the reciprocity of each citizen's duty to obey the law with the expectation that all others do the same.

The norms include the establishment of hierarchical role structures, chains of command, and authority.

According to this schema interpersonal relationships and even respect for other people are less important than upholding the system itself. One obeys authority out of respect for the system, not for the personal qualities of the officeholder. This schema centers so much on law and order that it is inconceivable that order would exist without upholding the law. Without the law and one's duty to uphold it and the roles that derive from order, there would be anarchy. There is no felt need to appeal to moral criteria beyond the law itself. The maintaining norms schema offers a sense of moral certainty, invigorating many of its adherents with missionary zeal.

The development of the *postconventional schema* is a breakthrough in cognitive development, marking one of the primary features of late-adolescent development, and has become one of the best indicators of college student development (McNeel, 1994; Pascarella & Terenzini, 1991; Rest & Narvaez, 1991). The postconventional schema is more advanced in a normative ethical sense as well as in terms of developmental complexity. Four elements constitute the postconventional schema: (1) primacy of moral criteria in making decisions about social cooperation, in that conventions are not inviolate (i.e., a law does not trump moral goals; laws are instruments of morality, not moral themselves); (2) appeal to an ideal rather than a rejection of the status quo for its own sake; (3) moral obligations based on sharable ideals rather than ethnocentric preference or personal intuition (this requires an openness to scrutiny and debate, in contrast to the ideals of conventional thinking, which are shielded by the privileges of authority); and (4) full reciprocity that views the application of laws uniformly, like conventional thinking, but also scrutinizes the laws themselves for fairness (laws are subjected to tests of logical consistency, coherence with accepted practice, and community experience).

With DIT data, we are able to focus on the chasm between conventionality and postconventionality. We see the effects of this chasm in the polarization of views on public policy issues such as religion in public schools, abortion, euthanasia, and the rights of homosexuals, about which more will be said later.[2]

THE VALIDITY OF THE DIT

The validation strategy for the DIT has made it one of the best-validated measures in psychology. The DIT meets all the criteria that a test of moral judgment should meet (a thorough discussion is available in Rest, Narvaez, Bebeau, & Thoma, 1999b). A brief outline of several validation criteria and research findings follows.

1. *The* DIT *differentiates groups with different levels of expertise.* Several large composite samples of DIT respondents have been compiled and show that postconventional thinking increases through college and postgraduate education. When comparing the performance of high and low scorers in postconventional thinking, the high scorers perform more like experts do in other domains (see Narvaez, 1999, 2001). The DIT does not discriminate on irrelevant factors such as sex. These are minimal and, if they occur at all, generally favor females (< 0.1% of variance).

2. *Longitudinal studies show significant upward gains.* Longitudinal studies indicate that individuals do develop through different types of thinking. They move from more egocentric to more sociocentric thinking. Their thought structures become more complex, and they are able to solve more complex problems. Using Kohlberg's theory, we can see that individuals do move from lower-stage thinking to higher-stage thinking. The greatest shifts occur in adolescence, when the individual becomes aware of the larger society, moving into the maintaining norms schema, social order thinking, and then in college, moving into the postconventional schema.

3. *The data show evidence of a developmental hierarchy.* Moral comprehension studies (e.g., Rest, 1969, 1973; Rest, Turiel, & Kohlberg, 1969) show that comprehension of moral reasoning is cumulative. Respondents with higher-stage thinking abilities are able to understand reasoning pitched at lower levels. Although they can understand reasoning at stages lower than those that they can paraphrase, they tend to disparage it, preferring reasoning that is at or above the stage they can articulate.

4. DIT *scores are sensitive to interventions designed to improve moral judgment.* Schlaefli, Rest, and Thoma (1985) performed a meta- analysis of 55 intervention studies and found an effect size of .41 (modest) for experimental groups in contrast with an effect size of .09 for control groups. Interventions need to last longer than 3 weeks, and

a dilemma-discussion approach works best (in contrast with lectures and readings alone).

Let me summarize what we know about what fosters development in moral judgment. (1) In a composite sample of 56 studies ($N =$ 6,863), Thoma found over 52% of the variance explained by education. Across studies, education is the most powerful demographic correlate with DIT scores, accounting for 30%–50% of the variance (Rest, Narvaez, Bebeau, & Thoma, 1999b). (2) The richer the social environment, and the greater the general social experience (including multicultural experience; Endicott, Bock, & Narvaez, 2003), the greater the gains in postconventional thinking (Rest, 1986).

5. DIT *data significantly predict to real-life moral behavior*. Does a moral judgment score predict to anything beyond itself? Higher postconventional scores on the DIT are linked to prosocial behaviors such as community involvement ($r = .31$, $p < .01$) and civic responsibility ($r = .44$, $p < .01$) (Rest, 1986). In a review of studies, Thoma, Rest, and Barnett (1985) found 32 of 47 statistical analyses of behavioral measures significant, both prosocial and antisocial. Interestingly, high postconventional scores are not all sweetness and light. Moral judgment sophistication appears independent of happiness (Schiller, 1999) and can strain friendships (Thoma, Malone Beach, & Ladewig, 1997), and, from Kohlberg's work, postconventional reasoning can lead you to behave in ways that make others want to kill you (Kohlberg, 1981).

6. DIT *scores significantly predict to political attitudes and choices.* Our research shows that moral judgment cannot be reduced to cultural ideology, or vice versa. Narvaez, Getz, Rest, and Thoma (1999) measured religious ideology, political identity, and moral judgment. When each construct is measured separately, then combined, the product predicts powerfully to attitudes toward human rights (Narvaez, Getz, et al., 1999)—as much as 67% of the variance. We argue that what occurs through development is an interaction between autonomous and heteronomous moral processes (not the move from one to the other, as Piaget maintained). That is, individual conceptual development in moral judgment and socialization into cultural ideology co-occur, simultaneously and reciprocally, in parallel, and not serially. Individual development in moral judgment provides the epistemological categories for cultural ideology, which in turn influences

the course of moral judgment, all of which influence moral thinking about social issues (e.g., opinions about abortion, free speech).

In fact, our work provides some insight into the clash between orthodoxy and progressivism that is on the rise in this country and elsewhere (Hunter, 1991) and is considered by some to be the most important clash in ideology since the cold war (see Marty & Appleby, 1993). By definition, religious fundamentalism regards the questioning of its authority as beyond human scrutiny, forbidden to inquiry and debate. Religious authoritarianism is related to high maintaining norms scores on the DIT. If at the point when most people shift to postconventional thinking a person is embedded in a fundamentalist social context, chances are that he or she will be blocked from progression into postconventional thinking, which is based on open scrutiny and debate. Therefore in orthodoxy we have an example of moral judgment influencing cultural ideology, and vice versa.

Regardless of how you study them or name them, Kohlbergian stages and neo-Kohlbergian schemas are global structures that do not offer specific help in deciding about particular situations. This has been noted especially in the professions that aspire to teach ethics (e.g., Strike, 1982). Neo-Kohlbergian theory emphasizes the importance of studying intermediate ethical concepts, the concepts that guide everyday decisionmaking. For example, Bebeau and Thoma (1999) found differences between novices (freshman dentistry students) and experts (senior students) in the identification and application of intermediate ethical constructs within dentistry, such as *patient autonomy* and *informed consent*.

The Shift Toward Cognitive Science

Neo-Kohlbergian theory as described in Rest, Narvaez, Bebeau, and Thoma (1999b) began to bridge the gap between current trends in psychology, such as cognitive science, and moral psychology. As part of this transformation, neo-Kohlbergian theory integrated schema theory into its reconceptualization of moral judgment development. Kohlberg sought to measure cognitive structure apart from particular content. But, when studying expertise in a particular domain, it is not so easy to separate structure from content. Experts have more and better-organized domain knowledge that is often characterized as schemas.

Schemas play an important role in my work, so let me spend a little time discussing them. What are schemas? The notion of schemas is one that has driven research in cognitive psychology for decades and underlies most theories of knowledge acquisition. Piaget described cognitive structures as schemas that organize an individual's operational activities (Piaget, 1970). Classic schema theorists (e.g., Rummelhart, 1980; Taylor & Crocker, 1981) describe schemas as general knowledge structures residing in long-term memory. According to Marshall (1995) schemas have three key sets of features: their form; their creation; and their application.

Form Schemas are basic storage devices represented by a tightly organized network structure. Schemas vary in size and can be embedded in or overlap with other schemas. Schemas are noted for their flexibility in accessibility and adaptation. There are usually several routes available for accessing a schema. No instantiation of the schema is identical to another, and each instantiation alters the schema.

Creation Schemas are not memorized but constructed from understandings, from prior knowledge. A schema will develop in response to repeated opportunities to solve a particular kind of problem. Although individuals experience life uniquely, the similarity of their experiences brings about the development of similar schemas.

Application Schemas include both procedural knowledge (rules) and declarative knowledge (concepts and facts). Schemas can be applied subconsciously and automatically or in a consciously and controlled manner.

The DIT is now understood as a device that activates moral judgment schemas from long-term memory. That is, it activates the schemas that are present in the mind of the respondent. Subsequent processing of considerations is concept-driven (top-down) processing based on the networks of ideas that have been activated. The DIT presents a dilemma about which the respondent makes a decision (e.g., for "Heinz and the drug," the respondent decides whether or not Heinz should steal the drug). The respondent is then presented with 12 considerations and asked to rate how important each was in his or her decisionmaking and which were the most important. From the rating and rankings of items, several scores are constructed, including the postconventional score, which is the most widely used.

DIT items strike a balance between too much and too little information, necessitating the activation of existent schemas. Humans work most of the time with partial information from the stimulus array or environmental input. Schemas help fill in the blanks. When the respondent is presented with an item that relates to a schema that the participant has, that item is given a high rating. When an item does not fit an activated schema, the item is rated of low importance.

Schemas facilitate information processing, allowing a person to more rapidly process information by providing a framework for analyzing stimuli (Taylor & Crocker, 1981). Schemas focus attention and affect processing time, speed of information flow, and speed of problem solving, including during reading (Gernsbacher, 1994). In fact, speeded recognition or reaction time is a method widely used by cognitive psychology to measure activated mental information (e.g., Higgins & Kruglanski, 1996). Respondents react more quickly when tested with a concept that is activated than when tested with a concept that is not activated. We find that this is the case when we compare more and less expert reasoners by timing their ratings of DIT items. Those who prefer the maintaining norms schema are significantly faster in responding to items representing this schema, while those who score high on the postconventional schema are significantly faster in rating items representing that schema (Narvaez, Endicott, & Thoma, 2001).

SCHEMAS AND MORAL DISCOURSE PROCESSING

I have been testing moral schemas in action with various studies in moral discourse processing. I have studied schema activation both during and after reading moral texts. In each case schemas structure experience, often determining which information will be encoded during reading and what will be retrieved from long-term storage at recall. Narvaez (1998) asked groups with different levels of moral judgment development—eighth graders and college students—to read and recall narratives about moral situations. Fragments of moral reasoning at Kohlberg's stages 2–5 were embedded in the narratives. The results indicated that both groups recall equally the lower-stage moral arguments (Kohlberg's stages 2, 3, and 4). Yet only readers with higher postconventional scores were more likely to recall postconventional (stage 5) reasoning (Narvaez, 1998).

Another finding with schemas is that readers will distort information to conform with preexisting schemas (e.g., Bartlett, 1932). This occurred in this study as well. Those with higher postconventional scores were significantly more likely to reconstruct stage 5 moral arguments during recall, including stage 5 arguments that were not included in the original text. Whereas both high and low reasoners were equally like to construct stage 1–4 reasoning *not* in the text, only higher-level reasoners constructed stage 5 reasons that were not in the text.

Schemas drive on-line processing of information. Those with the appropriate schemas are able to apply them to problem solving. For example, I have compared the performance of groups with more expertise to that of groups with less expertise in moral judgment and find that the more expert group performs like experts from other domains (Narvaez, 1999). For example, in one study I asked participants to think aloud (saying everything that comes to mind) while reading two moral narratives embedded with moral reasoning. Those with more moral judgment expertise (graduate students in philosophy and political science) performed like experts in other domains (Pressley & Afflerbach, 1995). They gave more explanations and total expressions, indicating a deeper understanding of and engagement with the texts. They also made more predictions and evaluations, further evidence for task engagement. In addition they expressed more coherence breaks (e.g., disagreeing with the logic of events). Like experts in other domains they performed as if they had more and better-organized knowledge (Chi & Ceci, 1987).

As a result of my studies with groups differing in expertise, I believe that moral judgment is a domain that is similar to that of music. Most people have some knowledge of music. For example, they can sing songs, having learned from general experience how to carry a tune. Yet general experience does not lead to expertise in music. Rather, expertise in music—whether it be composition or performance—requires extensive, deliberative, focused study (e.g., Ericsson & Smith, 1991). Likewise, although one can learn a great deal about moral reasoning in everyday life, in order to reach the highest levels one must undergo deliberative, focused study. Like Edelstein and Krettenauer (2004), I see moral judgment development comprising two kinds—normative and specialized.

The lower end of moral judgment development is not tapped by the DIT because the DIT is written at a 12-year-old reading level. So how might one study tacit moral judgment in younger children? I begin with stories. When readers processes a text, not only do they decode the data before their eyes, but they also apply their world knowledge to what they are reading. That is, their preexisting schemas interpret and drive their reading and understanding as they make meaning of the text. As a result of individual active and constructive reading, readers do not form the same mental representation from a text. Schema effects on reading comprehension have been documented with culturally specific texts (Bartlett, 1932; Harris, Lee, Hensley, & Schoen, 1988) and with level of reader familiarity with text material (e.g., Chiesi, Spilich, & Voss, 1979; Crafton, 1983; Spilich, Vesonder, Chiesi, & Voss, 1979). When pondering the effect of schemas on reading some years ago, I wondered how moral development affected children's understanding of moral stories. Some traditionalists, like William Bennett, have convinced parents and teachers that reading moral stories to children will build their moral literacy and, consequently, their moral characters (e.g., Bennett, 1993). This assumes that readers come to a text with similar schemas and create the same meanings. For anyone who knows about reading comprehension, Bennett's premise and the conclusion are dubious.

To examine the effects of moral schemas on reading moral stories, my colleagues and I conducted several studies (Narvaez, Bentley, Gleason, & Samuels, 1998; Narvaez, Gleason, Mitchell, & Bentley, 1999). We tested third-grade, fifth-grade, and college students using stories about getting along with others. For example, "Kim" concerns a girl whose family, while moving across the country, stops at a gas station where Kim receives too much change from the cashier. The moral messages concern honesty and self-control. After reading a story, participants were asked to rate and select the best matches to the original story theme from a set of paragraph-long stories and from a list of themes. We measured and controlled for reading comprehension. There were vast developmental differences in theme comprehension. For example, the 8-year-olds were much less likely to select the correct theme (11% of the time across stories), and they were consistently attracted to vignettes with the same actions (all groups were more attracted to this type of distractor, but the attraction decreased with age). In contrast to the younger children, the 11-year-olds selected the theme about half the time (45%), and the college students selected the theme nearly all the time (91%). When selections and ratings were combined into an overall *theme comprehension score* and reading comprehension was controlled, the statistical significance was large ($F(2,129) = 74.65$, $p < .0001$, effect size = 1.00).

In summary, discourse-processing techniques are useful for examining the effects of schemas on moral cognition. Discourse processing focuses on a more everyday kind of moral thinking than the more global approaches (e.g., the DIT, the Moral Judgment Interview), in which individuals process moral information that is mixed with other kinds of information, as is often the case in real life. Moral discourse research also allows more control over stimuli so that differences between input and output can be compared.

The Shift Toward a Social-Cognitive View of Moral Personality and Expertise

The Kohlbergian tradition avoided speaking of personality and virtues, yet research into moral exemplars indicates that those who are nominated by their communities to moral exemplary status are not nominated because of their moral reasoning. (And, although most nominees are conventional reasoners by interview standards (Colby & Damon, 1992; Hart, Yates, Fegley, & Wilson, 1995), it is likely that their DIT scores would indicate postconventional reasoning.) Despite the importance of moral reasoning and its relation, for example, to professional conduct, in everyday life other things matter more. Most researchers point to virtues or traits of character as the key to exemplary status. I would like to suggest a correction to this view.

Remember the four processes moral sensitivity, moral judgment, moral focus, and moral action? Briefly, moral sensitivity has to do with noticing and interpreting events, moral motivation with prioritizing ethical action, and moral action with carrying it out. It was ingenious of Rest (1983) to focus attention on the processes needed for a particular moral behavior. Unlike most analyses of moral behavior, his avoids talk of virtues or personality traits. This is appropriate for two reasons that I mention here. First, it fits with a sociocognitive understanding of personality (Cantor, 1990; Mischel, 1990, 1999). According to this perspective personality is not a static set of traits that is exhibited in some constant fashion across situations. Rather it is a shifting set of dispositional ways of acting that correspond to context-specific features (Lapsley & Narvaez, 2004b, in press; Narvaez & Lapsley, in press). Second, it fits with our understanding of human learning. We learn in increments; we learn responses in particular situations to particular content. We develop declarative, procedural, and conditional knowledge in each domain that we experience, developing more and more complex schemas (Derry, 1996; Schank & Abelson, 1977). Now let me say more about these two points.

Personality is more like a set of evolving schemas than like static traits. A social-cognitive view considers the construction of a moral personality as a construction of schemas and their accoutrements. For example, Cantor (1990) suggests that the cognitive substrate of personality consists of schemas, tasks, and strategies. Schemas are organized around specific life experiences. Tasks are integrations of our cultural goals and schemas into personal goals. Strategies are a complex network of feelings, thoughts, efforts, and actions that work together to bring about our life tasks. So here again schemas are "meat-and-potatoes" constructs. Schema theories are fundamental constructs, not only in social-cognitive personality theory (Cantor, 1990), but also in social perception (e.g., Fiske & Taylor, 1991) and in expertise literature (Chi, Glaser, & Farr, 1988).

Cantor (1990) suggests that the notion of expertise is applicable to the formation of personality. Three features of schemas underlie this proposal. First, individuals have chronically accessible schemas that influence information processing, directing attention, and filtering and organizing stimuli. Each person functions as an expert with the chronically accessible schemas that he or she has, tuning into key information that others miss. Second, chronically salient schemas will influence the selection of life tasks and goals. Third, chronic schemas translate into behavioral routines that become highly practiced and automatic. In a way, then, we are each experts in our own personalities. Our personal schemas guide our attention, our selection of life tasks, and our behavioral routines.

Experts are qualitatively different from novices. First, experts have large, rich, organized networks of schemas, containing a great deal of knowledge about the domain of study (Chi, Feltovitch, & Glaser, 1981; Sternberg, 1998). Second, because they have more and better-organized knowledge in a domain, experts actually perceive the world differently: "Information can be picked up only if there is a developmental format ready to accept it. . . . Perception is inherently selection" (Neisser, 1976, p. 55). What you see depends on who you are (Meilaender, 1984). In other words, you see what you have a knowledge base to see. Third, the skills of experts differ from those of novices in several important ways. Unlike novices, experts know what knowledge to access, which procedures to apply, how to apply them, and when it is appropriate. Vicente and Wang (1998) point out that the memory of experts is facilitated by prior knowledge in part because it provides goals and constrains what they look for and see, limiting the complexity of what they see (the *constraint attunement hypothesis*).

So what is it that moral experts have? They are more expert in the kinds of schemas that we call *moral*. The four-process model allows us to view moral behavior as a set of responses to particular situational features. Experts in the skills of moral sensitivity are better at quickly and accurately "reading" a moral situation and determining what role they might play. Experts in the skills of moral judgment have many tools for solving complex moral problems. Experts in the skills of moral motivation cultivate an ethical identity that leads them to prioritize ethical goals. Experts in the skills of moral action know how to "keep their eye on the prize," enabling them to stay on task and take the necessary steps to get the ethical job done. Viewed this way, moral behavior is pried from the rigidity of personality temperament and put into the realm of learnable behavior. It appears more like behavior in other domains like football or chess, as a set of skills that can be learned. This is not a new idea. Repeatedly throughout *The Republic*, Plato draws analogies from professions and vocations as analogies of the just person—one who has certain skills that are cultivated to expertise. According to this perspective, the variability that we see in moral behavior across contexts can be explained as variability in schema development and skill application across contexts, not necessarily as poor temperament or a lack of virtue. A more advantageous approach to describing moral exemplars is to look at their characteristics, not as a bag of traits, but as a set of highly developed skills, or *techne*, as proposed by Plato.

Yet many character education programs use a trait understanding of character. This level of analysis is not helpful if one is desirous of specific guidelines on how to develop virtues in children. A belief in traits appears to drive the poor pedagogy that plagues many approaches to character education. If honesty, for example, is considered a trait, the best way to get children to be honest is to tell them to adopt the trait (hence the posters and assemblies emphasizing its importance). Of course this is not an instructional approach that an educator would consider using to teach math or reading. Math and reading are viewed as domains whose skills can be learned. Adults should overcome their wariness of adopting such an attitude toward moral behavior. It is time to consider much of moral behavior as skills.

Application: Deliberative Character Education

What schemas do moral experts have, and how do we cultivate them?[3] Let me address the "what" question first. The four-process model gives us a starting point (for brief descriptions, see Table 2). Experts in moral sensitivity are better at generating usable solutions to problems because of their greater understanding of the consequences of possible actions. Experts in moral judgment can see the crux of a problem quickly and bring with them many schemas for reasoning about what to do. Their information-processing tools are more complex but also more efficient. Experts in moral motivation are directed by an organized structure of moral self-identity. Experts in moral action demonstrate superior performance when completing an ethical action.

And now I am going into the classroom to teach, but what do I teach? As you can tell, the four-process model is not specified enough for instruction. In 1998 the Minnesota Department of Education was given a federal Character Education Partnership grant for work with middle school teachers. I was the designer of the project and adopted the four-process model as a foundational framework for developing a new model of character development. My student colleagues and I collaborated with teachers and education leaders over the 4 years of the project as we developed a framework for guiding character education. We combed the literature to identify the features of moral personhood. We grounded our work in three areas: (1) common understandings of what it means to be good; (2) conclusions from the social sciences about what helps humans develop into flourishing prosocial beings; and (3) the consensus among leaders worldwide on the necessary characteristics for citizens in the 21st century.

Table 2. *The Process Model of Ethical Behavior*

Ethical Sensitivity: NOTICE!
Involves picking up on the cues related to ethical decisionmaking and behavior
Interpreting the situation according to who is involved, what actions to take, what possible reactions and outcomes might ensue

Ethical Judgment: THINK!
Involves reasoning about the possible actions in the situation and judging which action is most ethical

Ethical Focus: AIM!
Involves prioritizing the ethical action over other goals and needs (either in the particular situation or as a habit)

Ethical Action: ACT!
Involves implementing the ethical action by knowing how to do so and following through despite hardship

First, following Blasi (1990), we define *goodness* according to common understandings and ordinary language. According to this view, "We know it when we see it." The individual recognizes "(1) when the conditions for a certain meaning have or have not been fulfilled and (2) when an interpretation corresponds to his experience" (Blasi, 1990, p. 62). Etzioni (1996) states: "Certain concepts present themselves to us as morally compelling in and of themselves" (p. 241). We do not explain the nature of a good person precisely. Instead, we delineate the skills that a person needs to have in order to function as a moral being in the world, and we call this the ethical expertise model. The ethical expertise model offers a framework of skills that are based on universals such as human rights (e.g., the United Nations Declaration of Human Rights), common notions of democratic citizenship, and the elements that foster human flourishing, individually and within a given community. These are based on the perspective that we all breathe the same air and walk the same globe. Individuals are so interdependent that it is hard to separate individual flourishing from group flourishing. Personal flourishing enables others to flourish. Whitehead (1929) states: "We inhibit the world when we inhibit our own growth. We are each a potential for every becoming. We inhibit all other human beings with our own limitations. Immediate acts pass into universal experience. . . . Our decisions open and close other possibilities, we open and close the future" (p. 348). Moral being is a joint effort. Individuals cocreate the future, having much influence on one another's well-being and becoming. It should be noted that it is not always possible in the articulation of curriculum to make the fine distinctions of philosophy because what is analytic in philosophy becomes synthetic in educational practice. As one will notice, the skills of moral personhood overlap and are not orthogonal, but we tried to simplify the picture for the sake of educational practicality. Throughout the project we balanced theoretical purity with practical need, doing our best to make the framework user-friendly for teachers.

Second, the ethical expertise model is grounded fundamentally in a psychological description of human flourishing rather than in a philosophical one. But it is not unique in this regard. Recently, philosophers have emphasized the importance of integrating psychology into a moral philosophy (Flanagan, 1996; Johnson, 1996). We agree with McKinnon's (1999) proposal for a functionalistic naturalism: "Given their nature, humans have certain quintessentially human needs and human abilities. These [are] relevant in determining what counts as a good human life. The point of morality is to assist us in leading better human lives, so we need to understand how our nature constrains what counts as a good human life. . . . The normative component of ethics will be seen to emerge from certain natural facts about human beings and from the ways in which these facts constrain what counts as a good human life" (p. 6). The normative claims of a moral theory ought to relate the characteristics of a good person to the characteristics of optimally functioning individuals and communities. Individuals and communities may exist more or less optimally. When we identify the characteristics of an optimal life, we rule out choices that we know are harmful to humans (e.g., a violent upbringing) or to communities (extreme individualism). In *The Republic* (bk. 4, pt. 3) Plato suggested that actions that jeopardize well-being are unjust. Human well-being and potential go hand in hand with virtuous behavior. Virtue is its own reward in terms of personal flourishing.

What are human needs? What are humans able to do? What are the constraints on human achievement and morality? The philosophical and psychological foundations of a moral education theory must directly connect to the daily experience of an individual in a practical way. A practical focus requires an operationalization of optimal functioning that addresses human needs, capacities, and constraints.

In recent years, psychological science has learned quite a lot about human flourishing. Martin Seligman (2003) has initiated a positive psychology movement that focuses on optimal human functioning—what it is and how to foster it in persons and communities. Positive psychology identifies particular factors that are generally related to positive outcomes and mental health. Our model includes these skills, which are vital for social and psychological flourishing.

Third, it bears emphasizing that the good life is not lived in isolation. One does not flourish alone. The ethical expertise model is implemented in and with a community. It is the community that establishes and nourishes the individual's moral voice, providing a moral anchor. Indeed, both Plato and Aristotle agreed that a good person is above all a good citizen. Hunter (2000) suggests that we find the answers to our existential questions in the particularities that we bring to a civic dialogue: "Character outside of a lived community, the entanglements of complex social relationships, and their shared story, is impossible" (p. 227). It is in the community that students apply and hone their ethical competencies.

Citizenship education fosters skills, attitudes, and knowledge in students that enable them to participate in civic life effectively and responsibly. Davidson (2000) aptly points out that, in a global world, it is no longer feasible to consider citizenship "within the terms of the nation as something whose parameters are national" (p. 5). Rather, citizenship becomes a global "public" value. Consequently, citizenship in the 21st century must be considered in terms of what it means to be a citizen in a global society, rather than in a local or a national society.

The Citizenship Education Policy Study Project (Cogan, 1997) was undertaken to yield a global consensus on the demands of citizenship in the early 21st century from a global society perspective. Policy experts ($N = 182$) from nine countries and many different fields (e.g., government, business, science, education) participated in the project. They were asked to identify the global trends that will have a significant impact in the next 25 years and the characteristics necessary if citizens are to cope with these trends. The experts identified several global trends that should be treated as priorities by policymakers. Trends to be encouraged include more regional alliances,

Table 3. *Necessary Characteristics of Citizens in the 21st Century*

Listed in order of priority:

1. Approaches problems as member of a global society
2. Works cooperatively with others, and takes responsibility for own roles and responsibilities in society
3. Understands, accepts, and tolerates cultural differences
4. Thinks in a critical and systematic way
5. Resolves conflict in a nonviolent manner
6. Adopts a way of life that protects the environment
7. Respects and defends human rights
8. Participates in public life at all levels of civic discourse
9. Makes full use of information-based technologies.

Source: Citizenship Education Policy Study Project (Cogan, 1997).

fewer systematic mistreatments of marginalized groups, and the necessary adoption of environmentally friendly methods by business and industry. Trends to be assuaged include increased disparities among peoples, a deterioration of the environment, increased consumerism, and rising government control.

The policy experts in the Citizenship Education Policy Study Project identified the public virtues and values that a global citizen should have in the 21st century. It is anticipated that, if people around the world do not develop these characteristics, there will be more wars and threats of war. The experts agreed on the characteristics listed in Table 3, in descending order of importance.

Using these three sets of guidelines, common understandings of goodness, psychological flourishing, and citizenship requirements, we organized our review of literature following Marshall's (1995) guidelines for selecting schemas to guide instruction (outlined below). This method is intended to replace a longitudinal study of expert knowledge in identifying a basic set of expert schemas to guide instruction.

1. *Universe definition*. According to Marshall, one should define the universe of a skill as an expert understands it. We examined philosophical, psychological, and educational literatures for the sensitivities, motivations, and problem-solving skills that are considered important for a moral person to have. Some of these are rooted in simpler forms of knowledge and skills, which we included in our final developmental list.

2. *Situation description*. We followed the guideline to describe the

sets of situations to which expert schemas pertain. For example, we identified *emotional expression* as a skill area. But what does this mean? We tried to break skills into teachable units as subskills (e.g., reading emotions in others, expressing one's own emotions). Even these, however, are parsable (e.g., reading emotions in one culture or another, in one medium or another, in different sexes or ages). We spent most of our time outlining the big picture—the big list of skills and subskills. Still to be done is to take each subskill and note the characteristics and defining features of each within particular contexts, identifying the relations among elements. So we have not done the network mapping of features and their relations, although we are able to combine skills and subskills into more complex problems, as Marshall suggests.

3. *Status quo appraisal.* Take into account the schemas that students have already. What prior knowledge do they have? How do they use prior knowledge, and how is it organized? We aimed our skills at the middle school level with the understanding that some skills are simple and should be somewhat familiar to most children by that age, whereas some skills require years of study into adulthood if not lifelong practice.

4. *Source evaluation.* We examined existing instructional materials for matchup with identified features of domain. We collected ideas for teachers to use to teach each subskill. For areas untouched by existing materials we created suggestions for academic instructional activities.

5. *Theoretical verification.* We elaborated on the hypothetical schema structures to corroborate that they conform to schema theory by considering the four kinds of knowledge (identification, elaboration, planning, execution) and how they might be manifested in the newly identified schemas. We believe that the skills and subskills that we have identified can be characterized as schemas, and we present activities according to the four kinds of knowledge that Marshall has outlined.

6. *Practicality check.* Whether an individual can acquire the knowledge identified is an empirical question, largely answered in the affirmative for empirically based skills. Some skills, like "find meaning in life," are less clearly supported by available data, yet we believe that identifying adult exemplars for each of the skills and subskills is an indication of their learnability.

Table 4. *Four Processes of Moral Behavior, Their Skills and Suggested Subskills*

Sensitivity
ES-1: Understand Emotional Expression
  Identify and express emotions
  Fine-tune sources of information
  Manage anger and aggression
ES-2: Take the Perspectives of Others
  Take an alternative perspective
  Take a cultural perspective
  Take a justice perspective
ES-3: Connecting to Others
  Relate to others
  Show Care
  Be a friend
ES-4: Responding to Diversity
  Work with group and individual differences
  Perceive diversity
  Become multicultural
ES-5: Controlling Social Bias
  Diagnose bias
  Catch stereotyping, and overcome automatic responses
  Nurture tolerance
ES-6: Interpreting Situations
  Determine what is happening
  Perceive morality
  Respond creatively
ES-7: Communicate Well
  Speak and listen
  Communicate nonverbally and alternatively
  Monitor communication

Judgment
EJ-1: Understanding Ethical Problems
  Gathering information
  Categorizing problems
  Analyzing ethical problems
EJ-2: Using Codes and Identifying Judgment Criteria
  Characterizing codes
  Discerning code application
  Judging code validity
EJ-3: Reasoning Generally
  Reasoning objectively
  Using sound reasoning
  Make scientific method intuitive
EJ-4: Reasoning Ethically
  Judging perspectives
  Reason about standards and ideals
  Reason about actions and outcomes

EJ-5: Understand Consequences
Choose your environments
Predicting consequences
Responding to consequences
EJ-6: Reflect on the Process and Outcome
Reasoning about means and ends
Making right choices
Monitoring one's reasoning
EJ-7: Coping
Apply positive reasoning
Managing disappointment and failure
Developing resilience

Focus
EM-1: Respecting Others
Be civil and courteous
Be nonviolent
Show reverence
EM-2: Cultivate Conscience
Self-command
Manage influence and power
Be honorable
EM-3: Act Responsibly
Meet obligations
Be a good steward
Be a global citizen
EM-4: Be a Community Member
Cooperate
Share resources
Cultivate Wisdom
EM-5: Finding Meaning in Life
Center yourself
Cultivate commitment
Cultivate wonder
EM-6: Valuing Traditions and Institutions
Identify and value traditions
Understand social structures
Practice democracy
EM-7: Develop Ethical Focus and Integrity
Choose good values
Build your identity
Reach for your potential

Action
EA-1: Resolving Conflicts and Problems
Solve interpersonal problems
Negotiate
Make amends
EA-2: Assert Respectfully
Attend to human needs

Table 4 (*cont.*)

- Build assertiveness skills
- Use rhetoric respectfully

EA-3: Taking Initiative as a Leader

- Be a leader
- Take initiative for and with others
- Mentor others

EA-4: Planning to Implement Decisions

- Thinking strategically
- Implement successfully
- Determine resource use

EA-5: Cultivate Courage

- Manage fear
- Stand up under pressure
- Managing change and uncertainty

EA-6: Persevering

- Be steadfast
- Overcome obstacles
- Build competence

EA-7: Work Hard

- Set reachable goals
- Manage time
- Take charge of your life

Concurrently with identifying the skills of moral expertise, we fit them into the four-process model of moral behavior. As is necessary in educational application, we had to simplify the picture to make it manageable for teaching. Hence, for example, although a skill might feature in more than one process, we placed each skill and subskill in only one process. For the list of skills and subskills, see Table 4.

Here are the four processes outlined in more detail by schemas that cluster with each process. Moral sensitivity involves, not only moral perception (noticing and picking up a problem), but also what some philosophers call *moral imagination* (interpreting a situation according to who might be affected, what possible actions might be taken, what possible reactions and outcomes might ensue). Moral imagination requires perspective taking, empathy, and controlling social bias.

Moral judgment or reasoning concerns selecting the action to take that is the most moral of the choices at hand. It requires reasoning and reflection skills. Of course, the choices can be limited by one's moral imagination or sensitivity or may not occur unless moral perception is activated. One's disposition to reason morally is affected by habits of filtering the world, such as optimistic reasoning and other types of resilient coping strategies.

Moral focus has two aspects: the selection of priorities in the immediate situation (e.g., choosing to visit a friend in the hospital rather than taking a much-needed nap or giving money saved for a vacation to a needy friend) and the more long-term motivation secured by a code of ethics, either personal, religious, or professional. Moral motivation comprises many of the skills often referred to as *virtues*: respect, responsibility, conscience, integrity.

Ethical action has two parts as well, one involving the perseverance to stay the course until the ethical job is done, and the other concerning knowing how to reach the goal, what steps to take to get there. To complete an ethical action one must have skills in conflict resolution, assertiveness, leadership, and planning.

We have outlined moral expertise schemas, but how and what do we teach children? How do we get started, and what are we aiming for? We need to examine what kind of knowledge forms a schema and what kinds of instructional and learning environments facilitate learning schemas. According to Marshall (1995), there are four levels of knowledge in a fully developed schema, from less to more complex. These aspects come about more or less sequentially as a person builds a schema from experience.

With *identification knowledge*, the boundaries, or "big picture," of the domain are roughed out. The student becomes familiar with the essential nature of domain situations, learning to recognize essential elements in the dynamic context, simultaneously processing multiple elements. Identification or pattern recognition is made based on configuration of elements. Gijselaers and Woltjer (1997) note that, when solving domain problems, novices have superficial knowledge of problems (e.g., a label for the problem) that is the beginning of identification knowledge.

Elaboration knowledge is declarative knowledge that enables the creation of a situation or mental model. It includes individual experience, including sensory information, and general abstractions. Initially, students benefit from prototypical examples. Elaboration knowledge focuses on the details of the elements in particular situations (verbal and visual).

Planning knowledge refers to the way in which a schema can be used to make plans, create expectations, and set up goals and subgoals. The schema is updated with each usage. Given more than one situation in a problem, the student must acquire knowledge necessary for determining which situation to examine first and how the situations are related to one another. The student learns to formulate a plan of action. Planning knowledge is difficult to acquire; it is greatly dependent on having the right mental model and being comfortable working with it.

Marshall's outline of schema development is supported by Rummelhart and Norman's (1988) view that schemas change with the accretion of new knowledge (e.g., the increased knowledge depth of intermediate experts) and the tuning and reconstruction of prior schemas (e.g., experts' slightly changed representations of problems).

The ethical expertise model articulates a set of strategies for developing expertise. The development of moral expertise is seen to proceed in four levels of activities that correspond to these types of knowledge (see Table 5). Here is an example of a teacher using the four aspects of schema knowledge to structure a lesson. First, the teacher focuses the students' attention, thereby building concern (sensitivity and motivation) for it among students (if the teacher thinks it is important, it must be so). The teacher coaches the student in the subskills of a skill (e.g., motivation 3: acting responsibly; subskill 2: learning stewardship). The teacher immerses students in experiences of and the need for good stewardship (e.g., water conservation), designing lessons that draw student attention to aspects of the skill (e.g., for mathematics: keep a record of how much water your family uses in a week), and providing opportunities for practice (e.g., practice turning off the faucet when you are not using the water; see what effect it has on the amount of water used in a week).

HOW DO WE STRUCTURE DELIBERATIVE CHARACTER EDUCATION?

We have identified the skills and the nature of the schemas that underlie them. But how do we teach moral expertise to children? Identifying the skills to be learned is not enough. One must say something about how the skills are to be taught. Looking at the structure of education for experts provides us with some guidance that is well supported empirically. There are three elements that are critical to developing expert schemas: (1) the environment must provide the

Table 5. *The Ethical Expertise Approach to Instruction*

Level 1: Immersion in Examples and Opportunities
In this initial phase, attention is drawn to the big picture and to the recognition of basic patterns in the domain. Accordingly, the teacher plunges students into multiple, engaging activities. Students learn to recognize broad patterns in the domain and begin to develop gradual awareness and recognition of elements in the domain (comprising identification knowledge).

Level 2: Attention to Facts and Skills
In this phase of development, knowledge is built through a focus on detail and prototypical examples. The teacher focuses the student's attention on the elemental concepts in the domain in order to build more elaborate concepts. Skills are gradually acquired through motivated, focused attention (comprising elaboration knowledge).

Level 3: Practice Procedures
At this level, one sets goals, plans the steps of problem solving, and practices skills. The teacher coaches the student and allows the student to try out many skills and ideas throughout the domain to build an understanding of how skills relate and how best to solve problems in the domain. Skills are developed through practice and exploration (comprising planning knowledge).

Level 4: Integrate Knowledge and Procedures
At this level, one executes, plans, and solves problems. Deliberate practice at this level over a long period of time can lead to expertise. The student finds numerous mentors and/or seeks out information to continue building concepts and skills. There is a gradual systematic integration and application of skills and knowledge across many situations. The student learns how to take the steps in solving complex domain problems (comprising execution knowledge).

student with the correct feedback; (2) students must learn and use theory while they build domain-relevant intuitions; and (3) students must practice, practice, practice!

The Right Environment Every individual effortlessly learns from interaction with the environment, finding contingencies and regularities, creating representations such as schemas, building knowledge about what works and what does not. Human experience is by and large dependent on vast networks of this kind of tacit or implicit knowledge, learned inside and outside school. Because learning is automatic and operates on what is seen or experienced directly, it occurs in wicked as well as good environments, so it is common for individuals to learn inappropriate as well as appropriate intuitions. As Hogarth (2001, 85) says: "The process that leads to acquiring valid beliefs about the world is the same process that leads to acquiring superstitions and other erroneous beliefs." This means, for example, that a child raised in a white-supremacist environment will develop intuitions corresponding to that environment. The child is not able to develop appropriate intuitions about the hated groups if there is no direct positive experience with them. Hence intuitions garnered from the experienced and observed can be inappropriate intuitions that become firm beliefs (a self-fulfilling prophecy).

Tacit knowledge forms the rich base of practical intelligence within any domain (Sternberg, 1998). Experts in training learn in well-structured environments that provide them with the feedback needed to perform well. The key to developing moral character is selecting and designing the environments that influence the intuitions that the child develops (Hogarth, 2001). The most important conclusion that we can draw for education is that, if the child is learning constantly from the regularities in the environments, then the environments in which educators and parents place them must be designed or chosen carefully. The environment for learning is critical for skill development. The environment reinforces and rewards particular responses. Too often adults do not attend to the reward structures of the environments in which they place children, thinking that their intent is strong enough. If children do not get appropriate learning structures for character development either in school outside school, what is the result? Their character development is haphazard. Their moral personhood is spotty and opportunistic.

How do educators begin to foster in students the vast network of schemas that make up a domain's practical intelligence? Since so much of human processing and decisionmaking—including moral—occurs on an intuitive level built from long-term experience, this must be the focus of moral education. Deliberative, intentional character education is critical because children are going to automatically learn, and, if they don't learn ethical skills, they will learn vice (Kekes, 1990).

Learn and Use Theory It is not only an appropriate environment that contributes to the development of expertise. Learning from experience without reflection can be harmful, in part because one tends to engage in *single-loop* learning, learning that confirms what you already know or think you know (Argyris, 1991). Instead, the most effective learning is what Argyris calls *double-loop* learning, in which people question what they know or think they know. Another way to say this is to point out how the deliberative mind is needed to counteract the automatic responses of intuitions, to rethink behaviors associated with those intuitions. This has been demonstrated in research with older adults who do not wish to be racists. They may have automatic prejudiced responses, but their deliberative mind keeps them from acting on them (Gilbert, 1989; Quattrone, 1982).

Experts become experts in part because they learn to use explicit theory developed by previous generations of experts (Abernathy & Hamm, 1995). Along with the implicit learning that comes from immersion in a situation, they are given theoretical tools with which to perceive the domain. In expert education, the intuitive mind and the analytic mind are developed together.

Practice But there is more to building expertise than a well-structured environment and learning theory. Experts put in a lot of time and focused effort/practice in the domain (Ericsson & Charness, 1994). The standard amount of time that it takes to become a world-class expert is 10,000 hours, or approximately 10 years (Chase & Simon, 1973). This practice is not just time on task; it is focused on the key skills of the domain, and it is coached by an expert.

Practice should occur in authentic settings because real-world schemas involve multiple brain systems (e.g., visual, motor, language) and cognitive processes (Hogarth, 2001). Schemas can involve one kind of system, for example, procedural knowledge (e.g., how to introduce one friend to another) or declarative knowledge (what morality means), or a combination of systems. Schema application can involve different types of reasoning (Ericcson & Smith, 1991), such as analogical and/or intuitive reasoning (Hogarth, 2001); different types of processing such as linear and/or parallel processing (McClelland, 1995); different levels of awareness such as subconscious and automatic or conscious and controlled (Uleman & Bargh, 1989); and different types of knowledge (declarative, procedural). Essentially, a schema is a goal-oriented cognitive mechanism that operates in particular contexts using one or more of these systems (Neisser, 1976).

In summary, to build expertise you need a well-structured environment, explicit use and learning of theory, and an enormous amount of focused, deliberative practice (Ericsson & Smith, 1991).

Likewise, to become people of good character, students need opportunities to develop their intuitions in well-structured environments, explicit instruction about the theory behind the skills they are learning, and coached practice to develop their ethical skills properly. From all this, experts develop a whole set of skills, including reflective skills, routines, and superior processing capabilities (Abernathy & Hamm, 1995).

CHARACTER DEVELOPMENT DAY-TO-DAY

There are three aspects of character-development education that I want to emphasize. The model of skill development that I have just presented is intended to be incorporated into standards-driven academic instruction at school. A second aspect is the climate of the school: the way that adults treat one another and treat the students is fundamental to building caring school communities that nurture character and moral motivation (Solomon, Watson, & Battistich, 2001). The third aspect is related to both of these but focuses on the orientation of the adult. In other words, what should parents and teachers be doing moment to moment to foster character development in children?

Let me just mention two sets of actions that parents and teachers ought to take, based on research across psychology. Experts in training often experience these things in their training as their intuitions and schemas develop. These two areas stem from a longer list of preliminary suggestions that I am putting together (Narvaez, 2004) and are things that good parents and teachers do, but more often accidentally: marketing morality and fostering a moral personal narrative. Within the current social context, in which most of what children are experiencing encourages immoral character development, we must be intentional and deliberate in character-development education. Essentially what needs to be done is to select the schemas that you want children to have and build them from the ground up (Derry, 1996; Marshall, 1995).

Market Morality First, parents and teachers should market morality; that is, they should capture children's attention and influence preconscious and subconscious processing. Right now, children live in a world of marketing and branding (Quart, 2003). They are bombarded with messages, and most of these messages do not encourage morality. Parents and teachers need to offer a counterweight, conscientiously fighting back. This means far more than putting up posters. Marketers use many techniques to make a brand attractive. Some of these techniques are included here for parents and teachers to use.

a) Focus the child's attention on moral aspects of situations. We are easily led to believe in the importance of what our attention is drawn to by others, whether it is washing hands before a meal or watching the Super Bowl. Functioning like a spotlight, attention has the dominant function of facilitating all critical functions of the whole system: perception; storage; retrieval; focus; sequencing; and testing (Hogarth, 2001). Experts are coached to attend to certain features and to think in certain ways (Marshall, 1995). For deliberative character education, adults need to focus children's attention on being morally sensitive, reasoning morally, being morally motivated, and taking moral action.

b) Make moral processes familiar. We know from research in perception and social cognition that ease of processing breeds preference (Zajonc, 1980). The billions of dollars put into advertising attest to this effect. What is familiar becomes preferred. What kinds of things are children most familiar with these days? A few are fast-food products, movie merchandising, and violence.

c) Focus on morality so much that people will automatically orient themselves to it; build automaticity by frequent presentation of constructs and frequent experience. There is evidence that people chronically gauge events and other people by particular measurements, "chronically accessible constructs" such as thinness, intelligence, or income (Fiske & Taylor, 1991; Higgins, 1999). Chronically accessed constructs influence one's impressions of others, one's memory for and interpretation of social events (Higgins, 1999). This is true for moral constructs as well (Lapsley & Lasky, 1999). For example, a parent who is always worried about weight will likely raise a child with similar automatic orientations. Similarly, a parent who is explicitly concerned about being considerate of others will likely raise a child with a similar preoccupation. Right now, the U.S. culture is encouraging in its citizens the development of consumerism as a chronically accessible construct, and it is becoming the most elaborated schema that many children have.

d) Prime with prosocial thoughts/actions. Strong claims are made for "the automaticity of everyday life" (Bargh, 1997, 1). For example, there is evidence that nonconscious mental systems direct self-regulation (Bargh & Chartrand, 1999) and that evaluations, social perceptions, judgment, social interactions, and internal goal structures are similarly operative without conscious intention or acts of will (Bargh & Ferguson, 2000). Indeed, Bargh and Chartrand (1999) argue that we are not normally engaged in active planning, selecting, choosing, or interpreting when processing information. Moreover: "The ability to exercise such conscious, intentional control is actually quite limited" (p. 462). We are primed by the actions of others, by the images and messages that surround us. Too often children are primed with violence and cruelty rather than with concern and helpfulness.

e) Influence processing at all times with a prosocial, proactive bias. Bruner (1957) noted that a lot of social information is inherently ambiguous. The ambiguity about what was happening to Kitty Genovese as she was murdered played into the inaction of the many spectators who succumbed to the paralysis of the bystander effect (Staub, 1978)—the belief that someone else would act if action was worthwhile (as the Genovese witnesses indicated). Bargh (1989), Fiske and Taylor (1991), and others suggest that, because of this ambiguity, social perception is driven by category accessibility, ease of category activation. As a result, cue processing is affected by chronic accessibility constructs, priming, and well-rehearsed schemas. Better-rehearsed schemas may be initially selected and held on to despite evidence against them (Bargh, 1989). In order to counter the bias toward inaction, we need to prepare our children to take action under ambiguity. We should teach them to be proactive regardless of what others do or do not do, with an attitude of, "What can I do to help?"

Provide Narrative Elaboration We learn who we are from stories, the stories told about us and the stories we tell ourselves (e.g., Schank, 1999). Parents and adults need to use narrative elaboration to develop the child's sense of self and, through it, the child's moral motivation. Children hear many self-engrossing narratives from current society, and most of them focus on hedonism, consumerism, and status. If parents and teachers do not provide children with a scaffolded narrative, marketers are all too happy to do so.

a) Verbalize and interpret things for the child. The child internalizes adult speech and adult cultural knowledge (Rogoff, 1990; Vygotsky,

1987). Put moral thinking into words. Talk; reason; tell stories about moral goals. Develop the child's moral imagination.

b) Foster a prosocial moral narrative. Individuals operate in a narrative world framework that they themselves have structured and in which they make behavioral choices (McAdams, 1993; Schank, 1999). Adults influence this world by what they emphasize, by what they expect, and by what environments they set up for children.

c) Fill memories with moral schemas. Not only is more of an experience remembered when it is accompanied by words, but the way in which the adult helps the child remember events—for example, the types of questions an adult asks—also actually structures the child's memory (Fivush, 1991; Nelson, 1986). To foster personal moral schemas, adults can remind children how they helped and how they were good, teaching children to automatically self-assess in these ways.

d) Teach metacognitive skills. Children can learn the metacognitive skills that moral experts have, including those of self-control (Mischel, 1990): (i) self-monitoring of attention away from temptations; (ii) top-down executive control of negative impulses; (iii) awareness of susceptibilities to particular stimuli; and (iv) self-cheerleading when energy flags.

Conclusion

Piaget and Kohlberg gave life to the psychological study of moral development. They provided us with routes to study the deliberative moral mind. We have looked at the transformation of moral development theory from a focus on moral judgment stages to moral judgment schemas, from a focus on moral judgment schemas to a broader focus on the schemas of moral personality. We discussed the importance of schemas in human information processing, including multiple moral processes. I outlined the kinds of skills and schemas that moral experts have and made suggestions for how to nurture them in children. This requires an emphasis on creating good environments for intuition development, providing analytic tools, and providing extensive coached practice. It is time to focus on developing the intuitive moral mind. It is time to be deliberative about helping children develop prosocial intuitions. It is time to coach children on developing character skills. With such an education, students will develop schemas of goodness, of justice, of compassion. They will learn routines of helping, reasoning, and following through. They will learn skills of leadership, commitment, and respect. They will build memories of personal ethical action and build empathic reactions to others. With such an education, they will become the citizens we need for the 21st century.

Notes

1. The topics discussed in this section are fully described in Rest, Narvaez, Bebeau, and Thoma (1999b).

2. It is necessary to point out that the distinction between the maintaining norms and the postconventional schemas is not the same as a left-right political distinction. Rather, it is possible to be right-wing conventional (e.g., those who argue that it is unpatriotic to criticize one's government when it is at war) or left-wing conventional (e.g., those who argue that it is illiberal to criticize the philosophical positions taken by the traditionally oppressed). And it is possible to be left-wing postconventional (e..g., John Rawls, 1971) or right-wing postconventional (e.g., as a libertarian like Robert Nozick, 1974, or a communitarian like Michael Walzer, 1983).

3. The topics discussed in this section are more fully developed in Narvaez (2004).

References

Abernathy, C. M., & Hamm, R. M. (1995). *Surgical intuition*. Philadelphia: Hanley & Belfus.

Adelson, J. (1971). The political imagination of the young adolescent. *Daedalus, 100,* 1013–1050.

Argyris, C. (1991, May–June). Teaching smart people how to learn. *Harvard Business Review,* 44–54.

Bargh, J. A. (1989). Conditional automaticity: Varieties of automatic influence in social perception and cognition. In J. S. Uleman & J. A. Bargh (Eds.), *Unintended thought* (pp. 3–51). New York: Guilford.

Bargh, J. A. (1997). The automaticity of everyday life. In R. S. Wyer Jr. (Ed.), *The automaticity of everyday life: Advances in social cognition* (Vol. 10, pp. 1–61). Mahwah NJ: Erlbaum.

Bargh, J. A., & Chartrand, T. L. (1999). The unbearable automaticity of being. *American Psychologist, 54,* 462–479.

Bargh, J. A., & Ferguson, M. J. (2000). Beyond behaviorism: On the automaticity of higher mental processes. *Psychological Bulletin, 126,* 925–945.

Bartlett, F. A. (1932). *A study in experimental and social psychology*. New York: Cambridge University Press.

Beauchamp, T. L., & Childress, J. F. (1994). *Principles of biomedical ethics* (4th ed.). New York: Oxford University Press.

Bebeau, M., Rest, J. R., & Narvaez, D. (1999). Beyond the promise: A framework for research in moral education. *Educational Researcher, 28*(4), 18–26.

Bebeau, M. J., & Thoma, S. J. (1999). "Intermediate" concepts and the connection to moral education. *Educational Psychology Review, 11,* 343–360.

Bennett, W. (1993). *The book of virtues.* New York: Simon & Schuster.

Blasi, A. (1980). Bridging moral cognition and moral action: A critical review of the literature. *Psychological Bulletin, 88,* 1–45.

Blasi, A. (1990). How should psychologists define morality? or, The negative side effects of philosophy's influence on psychology. In T. Wren (Ed.), *The moral domain: Essays in the ongoing discussion between philosophy and the social sciences* (pp. 38–70). Cambridge: MIT Press.

Bruner, J. S. (1957). On perceptual readiness. *Psychological Review, 64,* 123–152.

Cantor, N. (1990). From thought to behavior: "Having" and "doing" in the study of personality and cognition. *American Psychologist, 45,* 735–750.

Chase, W., & Simon, H. (1973). Perception in chess. *Cognitive Psychology, 4,* 55–81.

Chi, M. T. H., & Ceci, S. J. (1987). Content knowledge: Its role, representation, and restructuring in memory development. In H. W. Reese (Ed.), *Advances in child development and behavior* (Vol. 20, pp. 91–142). San Diego: Academic.

Chi, M. T. H., Feltovich, P. I., & Glaser, R. (1981). Categorization and representation of physics problems by experts and novices. *Cognitive Science, 5,* 121–152.

Chi, M. T. H., Glaser, R., & Farr, M. J. (1988). *The nature of expertise.* Hillsdale NJ: Erlbaum.

Chiesi, H., Spilich, G., & Voss, J. (1979). Acquisition of domain-related information in relation to high and low domain knowledge. *Journal of Verbal Learning and Verbal Behavior, 18,* 257–273.

Clouser, K. D., & Gert, B. (1990). A critique of principlism. *Journal of Medicine and Philosophy, 15,* 219–236.

Cogan, J. (1997). *Multicultural citizenship: Educational policy for the 21st century.* Minneapolis: University of Minnesota.

Colby, A., & Damon, W. (1992). *Some do care: Contemporary lives of moral commitment.* New York: Free Press.

Crafton, L. K. (1983). Learning from reading: What happens when students generate their own background information? *Journal of Reading, 26,* 586–593.

Davidson, A. (2000). Fractured identities: Citizenship in a global world. In E. Vasta (Ed.), *Citizenship, community, and democracy* (pp. 3–21). New York: St. Martin's.

Davidson, P., Turiel, E., & Black, A. (1983). The effect of stimulus familiarity on the use of criteria and justifications in children's social reasoning. *British Journal of Developmental Psychology, 1,* 49–65.

DeGrazia, D. (1992). Moving forward in bioethical theory: Theories, cases, and specified principlism. *Journal of Medicine and Philosophy, 17,* 511–539.

Derry, S. J. (1996). Cognitive schema theory in the constructivist debate. *Educational Psychologist, 31,* 163–174.

Edelstein, W., & Krettenauer, T. (2004). Many are called, but few are chosen: Moving beyond the modal levels in normal development. In D. Lapsley & D. Narvaez (Eds.), *Moral development, self, and identity* (pp. 213–238). Mahwah NJ: Erlbaum.

Eisenberg, N. (Ed.). (1982). *The development of prosocial behavior.* New York: Academic.

Endicott, L., Bock, T., & Narvaez, D. (2003). Multicultural experience, moral judgment, and intercultural development. *International Journal of Intercultural Relations, 27,* 403–419.

Ericsson, K. A., & Charness, N. (1994). Expert performance: Its structure and acquisition. *American Psychologist, 49,* 725–747.

Ericsson, K. A., & Smith, J. (Eds.). (1991). *Toward a general theory of expertise.* New York: Cambridge University Press.

Etzioni, A. (1996). *The new golden rule.* New York: Basic.

Fiske, S. T., & Taylor, S. E. (1991). *Social cognition* (2d ed.). New York: McGraw-Hill.

Fivush, R. (1991). The social construction of personal narratives. *Merrill-Palmer Quarterly, 37*(1), 59–81.

Flanagan, O. (1996). Ethics naturalized: Ethics as human ecology. In L. May, M. Friedman, & A. Clark (Eds.), *Mind and morals: Essays on cognitive science and ethics* (pp. 19–44). Cambridge: MIT Press.

Gernsbacher, M. A. (Ed.). (1994). *Handbook of psycholinguistics.* San Diego: Academic.

Gibbs, J. (1979). Kohlberg's moral stage theory: A Piagetian revision. *Human Development, 22,* 89–112.

Gielen, U. P., & Markoulis, D. C. (1994). Preference for principled moral reasoning: A developmental and cross-cultural perspective. In L. L. Adler & U. P. Gielen (Eds.), *Cross-cultural topics in psychology* (pp. 73–87). Westport CT: Praeger.

Gijselaers, W. H., & Woltjer, G. (1997). *Expert novice differences in the representation of economics problems.* Paper presented at the annual meeting of the American Educational Research Association, Chicago.

Gilbert, D. T. (1989). Thinking lightly about others: Automatic components of the social inference process. In J. S. Uleman & J. A. Bargh (Eds.), *Unintended thought* (pp. 189–211). New York: Guilford.

Gilligan, C. (1982). *In a different voice: Psychological theory and women's development.* Cambridge: Harvard University Press.

Gleason, T., & Narvaez, D. (2003). *Expertise differences in comprehending moral narratives.* Manuscript in preparation.

Hare, R. (1963). *Freedom and reason.* New York: Oxford University Press.

Harris, R. J., Lee, D. J., Hensley, D. L., & Schoen, L. M. (1988). The effect of cultural script knowledge on memory for stories over time. *Discourse Processes, 11,* 413–431.

Hart, D., Yates, M., Fegley, S., & Wilson, G. (1995). Moral commitment in inner-city adolescents. In M. Killen & D. Hart (Eds.), *Morality in everyday life* (pp. 371–407). Cambridge: Cambridge University Press.

Higgins, E. T. (1999). Persons and situations: Unique explanatory principles or variability in general principles? In D. Cervone & Y. Shoda (Eds.), *The coherence of personality: Social-cognitive bases of consistency, variability, and organization* (pp. 61–93). New York: Guilford.

Higgins, E. T., & Kruglanski, A. W. (Eds.). (1996). *Social psychology: Handbook of basic principles.* New York: Guilford.

Hogarth, R. M. (2001). *Educating intuition.* Chicago: University of Chicago Press.

Hunter, J. D. (1991). *Culture wars: The struggle to define America.* New York: Basic.

Hunter, J. D. (2000). *The death of character: Moral education in an age without good or evil.* New York: Basic.

Jensen, L. A. (1996). *Different habits, different hearts: Orthodoxy and progressivism in the United States and India.* Unpublished doctoral dissertation, University of Chicago.

Johnson, M. L. (1996). How moral psychology changes moral theory. In L. May, M. Friedman, & A. Clark (Eds.), *Mind and morals: Essays on cognitive science and ethics* (pp. 45–68). Cambridge: MIT Press.

Keil, F. C., & Wilson, R. A. (1999). *Explanation and cognition.* Cambridge: MIT Press.

Kekes, J. (1990). *Facing evil.* Princeton: Princeton University Press.

Kohlberg, L. (1976). Moral stages and moralization: The cognitive developmental approach. In T. Lickona (Ed.), *Moral development and behavior* (pp. 31–53). New York: Holt, Rinehart & Wilson.

Kohlberg, L. (1981). *Essays on moral development: Vol. 1. The philosophy of moral development.* New York: Harper & Row.

Kohlberg, L., Levine, C., & Hewer, A. (1983). *Moral stages: A current formulation and a response to critics* (Vol. 10 of Contributions to Human Development, J. A. Meacham, Ed.). Basel: Karger.

Lapsley, D. K. (1996). *Moral psychology.* New York: Westview.

Lapsley, D. K., & Lasky, B. (1999). Prototypic moral character. *Identity, 1*(4), 345–363.

Lapsley, D., & Narvaez, D. (Eds.). (2004a). *Moral development, self, and identity.* Mahwah NJ: Erlbaum.

Lapsley, D., & Narvaez, D. (2004b). A social-cognitive approach to the moral personality. In D. Lapsley & D. Narvaez (Eds.), *Moral development, self, and identity* (pp. 189–212). Mahwah NJ: Erlbaum.

Lapsley, D., & Narvaez, D. (in press). Moral psychology at the crossroads. In D. Lapsley & C. Power (Eds.), *Character psychology and character education.* Notre Dame IN: University of Notre Dame Press.

Lourenço, O., & Machado, A. (1996). In defense of Piaget's theory: A reply to 10 common criticisms. *Psychological Review, 103*(1), 143–164.

Marshall, S. P. (1995). *Schemas in problem solving*. Cambridge: Cambridge University Press.

Marty, M., & Appleby, S. (1993). *Fundamentalisms and the state*. Chicago: University of Chicago Press.

McAdams, D. P. (1993). *The stories we live by: Personal myths and the making of the self*. New York: Morrow.

McClelland, J. L. (1995). A connectionist approach to knowledge and development. In T. J. Simon & G. S. Halford (Eds.), *Developing cognitive competence: New approaches to process modeling* (pp. 157–204). Mahwah: Erlbaum.

McKinnon, C. (1999). *Character, virtue theories, and the vices*. Toronto: Broadview.

McNeel, S. P. (1994). College teaching and student moral development. In J. Rest & D. Narvaez (Eds.), *Moral development in the professions: Psychology and applied ethics* (pp. 27–50). Hillsdale NJ: Erlbaum.

Meilaender, G. (1984). *The theory and practice of virtue*. Notre Dame IN: University of Notre Dame Press.

Mischel, W. (1990). Personality dispositions revisited and revised: A view after three decades. In L. A. Pervin (Ed.), *Handbook of personality: Theory and research* (pp. 111–134). New York: Guilford.

Mischel, W. (1999). Personality coherence and dispositions in a cognitive-affective personality system (CAPS) approach. In D. Cervone & Y. Shoda (Eds.), *The coherence of personality: Social cognitive bases of consistency, variability, and organization* (pp. 37–60). New York: Guilford.

Narvaez, D. (1998). The effects of moral schemas on the reconstruction of moral narratives in 8th grade and college students. *Journal of Educational Psychology, 90*(1), 13–24.

Narvaez, D. (1999). Using discourse processing methods to study moral thinking. *Educational Psychology Review, 11*(4), 377–394.

Narvaez, D. (2001). Moral text comprehension: Implications for education and research. *Journal of Moral Education, 30*(1), 43–54.

Narvaez, D. (2004). *Educating moral intuition*. Manuscript in preparation.

Narvaez, D., Bentley, J., Gleason, T., & Samuels, J. (1998). Moral theme comprehension in third grade, fifth grade, and college students. *Reading Psychology, 19*(2), 217–241.

Narvaez, D., & Bock, T. (2002). Moral schemas and tacit judgement; or, How the Defining Issues Test is supported by cognitive science. *Journal of Moral Education, 31*(3), 297–314.

Narvaez, D., Endicott, L., & Thoma, S. J. (2001, August). *Expertise and the speed of moral information processing*. Paper presented at the meeting of the American Psychological Association, San Francisco.

Narvaez, D., Getz, I., Rest, J. R., & Thoma, S. (1999). Individual moral judgment and cultural ideologies. *Developmental Psychology, 35*, 478–488.

Narvaez, D., Gleason, T., Mitchell, C., & Bentley, J. (1999). Moral theme comprehension in children. *Journal of Educational Psychology, 91*(3), 477–487.

Narvaez, D., & Lapsley, D. (in press). The psychological foundations of moral expertise. In D. Lapsley & C. Power (Eds.), *Character psychology and character education*. Notre Dame IN: University of Notre Dame Press.

Narvaez, D., & Rest, J. (1995). The four components of acting morally. In W. Kurtines & J. Gewirtz (Eds.), *Moral behavior and moral development: An introduction* (pp. 385–400). New York: McGraw-Hill.

Neisser, U. (1976). *Cognitive psychology*, New York: Appleton-Century-Crofts.

Nelson, K. (1986). Event knowledge and cognitive development. In K. Nelson (Ed.), *Event knowledge: Structure and function in development*. Hillsdale NJ: Erlbaum.

Nozick, R. (1974). *Anarchy, state, and utopia*. New York: Basic.

Nunner-Winkler, G. (1984). Two moralities? A critical discussion of an ethic of care and responsibility versus an ethic of rights and justice. In W. Kurtines & J. Gewirtz (Eds.), *Morality, moral behavior, and moral development: Basic issues in theory and research* (pp. 348–361). New York: Wiley.

Pascarella, E. T., & Terenzini, P. (1991). *How college affects students: Findings and insights from twenty years of research*. San Francisco: Jossey-Bass.

Piaget, J. (1970). *Genetic epistemology* (E. Duckworth, Trans.). New York: Columbia University Press.

Piaget, J., & Inhelder, B. (1969). *The psychology of the child* (H. Weaver, Trans.). New York: Basic.

Pressley, M., & Afflerbach, P. (1995). *Verbal protocols of reading*. Hillsdale NJ: Erlbaum.

Quart, A. (2003). *Branded: The buying and selling of teenagers*. Cambridge: Perseus.

Quattrone, G. A. (1982). Overattribution and unit formation: When behavior engulfs the person. *Journal of Personality and Social Psychology, 42*, 593–607.

Rawls, J. (1971). *A theory of justice*. Cambridge: Harvard University Press.

Rest, J. R. (1969). *Hierarchies of comprehension and preference in a developmental stage model of moral thinking*. Unpublished doctoral dissertation, University of Chicago.

Rest, J. (1973). The hierarchical nature of stages of moral judgment. *Journal of Personality, 41*, 86–109.

Rest, J. (1983). Morality. In P. H. Mussen (Series Ed.), J. Flavell & E. Markman (Vol. Eds.), *Handbook of child psychology: Vol. 3. Cognitive development* (4th ed., pp. 556–629). New York: Wiley.

Rest, J. (1986). *Moral development: Advances in research and theory*. New York: Praeger.

Rest, J., & Narvaez, D. (1991). The college experience and moral development. In W. Kurtines & J. Gewirtz (Eds.), *Handbook of moral behavior and development* (pp. 229–245). Hillsdale NJ: Erlbaum.

Rest, J., Narvaez, D., Bebeau, M., & Thoma, S. (1999a). A neo-Kohlbergian approach to moral judgment: An overview of Defining Issues Test research. *Educational Psychology Review, 11*(4), 291–324.

Rest, J. R., Narvaez, D., Bebeau, M., & Thoma, S. (1999b). *Postconventional moral thinking: A neo-Kohlbergian approach.* Mahwah NJ: Erlbaum.

Rest, J. R., Narvaez, D., Bebeau, M., & Thoma, S. (2000). A neo-Kohlbergian approach. *Journal of Moral Education, 29*(4), 381–395.

Rest, J., Turiel, E., & Kohlberg, L. (1969). Level of moral development as a determinant of preference and comprehension of moral judgments made by others. *Journal of Personality, 37*, 225–252.

Rogoff, B. (1990). *Apprenticeship in thinking: Cognitive development in social context.* London: Oxford University Press.

Rummelhart, D. E. (1980). Schemata: The building blocks of cognition. In R. Spiro, B. Bruce, & W. Brewer (Eds.), *Theoretical issues in reading comprehension* (pp. 33–58). Hillsdale NJ: Erlbaum.

Rumelhart, D. E., & Norman, D. A. (1988). Representation in memory. In R. C. Atkinson & R. J. Herrnstein (Eds.), *Handbook of experimental psychology: Vol. 2. Learning and cognition* (2d ed., pp. 511–587). New York: Wiley.

Schank, R. C. (1999). *Dynamic memory revisited.* Cambridge: Cambridge University Press.

Schank, R. C., & Abelson, R. (1977). *Scripts, plans, and goals.* Hillsdale NJ: Erlbaum.

Schiller, R. (1999). The relationship of developmental tasks to life satisfaction, moral reasoning, and occupational attainment at age 28. *Journal of Adult Development, 5*(4), 239–254.

Schlaefli, A., Rest, J., & Thoma, S. (1985). Does moral education improve moral judgment? A meta-analysis of intervention studies using the Defining Issues Test. *Review of Educational Research, 55*(3), 319–352.

Seligman, Martin E. P. (2003). Positive psychology: Fundamental assumptions. *American Psychologist, 16*(3), 126–127.

Shweder, R. A. (1982, June). Review of Lawrence Kohlberg's *Essays on moral development: Vol. 1. The philosophy of moral development. Contemporary Psychology*, 421–424.

Shweder, R. A. (1991). *Thinking through cultures.* Cambridge: Harvard University Press.

Shweder, R. A., Mahapatra, M., & Miller, J. G. (1987). Culture and moral development. In J. Kagan & S. Lamb (Eds.), *The emergence of morality in young children* (pp. 1–83). Chicago: University of Chicago Press.

Siegler, R. S. (1997). Concepts and methods for studying cognitive change. In E. Amsel & K. A. Renninger (Eds.), *Change and development: Issues of theory, method, and application* (pp. 77–98). Mahwah NJ: Erlbaum.

Snarey, J. (1985). The cross-cultural universality of social-moral development. *Psychological Bulletin, 97*(2), 202–232.

Solomon, D., Watson, M. S., & Battistich, V. A. (2001). Teaching and schooling effects on moral/prosocial development. In V. Richardson (Ed.), *Handbook of research on teaching* (4th ed., pp. 566–603). Washington DC: American Educational Research Association.

Spilich, G., Vesonder, G., Chiesi, H., & Voss, J. (1979). Text processing of domain-related information for individuals with high and low domain knowledge. *Journal of Verbal Learning and Verbal Behavior, 18,* 275–290.

Staub, E. (1978). *Positive social behavior and morality: Vol. 1. Social and personal influences.* New York: Academic.

Sternberg, R. (1998). Abilities are forms of developing expertise, *Educational Researcher, 3,* 22–35.

Strike, K. A. (1982). *Educational policy and the just society.* Urbana: University of Illinois Press.

Taylor, S. E., & Crocker, J. (1981). Schematic bases of social information processing. In E. T. Higgins, C. P. Herman, & M. P. Zanna (Eds.), *Social cognition: The Ontario symposium* (Vol. 1, pp. 89–134). Hillsdale NJ: Erlbaum.

Thoma, S. J., Malone Beach, E., & Ladewig, B. (1997). *Moral judgment and adjustment in late adolescence.* Unpublished manuscript, University of Alabama.

Thoma, S. J., Rest, J. R., & Barnett, R. (1986). Moral judgment, behavior, decision making, and attitudes. In J. Rest (Ed.), *Moral development: Advances in research and theory* (pp. 133–175). New York: Praeger.

Tisak, M., & Turiel, E. (1988). Variation in seriousness of transgressions and children's moral and conventional concepts. *Developmental Psychology, 24,* 352–357.

Toulmin, S. (1981). The tyranny of principles. *Hastings Center Report, 11,* 31–39.

Turiel, E. (1983). *The development of social knowledge: Morality and convention.* Cambridge: Cambridge University Press.

Uleman, J. S., & Bargh, J. A. (Eds.). (1989). *Unintended thought.* New York: Guilford.

Vicente, K. J., & Wang, J. H. (1998). An ecological theory of expertise effects in memory recall. *Psychological Review, 105,* 33–57.

Vygotsky, L. S. (1987). Thinking and speech. In R. W. Rieber & A. S. Carton (Eds.), N. Minick (Trans.), *The collected works of L. S. Vygotsky* (pp. 37–285). New York: Plenum.

Walzer, M. (1983). *Spheres of justice.* New York: Basic.

Whitehead, A. N. (1929). *The aims of education and other essays.* New York: Macmillan.

Youniss, J., & Yates, M. (1997). *Community service and social responsibility in youth.* Chicago: University of Chicago Press.

Zajonc, R. B. (1980). Feeling and thinking: Preferences need no inferences. *American Psychologist, 35,* 151–175.

The Development of Moral Identity

Daniel Hart
Rutgers University

Moral identity joins two traditions of theorizing. Attempts to characterize the essences of morality, to understand the origins of moral inclinations, and to promote the pursuit of a moral life are found throughout the histories of philosophy and psychology. A great deal of progress has been made along the way. The questions concerning moral life to which answers are sought are much clearer; weaknesses in early philosophical and psychological theories seeking to explain moral life have been revealed; and there is an accumulating store of information about human nature that can inform efforts to understand the moral domain. The conceptual and empirical progress makes the moral domain ripe for study. But so does its enduring relevance for our lives; moral questions and moral issues pervade our experience. Events at the scale of nations have moral facets, as do our daily interactions with others.

The notion of identity also fascinates philosophers and psychologists, many of whom believe that the importance of identity for understanding human affairs increases as cultures are transformed by modernity (e.g., Baumeister, 1986; Taylor, 1989). Identity concerns

I thank Robert Atkins, Samuel Hardy, Gus Carlo, and Carolyn Edwards for their careful reading of several drafts and the W. T. Grant Foundation for its support of the research described in this chapter.

our fundamental notions of ourselves: who we are, what we are doing in this world, and where we are going. These kinds of concerns are connected in some fashion to our moral values, appraisals, emotions, and actions. As Flanagan has pointed out: "The connection with either or both social peace, harmony, and welfare, on the one hand, and self-esteem and personal identity, on the other, is probably a necessary condition for something—a value, a virtue, a kind of action, a principle, or a problem—to fall under the concept of 'morality'" (1991, p. 18). Bringing together the notions of morality and identity offers opportunities for broadening our understanding of morality and identity as well as deepening our appreciation of the complexity of human life. Before examining why the two should be brought together, it is worthwhile to discuss briefly the broad outlines of each.

The Moral Domain

Moral theories seek to provide answers to three broad questions (Williams, 1995). The first of these questions is, What is the right thing to do? Deontological theories attempt to identify principles or processes that can be applied in the search for the morally correct line of action. The goal is to act in a way that protects others' autonomy and rights (Williams, 1995, p. 551). For example, Kant (1875/1964) believed that the categorical imperative, a principle by which an individual measures the moral worth of an intended action by judging whether the action could be made obligatory for all persons in the same context, could ensure that individuals were always treated as means rather than ends.

Second, moral theories address the question, How is the best possible state of affairs achieved? Utilitarian theories, which seek to offer single principles that can be applied in all moral contexts to yield the correct answer to moral dilemmas, constitute one line of theorizing in this tradition.

Third, the question, What qualities make for a good person? orients theories that focus on virtue. Aristotle is generally considered to be a theorist in this tradition, as are a number of recent philosophers.

Williams (1995) points out that the three traditions—deontological, utilitarian (or consequentialist), and virtue—are traditionally placed in competition with each other, with advocates seeking to demonstrate that a theory in one tradition is superior to those in the other two traditions. There are the debates between the deontological theorists and the utilitarians, and more recently the advocates of virtue approaches have decried the emphasis on the objective judgment at the heart of the deontological theories. But Williams (see also Watson, 1993) suggests that, because the three traditions are oriented by different questions, they can complement and inform each other, at least in some respects.

Identity

Identity refers to a variety of experiences associated with the self (for a review, see Hart & Yates, 1997). These include self-awareness, continuity through time and context, the self in relation to others, and the self as the basis for strong evaluations. Each of these is briefly considered below.

SELF-AWARENESS

Self-awareness refers to the ability to take oneself as the object of reflection. Self-awareness is usually accompanied by the sense of attachment to and investment in oneself. As William James pointed out, self-reflection is characterized by a "unique kind of interest" (1890, p. 289). An example of this "unique kind of interest" particularly relevant to the aim of this chapter concerns goals: one cares very much about one's own goals in life—how close one is to them and whether the distance is diminishing or growing—but much less about someone else's. Indeed, the extent to which an individual is emotionally invested in an aspect of the self is directly related to the centrality of the aspect to the sense of the identity.

COHERENCE AND INTEGRATION

The sense of identity is also associated with the experiences of integration among aspects of self and the continuity of the self over time and through contexts. Erikson has suggested: "The wholeness to be achieved at this stage I have called a sense of inner identity. The young person, in order to experience wholeness, must feel a progressive continuity between that which he has come to be during the long years of childhood and that which he promises to become in the anticipated future; between that which he conceives himself to be and that which he perceives others to see in him and to expect of him" (1968, p. 87). To plan for the future rests on the sense of personal continuity and coherence across time and context; for example, one saves for retirement on the basis of the assumption that one is caring now for the person one will become in the future. Similarly, our intuitions concerning moral and legal responsibility presuppose that the individual who acts today bears responsibility for that action tomorrow.

SELF IN RELATION

One of the strengths of Erikson's work on identity is its focus on the social-relational aspects of identity. As Erikson described it: "Identity includes, but is more than, the sum of all the successive identifications of those earlier years when the child wanted to be, and often was forced to become, like the people he depended on. Identity is a unique product, which now meets a crisis to be solved only in new identifications with age mates and with leader figures outside the family" (1968, p. 87). This suggests that identity is revised and reconstructed throughout life. Relationships and group processes influence which facets of self are judged to be at the core of identity; inspiration, the sense of being motivated to pursue goals and ideals by the example of another (see Thrash & Elliot, 2003), results in changes in identity. The openness of identity to social influence suggests that it is more plastic than personality traits, which change slowly and do not reflect social influences directly.

IDENTITY AS AN ORIENTATION

Identity is composed of the specific plans, goals, and values that matter to the individual. These form a basis for perceiving, judging, and acting. Charles Taylor has suggested: "Identity is defined by the commitments and identifications which provide the frame or horizon within which I can try to determine from case to case what is good, or valuable, or what ought to be done, or what I endorse or oppose" (1989, p. 27).

It is this notion of identity, identity as one's location in "moral space" (Taylor, 1989, p. 28), that helps bind the notion of identity to the moral domain. If the concern with moral functioning is broadened to include consideration of how an individual's life expresses answers to all three moral questions (What is the right thing to do? How is the best possible state of affairs achieved? What qualities make for a good person?), then moral identity may help us understand how individuals integrate these answers.

The Background to Moral Identity

The growing interest in identity among psychologists (e.g., Aquino & Reed, 2002; Bergman, 2002; Colby, 2002; Reimer, 2003) and philosophers (e.g., Flanagan, 1991; Flanagan & Rorty, 1993; Glover, 1999) interested in moral life has many sources. Rather than attempt an encyclopedic review of all the moral identity literature, I review below three lines of work that highlight different strengths that the concept of moral identity offers. These lines focus on moral collapse, the specificity of moral action, and reflective integration.

MORAL COLLAPSE

To be of relevance in the world, moral psychology must offer insights into the great moral calamities of our time. For example, how is it possible that in the 20th century there were, in no particular order, the moral failures of the Holocaust, the Cultural Revolution, the My Lai massacre, and the Khmer Rouge's destruction of Cambodia? These were moral disasters of the first order. Surely a rich moral psychology would be able to give some insights into the origins of these moral collapses and some suggestions as to how similar collapses can be prevented.

Philosophical and empirical psychologists do not often study moral collapses (for an important exception, see Staub, 2003), perhaps because they occur in historical and cultural contexts that complicate analysis. Moral psychology has probably focused too exclusively on hypothetical dilemmas and on the mundane conflicts of daily life. No doubt research with hypothetical dilemmas has been productive. Developmental psychologists such as Piaget (1932/1965) and Kohlberg (1984) contributed to a revolution in our understanding of development through their research in which children were asked to reason about hypothetical moral dilemmas. Hypothetical dilemmas have also been used effectively by game theorists (e.g.,

Nowak, Page, & Sigmund, 2000), who have used the "prisoner's dilemma" and the "ultimatum game" to illustrate enduring biases and preferences in reasoning about the fair distribution of penalties and assets. Similarly our understanding of the moral domain has been advanced by studies of modestly moral behaviors such as volunteering and donations. The field is much richer for these investigations, and certainly theorists have extrapolated from them to offer explanations for a variety of moral failures.

However, it is certainly possible that extrapolation from ordinary moral behavior cannot fully account for catastrophic moral collapses, so investigations of the latter are urgently needed. There is some work that examines moral collapses directly (see, e.g., Glover, 1999; Gourevitch, 1998). Consider, for example, the disaster of Rwanda. The broad outlines of the tragedy in Rwanda are well described by Gourevitch (1998), Powers (2002), Richburg (1997), and Staub (2003), on whose accounts the following description of the events is based. Rwanda, a country roughly the size of the state of Vermont, was home to two tribes: Hutus and Tutsis. In 1994, the president of Rwanda, a member of the Hutu tribe, was killed in a plane crash. His death marked the beginning of genocide in the country. In the course of 4 months Hutus killed approximately 800,000 Tutsis. Tutsis were shot, burned, stoned, drowned, and hacked to death with machetes.

If we are to avoid moral disasters, we must understand them. The Rwandan genocide illustrates the importance of identity in moral life. For those participating in the killing, being a Hutu, and belonging to the Hutus, eclipsed all other definitions of self. Once the Tutsis were perceived as a threat to the Hutus—a perception resulting from economic inequalities, a legacy of colonial rule, and years of government propaganda—many Hutus felt compelled to protect their identities by killing Tutsis. Particularly important for the goals of this chapter is the fact that the extermination of the Tutsis by the Hutus occurred even though the two groups shared many similarities. Tutsis and Hutus spoke the same language, shared the same towns, and worked and traded with each other. Indeed, there is evidence that tribal identities were permeable, with some Hutus becoming Tutsis, and vice versa. Moreover, lethal conflict between Tutsis and Hutus was unknown until recent history. Together, these facts highlight the crucial role of identity—of, in this case, the perception of oneself as Hutu or Tutsi—in contributing to moral collapses.

Identity, and the psychological processes that influence it, does not account fully for the Rwandan genocide. For example, the world's largest countries—including the United States—sought to avoid responsibility under international treaty to intervene in Rwanda by refusing to characterize the deliberate extermination of the Tutsis with the key term *genocide* (Powers, 2002). However, identity does seem to figure in the explanation for the moral calamity in Rwanda and for many of the moral disasters of the 20th century (Glover, 1999).

SPECIFICITY OF ACTION

Psychologists (e.g., Bergman, 2002) and philosophers agree that the moral life features moral action. Aristotle claimed: "The activity, not the possession, of virtue is paramount; possession without activity means a life where nothing gets done" (Doris, 2002, p. 17). Moral exemplars, individuals whom we admire for their moral achievements, often earn respect for their long-term dedication to particular causes and lines of action. Nelson Mandela, Martin Luther King, Mohandas Gandhi, all pursued political ends that advanced moral goals. All had characteristics that prepared them for success: intelligence; personality characteristics; and so on. Yet it would be difficult to claim that their moral achievements could be attributed specifically to qualities that predated their involvement with the causes that they advanced. There were other men as capable as King in making thoughtful judgments about moral issues, or as creative as Gandhi in imagining a country freed of colonial rule, or as sensitive as Mandela to social justice. Moreover, nothing in the psychologies of King, Gandhi, and Mandela propelled them inevitably to involvement with the specific causes that they advanced. For example, King's moral and intellectual qualities were consistent with many paths through life—he could have easily been a minister, a professor, and so on—not just the one that he traveled. One can neither predict the moral contributions of exemplars from their personalities and backgrounds nor deduce their personalities and backgrounds from their moral accomplishments.

The lifelong commitments to moral causes characteristic of many moral exemplars seem best explained through the consolidation of identity, a process explored in work by Colby and Damon (1992). In Colby and Damon's model, individuals' tentative engagements in moral pursuits become important facets of their views of themselves. These additions to the self-image in turn lead to changes both in the understanding of the activity and in one's identity that solidify commitment to and involvement in the moral pursuit. It is because identity can become defined in large part by engagement in particular activities that individuals can remain committed to causes over long periods of time despite many hardships.

REFLECTION AND EXPERIENCE

Finally, moral identity may be a construct that is at a level of consciousness and reflection that is consistent with both the findings of empirical psychology and the conceptual needs of philosophical psychology. Certainly one of the robust achievements of empirical psychology is the demonstration that the processes for thinking, emoting, and acting usually occur outside conscious awareness (Bargh & Chartrand, 1999). The moral domain is not exempt from this conclusion; moral decisions and moral behaviors often are not preceded by the rational, conscious calculations seemingly demanded by deontological and utilitarian theories. Few people experience moral deliberation throughout the course of day-to-day life.

The demonstration that moral emotions and moral actions usually occur outside consciousness has led some empirical psychologists to reject reflection as a significant constituent of moral life (e.g., Haidt, 2001). This is a mistake for any number of reasons (for a discussion, see Hart & Killen, 1995). It is a mistake in part because none of the traditional issues of moral inquiry—right action, the best possible state of affairs, and good character—can be fully imagined without deliberation. Even virtue theory, with its assumption that moral behavior directly follows from character traits, has always included an element of reflection. As Williams (1995, p. 573) points out, Aristotle claimed: "One cannot properly possess even one virtue unless one had the central capacity to make sense of what one is doing."

If an account of moral psychology is incomplete if it assumes a reflection-free, unconscious processing of stimuli, then there is a need for a construct in which occasional conscious moral deliberations can be integrated with action plans, emotions, and the structures of life. Moral identity can be that construct. Taylor (1989) has suggested that moral views both frame and are revealed in the narrative construction of identity. In Taylor's theory, modern life propels individuals to the consideration of their lives and the construction of identity, a process that cannot be accomplished "without an orientation to the good" (1989, p. 47). In other words, Taylor is suggesting that the formation of identity necessarily involves some consideration of what is of ethical value. This line of argument suggests that it is possible that the requirements for deliberation of traditional moral issues can be embedded within the construction, consolidation, and revision of identity.

SUMMARY

Because moral identity helps explain moral failure, accounts for the specificity of moral action, and exists at a level of awareness consistent with psychological and philosophical investigations, it may be a useful addition to theories of moral functioning.

Moral Identity and Psychological Research

Moral identity in all its richness cannot be translated completely into constructs that can be used in research. Compromises struck between the fullness of the notion of moral identity and the needs of empirical investigation are of three types. First, there are investigations of moral identity that rely on biographical analyses of individuals involved in remarkable moral (or immoral) projects (e.g., Colby & Damon, 1992; Glover, 1999; Jasper, 1997). This line of work is successful in examining multiple facets of moral identity in individual lives and makes a compelling case for the value of the construct. However, it does not yield findings that can be replicated, at least in the sense that empirical psychologists ordinarily understand replication, because there is no clear separation of analysis from findings.

Second, there is the type of compromise that focuses only on a single psychological quality of moral identity in order to develop measures that can be applied in traditional research. For example, Aquino and Reed (2002) developed a measure of moral identity defined as "a self-conception organized around a set of moral traits" (p. 1424). In a series of studies, they were able to show that self-ratings on trait-like qualities related to moral identity were both distinct from measures of related constructs and predictive of volunteering. While this kind of measure assesses one facet of moral identity—the centrality in the perception of oneself of moral traits—other facets such as the experiences of coherence and continuity escape from this sort of measure.

Third, moral identity research can begin with sustained moral actions and then seek to assess the characteristics of identity that distinguish those who participate and those who do not. Piliavin's fascinating research on blood donation is one example of this kind of research (e.g., Lee, Piliavin, & Call, 1999; Piliavin & Callero, 1991). The limitation of this kind of approach is that it tends to assume that, whatever the qualities that distinguish participants from nonparticipants, they must be components of moral identity; consequently the notion of moral identity can be stretched too far.

Moral Identity in Childhood and Adolescence

All three compromises are evident in our studies of moral identity in childhood and adolescence. Nonetheless together these studies can illustrate how moral identity forms in childhood and adolescence and the role that it may play in moral life. These studies are reviewed in the sections that follow.

CARE EXEMPLARS IN CAMDEN, NEW JERSEY

Moral identity may be particularly useful for understanding committed moral action, an advantage suggested in the previous section. Hart and Fegley (1995) studied a group of adolescents who had demonstrated genuine commitments to care for others in Camden, New Jersey. This study is reviewed here because the original results and the recent reanalysis of data from the study lay the foundation for more recent research.

To identify a group of genuinely caring adolescents, Hart and Fegley (1995) solicited nominations from schools, social service agencies, and churches in Camden, New Jersey. Camden is one of the poorest cities in the United States. It has all the problems that one expects of an extremely poor city. The infant mortality rate is double the national average; many children and adolescents lack health insurance, and consequently the incidence of chronic, subacute problems is much higher than it is in the suburbs; students fare very poorly on the state-mandated tests of academic achievement.

Poor cities typically have qualities that can make them quite interesting for developmental psychologists. For example, poor cities tend to be young cities, and this is true of Camden as well. The ratio of child to adult in Camden is nearly 1 to 2, while the ratio in neighboring suburbs is closer to 1 to 3 (Hart & Atkins, 2002). This means that, during the summer, Camden's streets teem with children and adolescents.

Finally, like most poor cities, Camden has a large population of talented, resourceful, caring adolescents—a group that is often eclipsed in the media by delinquent youths. The solicitation resulted in nearly 100 nominations of youths throughout the city who had demonstrated remarkable, sustained commitments to care for others. Fifteen adolescents were selected for intensive study from among those who were nominated, and they were matched with comparison adolescents of the same age, gender, ethnicity, and neighborhood. Most of the care exemplars were involved in community service. They had begun community gardens, led school efforts to address community problems, were involved in neighborhood political-organizing campaigns, led youth civil rights groups, and so on. They were an outstanding group.

Each care exemplar and matched comparison adolescent was individually interviewed in multiple sessions for a total of 4–6 hours. The interviews targeted qualities of self and identity. First, adolescents were asked to describe many different facets of their selves. These facets included their views of their actual selves, or the persons they really were; their views of themselves in the past and the future; and the kinds of persons they desired to be and feared becoming. Adolescents also described influential people in their lives, including their parents and friends.

The adolescents also responded to the Kohlbergian interview measure of moral judgment development (Colby & Kohlberg, 1987). Finally, the interviews were all coded with the California Adult Q-Sort (Block, 1961), which permitted each participant to be characterized in terms of the five-factor model of personality (for a description, see Saucier & Goldberg, 2001).

Moral Attributions to the Ideal Self Identity is in part composed of those characteristics central to the self described earlier. Our hypothesis was that exemplars would be more likely to believe that moral qualities are central to their visions of themselves—to their identities—than would be the case for the comparison adolescents. Indeed this turned out to be true. In one component of the interview the adolescents were asked to list characteristics that defined their ideal selves. These lists were checked for the presence of words that Walker and Pitts (1998) have identified as prototypically moral in meaning. These prototypically moral words include *fair*, *reliable*, and *honest*, along with 50 or 60 others. Eighteen percent of the characteristics ascribed to the ideal self by the care exemplars contained one or more of these prototypical words, in contrast to the 9% found in ideal self descriptions offered by the comparison adolescents. This suggests that moral features were more central to the identities of the care exemplars than to the identities of the comparison adolescents.

It is worth noting that, among the care exemplars, the ideal self is only partially composed of moral features. This means that unusually good adolescents' aspirations include material goods, popularity, romantic success, and so on. Owen Flanagan (1991) has pointed out that even saints have desires and goals that are nonmoral in nature.

Continuity and Coherence There is also evidence to indicate that the exemplar adolescents perceived greater continuity and coherence in their lives than did the comparisons. As mentioned above the participants were asked to attribute characteristics to many facets of self and to important others in their lives. After these characteristics were generated the participants were then asked to judge the extent to which each characteristic was descriptive of each facet of self and each important other. This resulted in a matrix of characteristics by facets of self and important others, with judgments of descriptiveness as the cell entries. The value of this time-consuming procedure—it required hundreds and even thousands of judgments for some participants—is that, for each participant, it permitted the measurement of the similarity between any two facets of self, whether past-current, current-current, or current-future (for a description of this procedure, see Hart, Field, Garfinkle, & Singer, 1997).

This similarity information can be analyzed in a number of ways. In this chapter I focus on the similarity of the adolescent's perception of the current self to past and future selves. We calculated the average resemblance of the current self to five temporal selves described by each participant: the self of 5 years ago; the self of 2 years ago; the self 2 years in the future; the self of 5 years in the future; and the self in adulthood. On average, the care exemplars perceived greater similarity between their current selves and their selves of the past and the future than did the comparison adolescents. This suggests that the exemplars perceived greater continuity and coherence in their identity than did the comparison adolescents.

Social Influence The resemblance of participants' descriptions of themselves to their descriptions of their mothers was also estimated. The resemblance of self-descriptions to descriptions of mothers was greater among care exemplars than it was among the comparison adolescents. This suggests that mothers are more significant within the identities of the care exemplars than within the identities of comparison adolescents.

This finding is consistent with previous research. Those who take on difficult moral commitments are often inspired by their parents. Rosenhan (1970), for instance, reported that those fully committed to the early civil rights movement "formed and maintained a positive cordial, warm, and respecting relationship with their parent (and often both parents)" (p. 261). Those who were less committed tended "to describe their parent (or both parents) in negative or ambivalent terms" (p. 262). Rosenhan also reported that the parents of those fully committed to the civil rights struggle were likely to have modeled sustained altruistic action when their sons and daughters were children.

London (1970) and Oliner and Oliner (1988) report similar findings from research focused on Christians who risked their lives to save Jews from death during the Second World War. London (1970) found that the Christians who saved Jews from the Nazis tended to express an intense identification with at least one parent, who was seen to have been a model of moral conduct. In a much more thorough study, Oliner and Oliner (1988) again found evidence for parental influence.

Moral Judgment and Personality Somewhat surprisingly, the care exemplars were not more sophisticated than the comparison adolescents in terms of their moral judgment, at least as measured by the Kohlberg scale. As noted above, since the publication of the original report, we have coded the interviews for the personality traits of the five-factor model. These traits are *neuroticism, extraversion, openness* *to experience*, *agreeableness*, and *conscientiousness*. Care-exemplar adolescents were higher on the trait of conscientiousness than were the comparison adolescents. There were no differences on the other four traits.

Summary of the Exemplar Study The study of care exemplars illustrates the connection of identity with dedicated community service. In comparison to other adolescents, the care exemplars attributed more moral characteristics to their ideal selves, perceived more self-continuity over time, and incorporated more of their images of their mothers within themselves (similar findings emerge in a study by Reimer, 2003).

Two questions arose from the exemplar study:

1. What sorts of characteristics prepare the way for the convergence of identity and action? In other words, are there identifiable personality characteristics, family environments, and so on that are precursors to moral commitments?

2. Does the poverty, and the associated challenges, of a place like Camden affect the development of moral identity?

A Model of Influences on Moral Identity Formation

The findings from the care-exemplar study, and the questions arising from them, led to the development of a model of moral identity formation (an earlier version of which appeared in Hart, Atkins, & Ford, 1998). This model is presented in Figure 1.

The model suggests that there are five influences on moral identity arranged in two layers. The first layer, at the left edge of the figure, is composed of enduring personality and social characteristics that form the foundation for much of child and adolescent development. The kinds of personality and social characteristics in this layer change slowly and may be largely outside children's and adolescents' volitional control. For example, there is little research to indicate that childhood personality traits can be affected in targeted interventions. Similarly, broad patterns of family functioning are difficult to alter.

The left edge of the model corresponds to what the philosopher Thomas Nagel (1979) has labeled *moral luck*. Nagel has suggested that each individual's moral status—whether he or she can be judged to

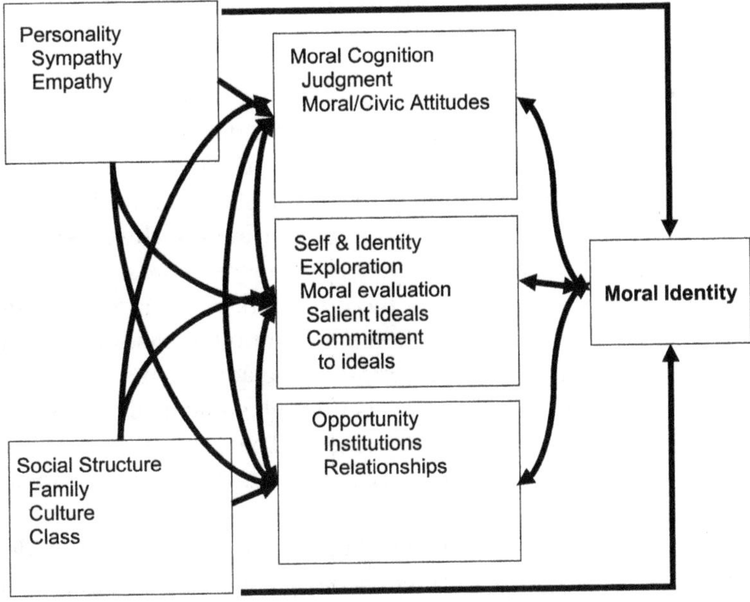

Figure 1. A model of moral identity formation.

be a moral success or a failure—is a consequence in part of contexts and influences that are not controlled by the individual. We judge the Hutu who participated in the slaughter of Tutsis to be responsible for great moral horror, yet, if that same person had been studying in England in 1994, it is certain that he would not have killed Tutsis on the streets of London. Enduring personality characteristics, one's family, one's culture and location in a social structure, all shape moral life. Some may be better positioned than others to avoid moral disaster owing to their good fortune with their personalities, families, cultures, and location in social structures.

The central elements of and influences on moral identity, located in the center column of the model, include moral judgments and attitudes, the sense of self, and opportunities for moral action. This layer is closer than the previous one to moral identity, and it is also more plastic; moral attitudes and judgments can more readily be changed, as can views about oneself.

Moral attitudes and judgments and features of the self, two of the three constituents in this middle layer, have been discussed to some extent in previous sections. The third component, the opportunity for action, has not been covered in previous sections and is in need of some explication.

Moral identity requires commitment to plans or lines of action. Often identity becomes invested in lines of action that are either evident in the lives of others or embedded in social institutions. For example, an adolescent may be inspired by the life of Mother Theresa to work with those in poverty or join an organization such as VISTA that results in an assignment to a helping role. In other words, attachment to a line of action may require the opportunity to join with others in the activity or to be called to the activity by others. In the care-exemplar study just discussed, most of the adolescents became involved in their moral commitments through social institutions such as churches, service agencies, and schools. These opportunities led to lines of action that became central constituents in the care exemplars' identities.

Another example of the importance of opportunity is provided by the research of Oliner and Oliner (1988), who compared Christians who hid Jews in Nazi Germany with a comparison group of Christians who did not. Hiding Jews was dangerous; those who did so believed that discovery of their actions by the Nazis would result in severe punishment. Why would anyone undertake such a burdensome, dangerous activity? Oliner and Oliner (1988) reported that most of those who hid Jews were *asked for help*; in contrast, only a minority of those in the comparison sample reported receiving such a request. It appears, therefore, that participation in genuinely admirable moral action is partly a consequence of an invitation to participate in it. Much the same lesson emerges from Halberstam's (1998) analysis of young adults who joined the civil rights movement in the 1960s.

Summary This model highlights personality, enduring social influences, moral judgment and moral attitudes, the self, and opportunity. The research with care exemplars is generally consistent with the model. In comparison to the comparison adolescents, the care exemplars had more moral elements in their sense of self. There was also some evidence that the two groups differed in terms of personality. Finally, it appeared to be the case that the exemplars entered into community service through community institutions and relationships, although this was not explicitly tested.

RESEARCH ON MORAL IDENTITY DEVELOPMENT

More recent research supportive of the model is reviewed in this section. The studies in question borrow data from three national studies and have large, nationally representative samples. They are used to identify precursors to and predictors of voluntary community service, which is used a proxy for the action component of moral identity. No doubt the working assumption in these studies that an individual reporting voluntary community service has a moral identity is often wrong as participation in voluntary service can arise for nonmoral reasons as well. However, there is enough evidence (for a review, see Hart, Atkins, & Donnelly, in press) suggesting that community service is integrated with moral beliefs and the sense of self—some of these findings are reviewed in the sections that follow—to suggest that making use of national samples is warranted.

ENDURING FEATURES

Personality My colleagues and I (Hart, Atkins, & Fegley, 2003) have used the Child data from the 1979 National Longitudinal Survey of Youth (C-NLSY) to examine the relation of childhood personality to cognitive and social development. The sample of the C-NLSY is composed of the children born to a nationally representative sample of young women who were between the ages of 14 and 21 in 1979. Beginning in 1986, and every 2 years since, children born to women in the original sample have been tested.

In recent research (Hart, Atkins, & Donnelly, in press) we have used two types of data in this longitudinal study relevant to testing the model depicted in Figure 1. First, mothers rated their children's personalities when the children were 5 and 6 years of age using a 20-item inventory. We have analyzed these maternal personality ratings using Q- (or inverse-) factor analysis and have identified three basic personality types.

These personality types are labeled *resilient, overcontrolled,* and *undercontrolled*. The resilient type is characterized by self-confidence, independence, verbal fluency, and an ability to concentrate on tasks; the overcontrolled type by shyness, quietness, anxiety, and dependability; and the undercontrolled type by impulsivity, stubbornness, and physical activity.

The types are replicable; we have conducted analyses with 28 different samples of 3-, 4-, 5-, and 6-year-olds and found the same three types in all the samples (Hart et al., 2003). Moreover, the types have predictable relations to measures of psychopathology and adjustment. Those in the resilient group have the lowest level of problem behaviors, overcontrolled children are most likely to be high in internalizing symptoms, and undercontrolled children have the highest rates of problem behavior in school and report the most delinquent behaviors (Hart et al., 2003; Hart, Hofmann, Edelstein, & Keller, 1997; Robins, John, Caspi, Moffitt, & Stouthamer-Loeber, 1996). Demographic information was also collected at this testing point.

When the participants in the C-NLSY reached 15 and 16 years of age, they responded to a self-report survey, one section of which concerned community service. As in previous research (Hart et al., 1998) we considered the respondents to be participating in voluntary community service if they reported (*a*) that they were actively involved in service and (*b*) that this service was not required by school or mandated by the courts.

To summarize, there was a measure of personality at ages 5 or 6 and a measure of voluntary community service administered 10 years later. There were approximately 1,000 participants with scores at the two testing periods.

The hypothesis was that childhood personality predicts adolescent community service. Specifically we anticipated that resilient children would be most likely to participate in community service as adolescents. The ability to interact effectively with others and the capacity for emotion modulation, both characteristic of resilient children, lay the foundation for the development of moral identity.

These hypotheses were tested using logistic regression. Community service was regressed on dummy variables for personality type and simultaneously on a number of control variables such as gender, age, race/ethnicity, academic achievement, home environment, maternal educational attainment, and family income. The dummy variable contrasting the resilient personality type to the other two types was significant. The nature of the relation of personality type with voluntary community service is illustrated in Figure 2.

Figure 2 indicates that teenagers who were judged to be resilient as children were more likely to be involved in voluntary community service than were teenagers who were assigned to the overcontrolled

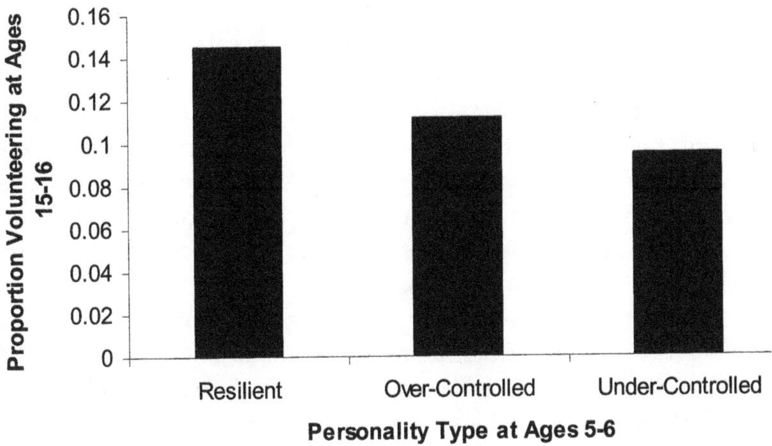

Figure 2. The estimated proportion of adolescents volunteering as a function of childhood personality type, controlling for background factors. These estimates are derived from analyses presented by Atkins, Hart, and Donnelly (in press).

or undercontrolled personality type in childhood. This is a meaningful effect and demonstrates that adolescent moral identity, at least as reflected in voluntary community service, has roots in personality.

Still, while the effect is real, personality does not by itself determine whether a child will become involved in community service as an adolescent. The magnitude of the association of membership in the undercontrolled type to community service is quite small. This means that childhood personality accounts for only a modest amount of the variability in volunteering in adolescence.

Social Structure There is also good evidence that the social structure of an adolescent's environs affects the development of moral identity. Some of our recent research (Hart, Atkins, Markey, & Youniss, 2004) examines the effects of social structure on children's and adolescents' voluntary community service. There is now a wealth of evidence to indicate that characteristics of a child's family—parental educational level, parental income, and parental occupational status—are powerful predictors of child outcomes (see, e.g., Leventhal & Brooks-Gunn, 2003). However, our interest in this research is not in the social structural characteristics of the family but instead in the neighborhoods in which children live. Our experiences in Camden directing programs for youths suggest that neighborhood- and city-level factors can be powerful influences on the development of moral identity (Atkins & Hart, 2003; Hart & Atkins, 2002; Hart et al., 1998).

Two qualities of neighborhoods seem particularly important: poverty and the percentage of the population constituted by children. Neighborhood poverty is generally found to have adverse effects on children's development (Leventhal & Brooks-Gunn, 2003). Our hypothesis was that neighborhood poverty would depress volunteering in childhood and adolescence.

Second, we believe that the youthfulness of a neighborhood or city is an important influence on development. The percentage of a neighborhood's population composed of children is usually correlated with neighborhood levels of poverty. In our view, however, the effects of the youthfulness of a neighborhood on development are different from those resulting from poverty. Our hypothesis was that a child or an adolescent in a community in which a large fraction of the population is composed of children and adolescents (*child-saturated environment*) will interact more often with peers, and consequently will be more influenced by them, than will an adolescent in a community with relatively few children and many adults (*adult-saturated environment*). This hypothesis rests on the notion that social influence is a product of the persons with whom an individual interacts on a daily basis (Latané, 1981).

If our hypothesis is correct, then child-saturated environments are better than adult-saturated ones for the acquisition by adolescents of behaviors and roles more common in adolescents than in adults. Volunteering is one such activity; in the United States it is more common among adolescents than among adults (Niemi, Hepburn, & Chapman, 2000). Consequently we predicted that adolescents in child-saturated environments would be more likely to volunteer than would adolescents in adult-saturated environments.

These hypotheses were tested using data from the National Household Educational Survey of 1999 (NHES-99). The NHES-99 was a telephone-interview study of nationally representative households from across the United States. Children and adolescents in grades 6–12 were asked if they had been voluntarily involved (i.e., not to meet a school-mandated requirement) in community service in the current school year. Demographic information was collected from the parents, and the parents were also asked to report their children's academic grades. The child saturation of each participant's community was estimated from the 1990 U.S. census. We divided the number of children (birth to age 16) by the number of adults (age 21 and older) in the postal (zip) code area corresponding to the participant's address. We also estimated the percentage of households in the postal code area below the poverty line.

Logistic regression was used to predict volunteering. The analysis included controls for variables found in previous research (for a review, see Hart, Atkins, & Donnelly, in press) to predict to individual differences in volunteering, such as participants' race/ethnicity, age, gender, and school grades; parents' educational attainment, income, and presence in the home; and language spoken at home.

To reiterate, our goals were to test the effects of neighborhood poverty and child saturation on volunteering. The main effect for neighborhood child saturation was positive and significant, but this main effect was qualified by an interaction with poverty. This interaction is illustrated in Figure 3. Among low-poverty neighborhoods (in which the poverty rate is 1 SD below the mean, or approximately 3%), the rate of volunteering was nearly twice as high in those with child-saturation levels of 0.4 than it was in those with child-saturation levels of 0.2. Among moderate-poverty neighborhoods (1 SD above the average, or approximately 21%), child saturation had no effect on volunteering. Finally, among extreme-poverty neighborhoods (+3 SD, 40% poverty), those with 0.4 child-saturation levels had extremely low rates of volunteering. The conjunction of extreme poverty and an extremely youthful populace appears to overwhelm a community's capacity to provide opportunities for children and adolescents to contribute through volunteering to the public good.

Summary Our research with the NLSY and the NHES demonstrates that personality and social structure are predictors of voluntary community service and, by extension, the development of moral identity. Children who have resilient personalities—effective in social interaction and capable of emotion modulation—are more likely than children lacking these qualities to volunteer 10 years later. Finally, children and adolescents who live in very poor, child-saturated neighborhoods are much less likely to volunteer than are those living in more affluent neighborhoods.

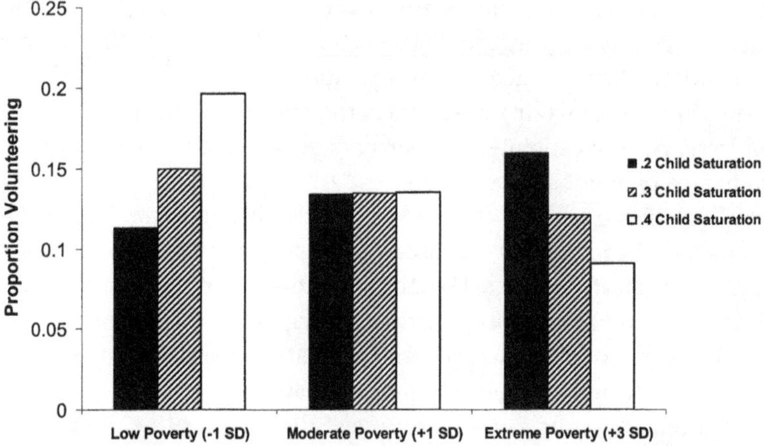

Figure 3. The estimated proportion of adolescents volunteering as a function of neighborhood poverty level and child saturation, controlling for background factors. These estimates are derived from analyses presented by Hart, Atkins, Markey, and Youniss (in 2004).

PLASTIC CHARACTERISTICS: OPPORTUNITIES

Opportunities to become involved in moral action are central to the model of moral identity that is presented in this chapter. Moreover, the provision of opportunities may be one route to guiding the development of moral identity. We have used the data from the NLSY to estimate the effects that two types of institutional opportunities have on voluntary community service. The first of these opportunities is membership in a club or a team. As described earlier adolescents' entry into a line of moral action often occurs in the context of a social institution. For example, boys and girls who join the Scouts often become involved in community service because this service is institutionalized in each troop. By becoming a member of the troop, an adolescent becomes involved in some type of community service, and this activity may become embedded in the adolescent's identity.

Religious institutions also connect adolescents to lines of moral action. Serving others in the community is a prominent theme in many religious denominations, and consequently adolescents who are active religiously are more likely to become involved in lines of moral action than are adolescents with no religious affiliation (for a review, see Hart & Atkins, 2004).

Atkins, Hart, and Donnelly (in press) used the C-NLSY data to test the prediction that club membership and religious affiliation would be related to voluntary community service, our proxy for moral identity. Personality, family functioning, academic achievement, and demographics were measured when the participants were 5 and 6 years old. Six years later, when the participants were 11 and 12 years old, they were asked if they were (*a*) members of a club or a team and (*b*) how frequently they attended religious services. Finally, 4 years later the participants reported whether they were involved in community service. We regressed community service on the age 5–6 measures and on the indicators of club membership and religious participation.

Consistent with predictions, both club membership and religious participation increase substantially the likelihood that adolescents will be involved in community service. Figure 4 illustrates the relation of club membership to volunteering; this effect is illustrated for each of the three personality types. Even after controlling for personality, academic achievement, and family environment, preadolescents who are members of clubs and teams are more likely than preadolescents who do not belong to clubs or teams to volunteer as adolescents. This suggests that clubs and teams help connect adolescents to lines of voluntary action.

An even more powerful effect is observed for religious participation. Figure 5 illustrates the relation of the frequency of religious attendance to voluntary community service, controlling for personality, family environment, academic achievement, and club and team memberships. Preadolescents who reported weekly religious participation were almost twice as likely as those who never attend to be involved in community service 4 years later.

MORAL IDENTITY IN ADULTHOOD

The model of moral identity presented in Figure 1 characterizes adults as well as children and adolescents. We have used data from the Midlife in the United States Survey (MIDUS), which was administered to a representative sample of middle-aged adults in the mid-1990s (Hart, Matsuba, Atkins, & Donnelly, 2004). The MIDUS had self-

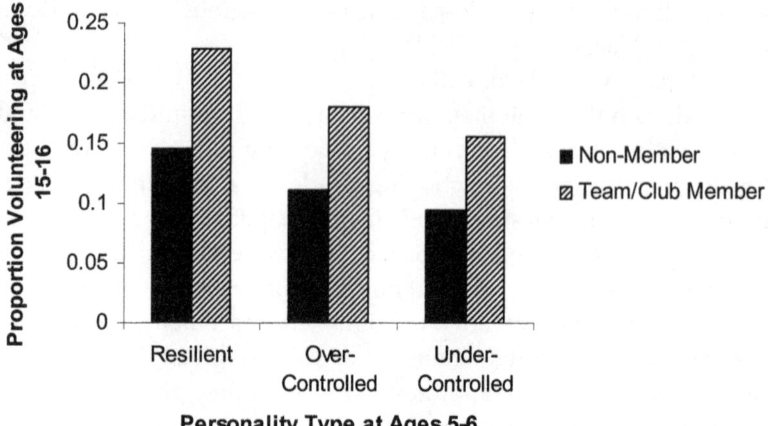

Figure 4. The estimated proportion of adolescents volunteering as a function of childhood personality type and preadolescent club/team membership. These estimates are derived from analyses presented by Atkins, Hart, and Donnelly (in press).

report items that correspond to all the items in the model of moral identity described in the chapter.

Personality was assessed in the MIDUS with self-ratings of the descriptiveness of 30 adjectives such as *outgoing* and *calm*. Cluster analysis of these self-ratings was used to assign participants to three groups, each corresponding to a personality type. The personality types can be labeled *resilient*, *overcontrolled*, and *undercontrolled* and correspond generally to the types used in the NLSY. We used household income and educational attainment as indicators of social structure.

A latent variable for civic obligation, corresponding to the moral attitude/moral judgment component of our model, was estimated from participants' ratings of their obligation to fulfill a number of responsibilities, such as to serve on a jury if called.

Three items on the MIDUS were used to estimate the latent variable of the *helping self*, the centrality to the self of contributing to the welfare of others. One question asked how large a contribution to the welfare of others the individual expects to make 10 years in the future, another asked how much control the individual exercises over his or her contribution to others, and the third asked for a judgment

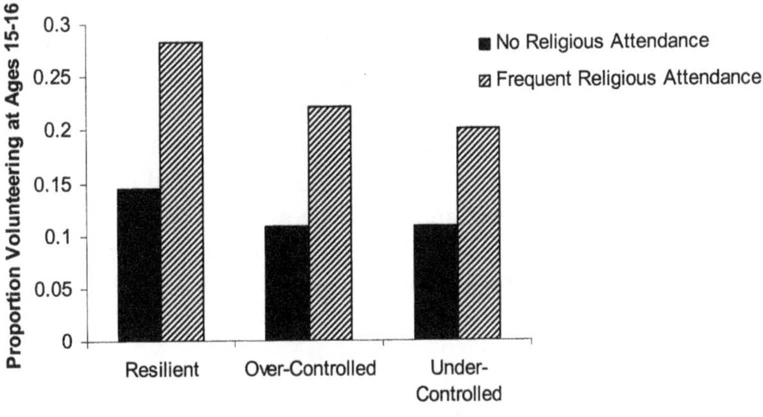

Figure 5. The estimated proportion of adolescents volunteering as a function of childhood personality type and preadolescent religious participation. These estimates are derived from analyses presented by Atkins, Hart, and Donnelly (in press).

of the extent of thought and effort the individual expended in promoting the welfare of others.

Opportunity for action was represented by a latent variable, estimated from three items in the MIDUS assessing frequency of interaction with friends, family, and neighbors. We expected that those who reported frequent interactions would be more likely than loners to become aware of opportunities for community service and consequently to become involved in it. Volunteers frequently report being recruited into their roles by friends and family (e.g., Independent Sector, 2001).

Finally, participants were asked to report how many hours they volunteered per month in each of four types of community service activities (health related, child related, political, or other). The sum of hours across the four types of service activities is the dependent measure in the model.

We used structural equation modeling to estimate the parameters for a model in which the enduring personality and social influences—from personality type, age, gender, household income, and educational attainment—were used to predict civic obligation, helping self, and frequency of interactions with others, and these three variables were then used to predict volunteering. The significant paths from the enduring characteristics to the plastic ones, and from the latter to volunteering, are depicted in Figure 6 (the covariances among the enduring influences and among the plastic constituents are omitted).

The results are consistent with the model that has been outlined. Enduring personality and social influences are related to civic obligation, to helping identity, and to the frequency of interaction with friends, with the latter three qualities all predictive of the number of hours spent monthly in voluntary community service.

Conclusion

Moral identity is composed of self-awareness and attachment to one's moral goals, a sense of self-coherence and self-continuity, and an orientation within "moral space" (Taylor, 1989), with the configuration of all these qualities open to social influence. Among its benefits for moral psychology, the notion of moral identity helps explain moral collapses and the specificity of moral action and may serve to integrate reflection and plans. Moral identity is, in some ways, a reflection of an individual's response to the three questions of moral life.

The model of moral identity formation reviewed in this chapter is consistent with research on a group of adolescents selected for their moral qualities, with two large, nationally representative samples of adolescents, and with a study with a large representative sample of adults.

IMPLICATIONS

The model of moral identity formation and the research guided by it have implications for our understanding of development and intervention.

Moral Luck First, the model and research suggest that moral identity is influenced by factors largely outside a child's or an adolescent's control. These factors include personality, home environment, and neighborhood. A child with an undercontrolled personality living in an impoverished, child-saturated environment is unlikely to become involved in community service. One might say that such a child has bad moral luck.

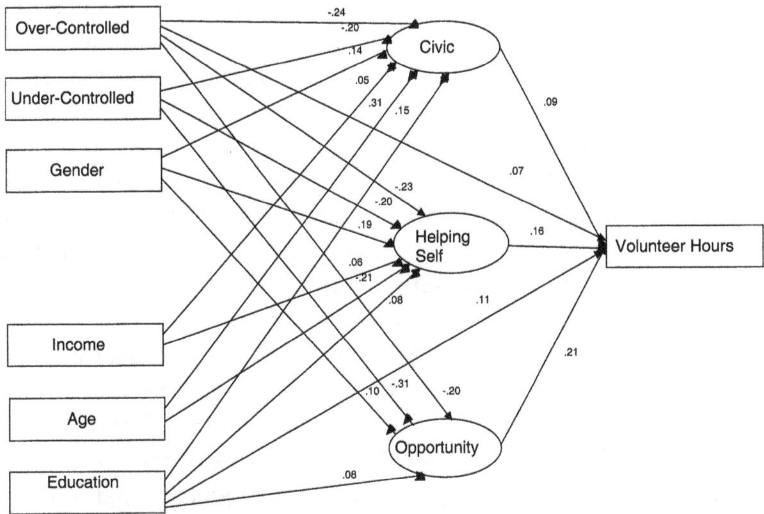

Figure 6. Path diagram of significant paths among indices in the MIDUS of constituents of moral identity. This diagram is based on analyses presented in Hart, Atkins, and Donnelly (in press).

Development In the review of the four studies, covering the age range 5–65, little was said about age-related change. This is because there is little indication of substantial age-related change over short periods of time in most of the components of the models. The only exception to this generalization is that moral judgment, measured in the care-exemplar study, was moderately correlated with age.

This pattern suggests that moral identity is constructed within the stable constraints of personality and location in a stable social structure but that, apart from these constraints, it is open to revision and reconstruction throughout adolescence and adulthood. These findings can be interpreted to mean that many adolescents with histories of problems can find their way back onto the path toward successful development. As a culture we need to offer opportunities to adolescents with bad moral luck and reserve long-term incarceration only for those who, even with support, cannot escape participating in moral collapse.

Interventions The demand for character education in schools reflects the public's generally negative perception of adolescents. Surveys conducted by the Public Agenda find that adults believe that children and teenagers lack moral character. For example, when asked to describe teenagers, 71% of adults use words such as *rude, irresponsible*, and so on (Duffett, Johnson, & Farkas, 1999). Only 15% of adults describe teenagers positively (Duffett et al., 1999). American adults believe that the failure to learn moral values is the most serious problem facing youths today (Duffett et al., 1999). Given these perceptions it is no surprise that Americans believe that the current generation of teenagers will either make America a worse place or do nothing to improve it.

Character education is intended to remedy these ills by fixing the character of American adolescents. For many American adults, this means changing the personalities of adolescents. However, the model of moral identity suggests that our efforts to intervene may be better directed toward other elements in the model and particularly toward offering opportunities for action. There is now a body of research to indicate that substantial transformations in identity can result from participation in moral activities. Adolescents who differed little from their peers prior to their active participation in the civil rights movement or the antiwar movement were substantially different in early and middle adulthood from their formerly similar peers (Jennings, 2002). Required community service in schools seems to effect the same beneficial changes in attitudes as does voluntary service, which suggests that "encouraged" involvement in moral lines of action can transform identity (Donnelly, Hart, Youniss, & Atkins, 2004).

Finally, the results suggest that institutions serving youths can have powerful effects on the development of moral identity. We need to strengthen these institutions and to encourage them to ask more of the adolescents they serve.

Balance Finally, while emphasis has been placed on the importance of opportunities for action in interventions with youths, this does not mean that moral reflection and the sense of self ought to be neglected. Moral reflection and a sense of the self as moral, bereft of action, is arid and cannot support moral life. A self committed to ideals joined with a line of action, but without moral reflection, can lead to extremism. In the absence of integration of moral goals and moral orientation into the self, there is no motivation to take on the hard work of moral action and moral reflection.

Moral identity can help us organize our theoretical work in philosophical and empirical psychology and can orient our research on moral functioning in children, adolescents, and adults. I hope that the notion of moral identity can also serve to alert us to the vagaries of moral luck, the fragility of moral life, the diversity of lives that integrate moral value, the opportunities for moral life that we can offer each other, and the effort and vigilance that moral success—and the avoidance of moral collapse—requires of us all.

References

Aquino, K., & Reed, A. (2002). The self-importance of moral identity. *Journal of Personality and Social Psychology, 83,* 1423–1440.

Atkins, R., & Hart, D. (2003). Neighborhoods, adults, and the development of civic identity in urban youth. *Applied Developmental Science, 7,* 156- 165.

Atkins, R., Hart, D., & Donnelly, T. (in press). The association of childhood personality type with volunteering during adolescence. *Merrill-Palmer Querterly.*

Bargh, J. A., & Chartrand, T. L. (1999). The unbearable automaticity of being. *American Psychologist, 54,* 462–479.

Baumeister, R. F. (1986). *Identity: Cultural change and the struggle for self.* New York: Oxford University Press.

Bergman, R. (2002). Why be moral? A conceptual model from developmental psychology. *Human Development, 45,* 104–124.

Block, J. (1961). *The Q-Sort method in personality assessment and psychiatric research.* Springfield IL: Thomas.

Colby, A. (2002). Moral understanding, motivation, and identity. *Human Development, 45,* 130–135.

Colby, A., & Damon, W. (1992). *Some do care: Contemporary lives of moral commitment.* New York: Free Press.

Colby, A., & Kohlberg, L. (1987). *The measurement of moral judgment* (Vol. 2). New York: Cambridge University Press.

Donnelly, T. M., Hart, D., Youniss, J., & Atkins, R. (2004). *High school predictors of adult civic engagement: The roles of volunteering, civic knowledge, extracurricular activities, and attitudes.* Manuscript in preparation.

Doris, J. M. (2002). *Lack of character: Personality and moral behavior.* New York: Cambridge University Press.

Duffett, A., Johnson, J., & Farkas, S. (1999). *Kids these days '99: What Americans really think about the next generation.* Retrieved 31 December 2003 from http://www.publicagenda.org.

Erikson, E. H. (1968). *Identity: Youth and crisis.* New York: Norton.

Flanagan, O. (1991). *Varieties of moral personality: Ethics and psychological realism*. Cambridge: Harvard University Press.

Flanagan, O., & Rorty, A. O. (1993). *Identity, character, and morality*. Cambridge: MIT Press.

Glover, J. (1999). *Humanity: A moral history of the twentieth century*. New Haven: Yale University Press.

Gourevitch, P. (1998). *We wish to inform you that tomorrow we will be killed with our families*. New York: Farrar, Straus, Giroux.

Haidt, J. (2001). The emotional dog and its rational tail: A social intuitionist approach to moral judgment. *Psychological Review, 108*, 814- 834.

Halberstam, D. (1998). *The children*. New York: Random House.

Hart, D., & Atkins, R. (2002). Civic development in urban youth. *Applied Developmental Science, 6*, 227–236.

Hart, D., & Atkins, R. (2004). Religious participation and the development of moral identity in adolescence. In T. Thorkildsen & H. Walberg (Eds.), *Nurturing morality* (pp. 157–172). New York: Kluwer.

Hart, D., Atkins, R., & Donnelly, T. M. (in press). Community service and moral development. In M. Killen & J. Smetana (Eds.), *Handbook of moral development*. Hillsdale NJ: Erlbaum.

Hart, D., Atkins, R., & Fegley, S. (2003). Personality and development in childhood: A person-centered approach. *Monographs of the Society for Research in Child Development, 68*(1, Serial No. 272).

Hart, D., Atkins, R., & Ford, D. (1998). Urban America as a context for the development of moral identity in adolescence. *Journal of Social Issues, 54*, 513–530.

Hart, D., Atkins, R., Markey, P., & Youniss, J. (2004). Youth bulges in communities: The effects of age structure on adolescent civic knowledge and civic participation. *Psychological Science, 15*(9), 591–597.

Hart, D., & Fegley, S. (1995). Altruism and caring in adolescence: Relations to moral judgment and self-understanding. *Child Development, 66*, 1346-1359.

Hart, D., Field, N. P., Garfinkle, J. R., & Singer, J. L. (1997). Representations of self and other: A semantic space model. *Journal of Personality, 65*, 77–104.

Hart, D., Hofmann, V., Edelstein, W., & Keller, M. (1997). The relation of childhood personality types to adolescent behavior and development: A longitudinal study. *Developmental Psychology, 33*, 195–205.

Hart, D., & Killen, M. (1995). Introduction: Perspectives on morality in everyday life. In M. Killen & D. Hart (Eds.), *Morality in everyday life: Developmental perspectives* (pp. 1–20). New York: Cambridge University Press.

Hart, D., Matsuba, K. M., Atkins, R., & Donnelly, T. M. (2004). *Psychological and social-structural influences on involvement in volunteering*. Manuscript in preparation, Department of Psychology, Rutgers University.

Hart, D., & Yates, M. (1997). Identity and self in adolescence. In R. Vasta (Ed.), *Annals of child development, 1996* (pp. 207–242). London: Jessica Kingsley.

Independent Sector. (2001, November). *Giving and volunteering in the United States*. Retrieved 17 October 2003 from http://www.independentsector.org/PDFs/GV01keyfind.pdf.

James, W. (1890). *The principles of psychology*. New York: Holt.

Jasper, J. M. (1997). *The art of moral protest: Culture, biography, and creativity in social movements*. Chicago: University of Chicago Press.

Jennings, M. K. (2002). Generation units and student protest movement in the United States: An intra- and inter-generational analysis. *Political Psychology, 23*, 303–324.

Kant, I. (1964). *Groundwork of the metaphysics of morals* (J. Paton, Trans.). New York: Harper Torchbooks. (Original work published 1785)

Kohlberg, L. (1984). *The psychology of moral development*. San Francisco: Harper & Row.

Latané, B. (1981). The psychology of social impact. *American Psychologist, 36*, 343–356.

Lee, L., Piliavin, J. A., & Call, V. R. A. (1999). Giving time, money, and blood: Similarities and differences. *Social Psychology Quarterly, 62*, 276–290.

Leventhal, T., & Brooks-Gunn, J. (2003). Children and youth in neighborhood contexts. *Current Directions in Psychological Science, 12*, 27–31.

London, P. (1970). The rescuers: Motivational hypotheses about Christians who saved Jews from the Nazis. In J. Macaulay & L. Berkowitz (Eds.), *Altruism and helping behavior* (pp. 241–250). New York: Academic.

Nagel, T. (1979). *Mortal questions*. Cambridge: Cambridge University Press.

Niemi, R. G., Hepburn, M. A., & Chapman, C. (2000). Community service by high school students: A cure for civic ills? *Political Behavior, 22*, 45–69.

Nowak, M. A., Page, K. M., & Sigmund, K. (2000). Fairness versus reason in the ultimatum game. *Science, 289*, 1773–1775.

Oliner, S., & Oliner, P. (1988). *The altruistic personality*. New York: Free Press.

Piaget, J. (1965). *The moral judgment of the child*. New York: Free Press. (Original work published 1932)

Piliavin, J. A., & Callero, P. L. (1991). *Giving blood: The development of an altruistic identity*. Baltimore: Johns Hopkins University Press.

Powers, S. (2002). *A problem from hell: America and the age of genocide*. New York: Basic.

Reimer, K. (2003). Committed to caring: Transformation in adolescent moral identity. *Applied Developmental Science, 7*, 129–137.

Richburg, K. (1997). *Out of America: A black man confronts Africa*. New York: Basic.

Robins, R. W., John, O. P., Caspi, A., Moffitt, T. E., & Stouthamer-Loeber, M. (1996). Resilient, overcontrolled, and undercontrolled boys: Three replicable personality types. *Journal of Personality and Social Psychology, 70*, 157–171.

Rosenhan, D. (1970). The natural socialization of altruistic autonomy. In J. Macaulay & L. Berkowitz (Eds.), *Altruism and helping behavior* (pp. 251-268). New York: Academic.

Saucier, G., & Goldberg, L. R. (2001). Lexical studies of indigenous personality factors: Premises, products, and prospects. *Journal of Personality, 69,* 847–879.

Staub, E. (2003). *The psychology of good and evil: Why children, adults, and groups help and harm others.* New York: Cambridge University Press.

Taylor, C. (1989). *Sources of the self: The making of the modern identity.* Cambridge: Harvard University Press.

Thrash, T. M., & Elliot, J. (2003). Inspiration as a psychological construct. *Journal of Personality and Social Psychology, 84,* 871–889.

Walker, L. J., & Pitts, R. C. (1998). Naturalistic conceptions of moral maturity. *Developmental Psychology, 34,* 403–419.

Watson, G. (1993). On the primacy of character. In O. Flanagan & A. O Rorty (Eds.), *Identity, character, and morality* (pp. 449–469). Cambridge: MIT Press.

Williams, B. (1995). Ethics. In A. C. Grayling (Ed.), *Philosophy: A guide through the subject* (pp. 546–582). New York: Oxford University Press.

Motivation and Moral Development: A Trifocal Perspective

F. Clark Power
Notre Dame University

I welcome this opportunity to address the issue of moral motivation from the perspective of my own research on moral development and education, research that has taken me down some of the less traveled paths in psychology over the last 3 decades. Working within the cognitive-developmental paradigm, I, like my mentors, did not explore in any systematic way the motivational framework underlying moral reasoning. On the other hand, on reflection, I can see that motivational issues have lurked in the background of my research on the moral atmosphere of the school, moral self-worth, and spiritual development.

In this chapter I propose an approach that locates moral motivation as part of a desire for the good. The *good* is a broad term that can include the nonmoral as well as the moral. We use the word *good*, for example, to speak of music, automobiles, and wine. What we regard as good for us changes as we develop our thinking, become more reflective, participate in different social organizations, and generally engage in a variety of activities that expand the breadth and depth of our experiences. Our notion of what is good influences the goals that we set for ourselves, the identity that we construct, and how we evaluate ourselves, our work, and our relationships.

How do we develop a sense of what is good in relation to what is right? In this chapter I will approach this issue by discussing three influences on moral motivation—the social environment, the self, and religion—through what I will call *spirituality*. Although these influences are distinctive, they interact with each other in intriguing ways. The social environment influences moral motivation from the outside. From the Piagetian, interactionist framework that I work out of in this chapter, the social environment provides a particular context out of which individuals construct their morality. There is no uniform social environment; individuals operate in very different contexts. I take up one such context—the school. I describe the just-community approach to moral education, which, I believe, offers important insights into the way in which an environment can nurture and support moral motivation. Just communities motivate individuals, not only to perform particular actions and habits of action, but also to develop sense of self through identification with the community's ideals. The self is a source of moral motivation insofar as it incorporates moral aspirations or ideals, which become the source of moral self-evaluation. Finally, religious or more generally spiritual outlooks can serve to support moral motivation by influencing one's perspective both on one's community and wider social environment and on one's self.

I do not intend this chapter to provide a comprehensive treatment of the psychology of moral motivation. By focusing on three strands of my research, I take up only a few of the many issues that arise when we look into the nature of and influences on moral motivation. The issues that I do address and the vantage point from which I address them do, however, raise foundational questions for a general psychological theory of moral motivation. The self, society, and religion involve motivational forces that are not necessarily moral and that may, in fact, undermine moral motivation. What kinds of influences do society and culture exert on moral development? What is the nature of these influences on moral motivation? Are our mainstream social science theories of socialization adequate as accounts of either moral knowledge or moral motivation? How do individuals develop a sense of themselves as moral? Can self-esteem be construed as a moral motive? Does moral self-evaluation factor into individuals' sense of self-esteem, and, if so, how? How do religious and moral sources of motivation relate to one another? Finally, how does the desire for the good, conceived of as the good society, self-fulfillment, and spiritual transcendence, influence individuals' desire to act morally and to be moral people?

The Desire for the Good and Rationality

The desire for the good includes the desire to know—and not only the desire to know what will bring personal satisfaction or happiness, but also the desire to know for the sake of truth itself. This desire to know leads scientists to test their ideas in symposia and publications. We are, I believe, motivated to make our work public, not primarily because we desire to see our point of view prevail or because we want others to agree with us. In spite of our vanity and defensiveness, our commitment to truth makes us willing to be corrected, to consider perspectives that we have not entertained, to search for new and better ideas. The truth that we seek is founded in part on the objectivity that comes when others see what we see and reach the same conclusions. This disinterested search for the truth may well be rooted in human cognition itself, as the research of Piagetian and post-Piagetian cognitive psychology indicates. It is not something acquired through formal education. Even children are, as Kohlberg (1968) put it, "philosophers" in the sense that they appear to love wisdom and seek after it for its own sake.

As I hope to show, the desire for the good brings together a desire for truth, justice, and happiness. While psychology cannot study morality without having a reasonable way of delimiting the moral domain, psychology cannot study moral motivation without locating the moral domain within the all-encompassing pursuit of the good. The abstraction of moral duty from desire leads to insights into the categorical, universal, and prescriptive features of the moral domain, which are important, not only for those who reflect on morality from a philosophical or scientific point of view, but also for any moral agent having to make a difficult moral judgment. On the other hand, moral duties do not operate in a vacuum; they regulate and direct desire in the context of human interaction. A theory of moral motivation must take into account how desire motivates moral reflection and action without reducing morality to ethical egoism.

I have long regarded the topic of moral motivation with some suspicion because I feared that behind the seemingly innocent question, Why be moral? was a request for a nonmoral answer. To do what is right simply because it is right appears puzzling to psychologists, who have long been accustomed to explaining behavior within a framework of drive states or reinforcement. Moreover, many psychologists, particularly in the past century, have regarded morality, not as motivated by a disinterested concern for doing what is judged to be right, but as motivated by conscious and nonconscious forces. Perhaps the most stunning scientific challenge to the notion of an intrinsically motivated morality was the Hartshorne and May (1928–1930) *Studies in the Nature of Character*. These studies suggested that individuals were motivated by their self-interest rather than standards of virtue or morality. For the next three decades (the 1930s, 1940s, and 1950s), mainstream psychologists simply did not entertain the premise of a self-motivated morality but assumed that so-called moral behavior was motivated by nonmoral factors. Kohlberg, of course, sharply criticized this assumption and argued, instead, for a view of morality motivated by a concern for justice alone.

As I noted earlier, cognitive developmentalists, including Kohlberg, devoted little attention to motivational issues other than to distance themselves from behavioral and psychoanalytic psychology. On the other hand, in support of their general view on motivation, they typically appealed to the theories of mastery and effectance motivation going back to White (1959), which describe motivation in terms of interacting competently with the environment. This kind of motivational account supports cognitive-developmental models based on metaphors of *adaptation* and *equilibration* (Heckhausen, 1991). These models focus on the relation between the cognitive structures of the individual and characteristics of the environment. They describe development as occurring as the result of resolving cognitive conflict between the individual and the environment through such metaphors such as *optimal mismatch* and *disequilibrium*. On the other hand, these theories, with varying degrees of success, try to account for the fact that children are motivated, not only by a desire to solve problems, but also by a desire to look for problems to solve.

The effectance theory of motivation helps account for the motivation behind the stages of moral development, yet the question, Why be moral? goes beyond the development of cognitive structures to moral action. Cognitive structures influence action but in a puzzling way. Kohlberg believed that, the higher the moral stage, the greater control reasoning exercised over behavior, and there is some support for this (e.g., Blasi, 1980). Yet, as I will later show, it is very clear in the work that we did together on the just-community approach to moral education, he held an implicit theory of moral motivation that went well beyond the framework of cognitive-developmental theory.

Knowledge and Motivation

As Blasi, Rest, Turiel, and many others have recognized, one of Kohlberg's lasting contributions to moral psychology was to use philosophical criteria to define the moral domain and a method of investigating it. Kohlberg demonstrated that the moral domain had particular normative features that distinguish it from the domain of prudence or social convention. Within Kohlberg's stage system, however, the moral domain did not become fully differentiated until the final postconventional stages. Turiel (1983) and his colleagues (e.g., Nucci & Nucci, 1982; Smetana, 1995) challenged that claim by reporting that, beginning in their third year and continuing until their 10th year, children distinguish with increasing proficiency moral obligations addressing welfare, rights, and justice from those of social convention, such as forms of address or manners. They also found that children justify their judgments on moral grounds, that is, by appealing to welfare, rights, and fairness.

Domain research clearly indicates that the system of moral judgment appears far earlier than Kohlberg recognized. Yet it is by no means clear that the categorical moral judgments that young children make around issues of welfare, fairness, and rights are adequate for resolving complex moral situations or for motivating moral behavior in conflict situations. Research by Damon (1977) suggests that indeed children do make moral judgments that are not only independent of the dictates of adult authority but also critical of the dictates of adult authority when these dictates conflict with simple moral demands. On the other hand Damon (1977) admitted that the task demands imposed on children make a vast difference in their level of performance. Young children do well in relatively clear-cut and familiar situations that are not too cluttered with self-interested concerns.

The fact that children do not follow rules that they recognize as binding raises questions about the way in which children experience the sense of moral obligation as well as their experience of moral responsibility. Moral judgments are preemptive by nature. Their universal, categorical demands supersede those of prudence or convention and, many philosophers and theologians would claim, even those of religion. In practice, of course, individuals put imperatives of self-interest, convention, and religious authority above moral imperatives. How they do this is a question for empirical research. At least some individuals appear to struggle with giving other claims a priority over the moral imperative and resort to the defense of rationalizations. Whatever the case, the rational claims of morality exert some force over some people, even if other individuals appear unaware of or impervious to such claims.

Moral Knowledge and the Moral Self

The research on early moral development, however, indicates that, although children develop sophisticated moral knowledge, this knowledge does not motivate them at the level of action in ways that would be expected of an adult with similar knowledge. As Blasi (1993) notes young children's sense of agency is limited by the external forces of authority and by inner wants and needs. These forces diminish children's sense of moral responsibility or rational control of their own behavior.

Nunner-Winkler (1993) argues persuasively, in my view, that moral development in its fullest sense involves a two-step learning process in which children first acquire moral rules and later become motivated to follow them by making them a "personal concern" (p. 287). According to Nunner-Winkler two separate processes are at work here: (1) a cognitive process, in which children develop their moral knowledge, and (2) a motivational process, in which children feel responsible for acting on that moral knowledge and giving a priority to moral concerns over more immediate needs and interests. In coming to this position Nunner-Winkler and Sodian (1988) drew on a series of studies of children's attributions of emotion to moral wrongdoers. They found, somewhat surprisingly, that a substantial proportion of 6- and 7-year-old children attributed positive emotions to wrongdoers who transgressed a moral rule in order to satisfy a concrete interest. The wrongdoers, in their judgment, were satisfied because they achieved what they desired. Although these children were aware that that the wrongdoers had violated a moral rule, this awareness did not lead them to judge that the wrongdoers would feel badly. Nunner-Winkler and Sodian (1988) concluded that these children had not yet achieved a genuine moral motivation because their moral knowledge had yet to influence their primary wants and needs.

Nunner-Winkler's (1993) understanding of moral motivation is based on an explicitly Kantian distinction between duty and inclination. In Nunner-Winkler's view moral motivation cannot be based on inclination alone. Spontaneous feelings of empathy can no more be a basis for moral behavior than can spontaneous feelings of acquisitiveness or anger. Moral motivation must be based on a recognition that one is acting in accord with one's moral duty or sense of what is morally right. This does not mean, as Nunner-Winkler (1993) makes clear, that moral motivation must in every case be based on a feeling of duty. One may be moved to act out of feelings of empathy or indignation. If these feelings are to be considered part of one's moral motivation, they must prompt an action that is judged to be in accord with one's moral duties. In this sense, as Nunner-Winkler (1993) explains, duty acts "as a filter through which other motives must pass" (p. 284).

Nunner-Winkler elaborates the nature of moral motivation by referring to Frankfurt's (1988, 1993) distinction between first-order and second-order desires. A first-order desire is experienced as an immediate or spontaneous need or wish. For example, I may experience a first-order desire to eat some chocolate candy. A second-order desire is a desire that is experienced as chosen after some deliberation. For example, I may have a second-order desire to lose weight to maintain my health. This second-order desire may lead me to limit myself to one piece of chocolate. Note that, in this example, my second-order desire modifies my first-order desire by subordinating my impulsive craving for chocolate to my rationally established desire for good health. Second-order desires thus involve the ability, not only to delay gratification, but also to deliberate about what one really wants to do (one's ultimate ends) and become (one's ideal self). Nunner-Winkler's research suggests that young children believe that happiness depends on meeting such desires whether or not they are in harmony with moral precepts. The development of moral motivation thus entails constructing a second-order desire to act morally or to become a moral person.

Although cognitive-developmental research has been enormously helpful in enabling us to map the trajectory of moral knowledge growth, it cannot provide a sufficient account for the development of specific second-order desires. While second-order desires depend on moral knowledge, they presume a commitment to follow a particular way of life and to be a particular kind of person. There is an element of personal commitment in the development of second-order desires that cannot be reduced to the cognitive dimension alone.

The development of second-order moral desires appears to involve two intersecting systems that function in different ways. There is a moral knowledge system that informs moral judgments and a self-system that informs self-understanding and responsibility. Cognitive development occurs in both systems whether one sees them as parts of a general structure or as partial structures (Damon, 1977). Research that my colleagues and I have undertaken (summarized in Hart, in this volume) as well as studies by Arnold (1993) and Blasi (1993) indicate that the self-system does not necessarily become more moral as it develops. Yet the fact that the two systems can diverge does not imply that they are altogether independent. Blasi (1993) states: "Morality seems to offer ideal ground for anchoring the successive forms of experienced identity" (p. 118). That identity can be and is anchored on grounds other than morality does not take away from morality's motivational power. What needs to be asked is why individuals do not choose to anchor their identities on moral grounds.

Moral Development and Desire

We cannot understand how individuals develop moral concerns, commitments, and goals without addressing the development of their desires (Blasi, 1993, in press; Nunner-Winkler, 1993). Moral judgments function, not only to regulate first-order desires that conflict with our sense of duty (see Nunner-Winkler, 1993), but also to shape or direct the formation of new desires. In other words moral judgment influences our sense of what is good by making our conception of the good less egocentric and more social. This is no more apparent than in the way in which moral judgment interacts with empathy, giving rise to sympathy and prosocial behavior (Carlo, Eisenberg, & Knight, 1992; Eisenberg, 1986; Eisenberg & Fabes, 1998).

Moral psychology throughout the past century has tended to equate the experience of morality with duty in the emphasis placed on the constraint of first-order desires conceptualized as impulses, interests, drives, needs, and the like. Psychoanalysis, behaviorism, and social-learning theory labored to explain how individuals acquired the internal controls necessary for inhibiting self-gratifying inclinations and resisting temptations to deviate from social expectations. Morality was an external structure imposed on individuals from without. Internalized moral norms could be effective only if they were enforced by strong negative emotions, such as guilt and shame.

Jerome Kagan (in this volume) stresses the importance of the emergence of these emotions, elaborating his earlier Humean position that "feelings, not reason, lie at the heart of morality" (Kagan, 1987, p. xiii). Kagan maintains that a "moral sense" emerges around the third year as children display the emotions that resemble shame and guilt in anticipation of "wrong" actions. Wrong actions for a 2- or 3-year-old appear to be actions that do not meet some standard of goodness. Kagan gives such examples as failing a task, breaking an object, soiling clothing, and causing emotional distress in another. Anticipatory moral emotions are, for Kagan, the essence of the moral sense insofar as they motivate children to do good and avoid evil. The content of the standards that define right and wrong, good and evil, varies with cultures.

Kagan offers an interesting alternative to the socialization theories that were so prevalent at the time Kohlberg began his research. Social-learning theorists maintained that standards of right and wrong were taught through reinforcement. Kagan believes that, prior to learning, there is a biologically based readiness to accept standards of right and wrong. Like the social-learning theorists, however, Kagan believes that the content of moral standards is socially transmitted. Kagan (1987, p. x) does, however, leave some room for children to transform environmental input and presumably impose their own standards on behavior. Distinctions between moral and conventional standards are rooted, not in features of the act itself, or in the intentions underlying the act, but in the strength of the emotions that are attached to standards. The strength of these emotions is a product of the way in which the standards are acquired.

Absent in Kagan's account is a description of moral development emerging through social interaction, reciprocity, and role taking. In Kagan's perspective children appear to be biologically predisposed for compliance. Within a hierarchical relationship dominated by adult authority, they acquire standards to maintain social ties, avoid punishment or disapproval, or identify with someone with power and resources.

Piaget and Kohlberg proposed an alternative view. They held that children take an active role in the process of moral development. Children construct their morality just as they construct their logic. In fact, Piaget (1932/1965) concludes *The Moral Judgment of the Child* by describing morality as "the logic of action" (p. 398). Morality, according to Piaget, arises within social interaction and, like logic, provides a normative system of regulation. The motivation to be moral is a desire, not for competence in general, but specifically for the social competence necessary for cooperative relationships. Moral motivation is inextricably tied to desires for social play, communication, mutual affection, and prosocial behavior generally. Morality enables even more than it constrains, and it constrains for the sake of reciprocal social relations.

What complicated Piaget and Kohlberg's approaches to moral development, however, was the fact that they elaborated their understanding of morality along the lines of Kant's philosophy in terms of rules and laws (Munzel & Power, in press). Although Kant's philosophy proved to be very helpful in defining features of the moral domain and of moral maturity, its rigid distinction between the right and the good poses significant problems for the study of moral motivation. Kant maintained that the categorical imperative could be derived from reason alone without any appeal to one's experience of happiness. Liberal moral theory more generally has relied on the distinction between the right and the good to sustain pluralistic societies. In liberal societies individuals are free to pursue happiness in any way that they choose as long as they do not infringe on the rights of others.

Kohlberg more so than Piaget allowed this Kantian philosophical understanding of morality to influence his psychology. Thus, in his psychological research (but not in his educational research, as I will later explain) Kohlberg did not examine the role that affections, desires, and the pursuit of the good played in moral development. In this respect Kohlberg diverged somewhat from Piaget, who thought of morality as regulating not only social interaction but also the affections. Piaget, moreover, described autonomous, golden-rule morality as based on a morality of the good, which he described as the "product" of cooperation (1932/1965, p. 195). This sense of duty, which arises in the context of constructing the social good, points, I believe, to what I have been calling *second-order desires*. These are desires that lead to perceived goods and happiness and that also subordinate and constrain other desires. The acknowledgment of second-order desires bridges the gap between the right and the good in ways that Kohlberg's Kantian theory failed to take into account of.

From Justice to the Just Community: The Right and the Good

Although Kohlberg did not give much attention to moral motivation in his psychological writings, in one of his most important educational articles, "Education for Justice: A Modern Statement of the Platonic View" (1970), he identified his understanding of development with Plato's theory of *anamnesis* or recollection. According to Plato, individuals possess a dim awareness of the good and are brought to knowledge of the good through a Socratic process of drawing out what is already within. As Reed (1997) notes, the Socratic process has two elements: "*elenchus* (refutation) and *psuchagōgē* (soul leading)" (p. 173). These two elements correspond with the two constructs used in both experimental and educational studies to understand stage change: cognitive conflict, as stimulated through disagreement, and preference for a higher stage of judgment, as stimulated through appeals based on higher-stage arguments.

Kohlberg's (1984) later elaboration of his theory as "constructivist" indicates that he did not literally subscribe to Plato's theory of recollection. Kohlberg did not believe that individuals had a knowledge of stage 6, the shadows of which they saw in the earlier stages. What Kohlberg wanted to convey with his allusions to Plato was, in my view, not an attribute of the knower's knowledge, but an attribute of the knower's knowing. As I noted earlier Kohlberg described children as philosophers. What motivates the philosopher's quest for the true, the good, and the beautiful is eros, which is a love based in desire that Plato in the *Symposium* describes as leading upward toward the height of good and beauty. Thus, a more defensible Kohlbergian motivational theory would claim that individuals' moral judgment development is motivated by an underlying eros, or what I earlier called *desire for knowledge or wisdom*.

One's experience of eros can be found, not only in one's restless pursuit of knowledge and truth, but also in one's pursuit of happiness itself. The moral discussion approach had as its aim the just resolution of moral conflicts. It did not address the deeper and more encompassing moral question of how to live one's life. The just-community approach, Kohlberg's most significant contribution to moral education, had as its aim the establishment of a social system that would meet one's moral desires. The just-community schools established a sense of community that went well beyond the demands of justice to benevolence in the pursuit of the common good. The just-community approach embodied a commitment, not only to fairness, but to happiness, which can in a qualified sense be understood in terms of what Ryan and Deci (2001) call *eudaimonic well-being*. Eudaimonic well-being has its roots in Aristotle's concept of happiness based on the cultivation of the human excellences or virtues. Ryan and Deci (2001) argue persuasively, in my view, that eudaimonic well-being follows when individuals experience autonomy, competence, and relatedness.

Kohlberg maintained a neutrality about theories of the good life and, as I have noted, tried to distance his moral theory from them. However, his just-community approach to moral education did more than develop students' moral reasoning. The just-community schools gave students meaningful control over their life in school, a strong sense of belonging to a community, and an expectation that they would achieve a relatively high level of academic success. In other words, the just-community schools met the conditions that Ryan and Deci (2001) hypothesized would lead to a sense of eudaimonic well-being, conditions that would motivate students, not only to attend just-community schools, but also to live up to the expectations for being a good member of these schools. Kohlberg, in fact, recognized that students would find the just-community schools appealing. To Ryan and Deci's three conditions for eudaimonic well-being—competence, autonomy, and relatedness—Kohlberg may well have added a fourth, a sense of moral purpose or a commitment to justice. Adding morality brings *eudaimonic* well-being much closer to the Aristotelian understanding of happiness than Ryan and Deci's (2001) formulation.

By analyzing the way in which a just-community school motivates its members to be moral, we can begin to see how the right and the good can be joined in the concrete experience of group membership. We cannot begin to understand moral motivation unless we situate individuals within particular social settings and take into account their relationships and life goals.

Moral Atmosphere: The Motivational Influence of the Environment

In his monumental synthesis of the psychological investigation of motivation, Heckhausen (1991, p. 4) outlines three general approaches to motivation: (1) those focusing on the person; (2) those focusing on the situation; and (3) those focusing on the interaction. The first is by far the most common in the history of motivational psychology and undergirds Kohlberg's moral judgment theory as well as the emerging-self paradigm that I described earlier. The second approach came out of the Hartshorne and May (1928–1930) studies of character and received considerable support from Latané and Darley's (1970) bystander-intervention studies. Piaget's and Kohlberg's developmental theories, while interactionist, emphasize the role of individual cognitive structures and processes over environmental influences.

Overlooked entirely in the recent reviews of moral motivation by Bergman (2002) and Shulman (2002) is the influence of the environment or moral atmosphere on moral development. Perhaps this is because Bergman and Shulman see the environment as having an extrinsic influence on moral behavior. Both Piaget (1932/1965), in his classic *The Moral Judgment of the Child*, and Kohlberg, in almost all his essays on education, believe that the environment plays a decisive role in children's moral functioning and development. Piaget argued that children develop heteronomous and autonomous thinking in response to hierarchical and egalitarian relationships. Kohlberg did not posit such a direct relation between social structure and individual reasoning, but he strongly maintained that the shared values and governance structure of schools influenced both moral reasoning and action (Power, Higgins, & Kohlberg, 1989).

The focus of my dissertation and subsequent research has been on the just-community approach to moral education. The just-community approach promotes moral development (broadly construed) by providing a group experience characterized by direct participatory democracy and a culture of civic friendship and collective responsibility. In this section I will review that work with attention to the motivational dynamics of the experience of being a member of a democratic community. Moral psychology, I believe, has much to learn from this kind of educational research, which looks at the influence of the environment on moral functioning.

Just communities motivate partly through the constraining power of their norms and the attracting power of their system of governance and close-knit community. Yet there is nothing inherently moral in this constraint or attraction. The motivation for group conformity and self-sacrifice for the group is in and of itself essentially amoral. On the other hand, if the group itself embodies ideals of fairness and benevolence and these ideals are at the basis of conformity and self-sacrifice, the motivation would seem to be moral. I will explore this claim in greater detail as I explain the theory behind and the practice of the just-community approach.

Durkheim's Collectivism: The Motivation of Group Attachment

Emile Durkheim was and, I believe, remains the major advocate for a theory of moral motivation based on group-level forces. His theory, I will argue, can and should serve as a foundational pillar for moral motivation and for what is called today *civic engagement*. A key question that runs throughout Durkheim's sociology is how moral motivation may be generated in a secularized society. Morality without God, he feared, would lack dignity and the power to compel. Durkheim hoped to replace God with society, as a quasi-collective being, a move that strikes us as particularly dangerous today, having witnessed the horrors of totalitarianism in Europe and the "tyranny of the majority" in the United States. Yet we should not dismiss his concerns too quickly. Durkheim calls our attention to a dimension of moral experience that secular social scientists tend to overlook. He noted that, if we do not find a way to tap into what he called the *religious dimension* of morality, our moral education efforts may be fruitless: "We will risk drying up the source from which the schoolmaster himself drew a part of his authority and also a part of the warmth necessary to stir the heart and to stimulate the mind" (Durkheim 1925/1973, p. 11). Without this religious dimension of the moral experience, "we risk having nothing more than a moral education without prestige and without life" (p. 11). Durkheim understood the religious dimension as both transcending and fulfilling the individual.

While Durkheim may have been mistaken in trying to substitute society for God, he was, I maintain, right in looking to membership in a moral community as a source of moral motivation and as a powerful context for acquiring habits that foster the moral life and character development. As we learned in the just-community studies, the moral community constrains as it challenges and enriches its individual members. It offers a sense of purpose, belonging, and support, even as it demands sacrifice.

The Value of the Group Experience: A Perspective from Sports

The closest that most children and adolescents in American society get to a Durkheimian moral community is in an extracurricular activity like a sports team, a band, or a drama club. Membership in such groups provides rich social bonds and demands considerable self-sacrifice. I will later argue that such experiences are a part of what I have called an *apprenticeship in democracy*. We do not normally think of these activities as constituting civic or moral education, but the intensity of the collective experience that they provide may well make them the most effective means at our disposal.

Clubs and teams provide their members with varied relational experiences, all of which are important. Power (1999) found that extracurricular activities influence high school students' planning and preparation for college by bringing them into closer contact with helpful adults than their classes do. My colleagues, Bredemeier, Shields, and LaVoi, and I have focused on sports as the single most popular of all the extracurricular activities. Remarkably, perhaps because of their focus on enhancing performance, sports psychologists have paid little attention to sports teams as a source of moral influence (Shields, Bredemeier, & Power, 2002). In fact, fact sports psychologists have only begun to explore the relational dimension of sports, having focused instead on physiological, attentional, and motivational factors directly influencing performance (LaVoi, 2002). In keeping with the expectations of the Ryan and Deci (2001) model, LaVoi (2002) finds that the quality of the coach—player relationship has a major influence on athletes satisfaction with their sports experience. LaVoi (2002) also notes that the athlete has a relationship with the team as a whole that provides not only personal satisfaction but also athletic motivation. My colleagues and I are building on LaVoi's research to show that teams also influence moral motivation. Teams can lead to respect and fair play or to the opposite, depending on their moral culture. Thus, beyond the interpersonal connection engendered by sports teams and extracurricular groups more generally is the collective connection to the group as a whole. Membership in a valued group fosters a willingness to accept the constraints of the group's discipline and to inspire self-sacrifice for the group.

Why do extracurricular activities generate more powerful group experiences than do classrooms or schools? In her review of the educational research, Power (1999) found that, in general, extracurricular activities put students on a more equal footing with adult authorities than do classrooms. This is because coaches, band leaders, and club moderators depend on students for the success of the activity. Students can be passive in the classroom and the lesson will go on. If students are passive on the athletic field, however, the team will fail. Even the most authoritarian coaches depend on their players to succeed. All the game preparation and exhortation in the world will not make a difference without the players' cooperation. Students are valued for their contributions to sports teams in ways in which they are not in the classroom. Students who win awards for their academic achievement are praised, not for their contributions to the school, but for their personal success. The opposite tends to be true for athletes who win awards in sports. At least in principle athletes are valued for their contributions to the team. In practice outstanding individual play can sometimes overshadow team play, but there is an awareness in sports, which is typically lacking in school, that athletes should be recognized for what they give to the team as a whole.

Although sports teams have great potential to become communities of character, Shields et al. (2002) point out that it is not sufficient that they generate a high degree of team solidarity or even a commitment to norms of fair play. Shields et al. (2002) propose that sports teams should, as far as is practical, involve athletes in decisions that affect the team as a whole. Because many coaches are notoriously autocratic, such a proposal may appear almost unrealistically radical. Yet there is nothing in research on sports to suggest that sports teams must be governed autocratically. In fact, many legendary coaches, such as Morgan Wooten from DeMatha High School and Tom Osborne from the University of Nebraska, used democratic coaching methods with great success.

DURKHEIM, DISCIPLINE, AND MORAL COMMUNITY

Before exploring the role of democracy in community, I return to Durkheim's insights into the collective dimension of discipline. In a passage that could have been written yesterday, Durkheim (1925/1973) makes a important distinction between discipline for the sake of order (classroom management) and discipline for the sake of moral education: "Too often, it is true, people conceive of school discipline so as to preclude it with an important moral function. Some see in it a simple way of guaranteeing superficial peace and order in the class. . . . In reality, however, the nature and function of school discipline is something altogether different. . . . It is the morality of the classroom" (p. 148). Elsewhere, Durkheim speaks of discipline as "essentially an instrument of moral education" (p. 149). The purpose of discipline is to foster respect for the rules and not simply to restrict external behavior. Respect for rules derives, according to Durkheim, from respect for the authority behind the rules. Many would equate the authority with the person of the teacher, but Durkheim believes that this is a dangerous mistake. The rules belong, not to the teacher, but to the class as a whole. In this sense the rules are impersonal.

Although Durkheim did not advocate democratic discipline, he did recognize the importance of securing the support of the students for rules and sanctions: a class in which justice is dispensed by the teacher alone, without securing the support of the group, would be like a society in which the judges render sentence against actions that the public does not condemn. Such judgments would lack both influence and authority. The teacher must gain the support of the class when he punishes or rewards (Durkheim, 1925/1973, p. 243).

Durkheim went on to recommend that each class have its "code of precepts, worked out in the course of everyday life—a sort of condensed summary of its collective experiences" (p. 244). How should teachers go about "securing the support of the group" for classroom rules and policies? A growing number of experts in classroom management and discipline believe that teachers should involve students in making and enforcing classroom rules.

Before turning to the just-community approach, which involves democracy, I will conclude my discussion of Durkheim with a comment on his conception of punishment. Many teachers rely on punishment to discourage students from breaking the rules. As Durkheim points out, whether or not punishment serves to deter unwanted behavior, such intimidation is hardly a "moralizing instrument" (1925/1973, pp. 161–162). Punishment, in his view, can, however, become a means of moral education if it is used to restore respect for the rule. This means that punishment must involve the whole group in a process of acknowledging the violation of the rule and the harm done to the community and of reconciling the offender while reasserting the duty to uphold the violated norm in the future. Durkheim may appear to be espousing a view of punishment as a form of expiation in his insistence that punishment redress the offense, but his point is far more complicated. He does not believe that those who break the rules should have to suffer to make up for their misdeeds. On the other hand he does believe that the community, including the offender, needs to take responsibility for what happened. He also believes that the group must reassert the importance of the violated rule so that students will not flaunt the authority of the group. "Vigorous disapproval," not suffering, is the "essence of punishment" (p. 167).

Punishment, according to Durkheim, should be a "palpable symbol, a notation, a language" for reaffirming respect for the rule by repudiating the misdeed (1925/1973, p. 167). As I discovered in the just-community programs, the mere verbal expression of disappointment is often enough, especially if the person expressing the disappointment speaks for the whole community. If punishment is to have moral influence, those breaking the rules must understand that their offense is against the whole community and not the teacher or another individual. Punishment, in this Durkheimian sense, has motivational significance insofar as it dramatizes the connectedness of the members of the community and the importance that the rules have for the community's identity. Just as individuals may be motivated by an anticipation of guilt to act in ways that are consistent with a moral identity, members of a community may be motivated by an anticipation of shame to act in ways that are consistent with the community's moral identity. It is possible, of course, that the anticipation of having to face the community may function as any other deterrent used in school (e.g., detention). Yet the purpose of punishment is not to motivate through fear of consequences but to motivate through moral reflection on the inconsistency between one's commitment to the community and one's actions. Violating the community's norms undermines the community itself. Durkheim's approach to punishment serves as a reminder that one cannot enjoy the fruits of community membership without upholding the norms that give one's community its character.

The extent to which Durkheim's approach to punishment involves moral motivation depends on the extent to which individuals freely and deliberately affirm the community and its norms. We might say that membership in a group unites one's second-order desires with those of others and in so doing enhances the motivational power of those second-order desires. If individuals were to violate the group's norms, they would experience others' reproach as self-reproach (assuming that the group's norms were genuinely shared). Individuals may in certain instances choose to violate a group norm because that norm is unjust. The motivation to violate a group norm must in some sense involve acknowledgment of a conflict between one's personal sense of justice and the practice of a group. It may also involve the acknowledgment of a conflict between one's perception of a group's ideals and its practices. In this case, punishment would undermine the well-being of the group.

THE JUST-COMMUNITY APPROACH TO MORAL EDUCATION

I have written extensively about the just-community approach elsewhere (e.g., Power, Higgins, & Kohlberg, 1989; Power, 2002), and I present only a brief outline here. The just-community approach actually originated, not in high schools, but in prisons (Hickey & Scharf, 1980). Prisons ironically provide an ideal situation for establishing just communities because they are "total environments" and also because they are expected to bring about moral rehabilitation through their environments. Hickey and Scharf (1980) focused on what they called the *moral atmospheres* of prison environments. They recognized that prisons created moral cultures, which had an effect on inmates for better or for worse. Punitive environments led to cultures that "pulled for" thinking and behavior that was actually below prisoners' moral reasoning competence. The just-community approach aimed to produce a culture that would pull upward. The key motivational component in both environments is the influence of the culture.

The Cluster School, an alternative school within a school, was the first of a series of just-community programs situated in high schools. The just-community approach, which was born in the prisons, grew up there and became fully articulated in Power, Higgins, and Kohlberg (1989), a study of three democratic alternative high schools. Kohlberg had probably been thinking about the just-community approach when he first spent time on a kibbutz after escaping from the British internment camp. Once he began thinking about the educational implications of his moral development theory, he looked to the kibbutz as a model. He concluded "Education for Justice" with a call to follow Plato's example in the *Republic* by restructuring schools to become ideal educational environments: "The Platonic view that I've been espousing suggests something still revolutionary and frightening to me if not to you, the schools would be radically different places if they took seriously the teaching of real knowledge of the good" (Kohlberg, 1970, p. 83). Kohlberg fleshed out his vision for the just-community approach after spending time in a kibbutz high school over twenty years later (Kohlberg, 1971). In fact, Kohlberg found the practice of democratic collective education on the kibbutz "to be better than anything that we can conceive from our theory" (Kohlberg, 1971, p. 358). It was at this time that Kohlberg took a deeper look at Durkheim's educational application of what we might think of as *collectivism* and found more there than a recipe for inducing conformity.

It is much easier to explain the just-community approach by pointing to a functioning just-community school than it is to present its key institutions and practices. This is because the just-community approach has as its primary aim the creation of a culture, of a certain kind of community. Cultures take time to develop and are subject to unforeseen events in the group life. All the just-community programs have two basic institutions: a weekly community meeting devoted to the democratic governance of the community and regular fairness committee meetings devoted to judicial matters pertaining to rule violations and conflict resolution. The community meetings involve all students and faculty in a direct participatory democracy with each member having an equal vote. The fairness committee meetings involve a rotating group of faculty and students who also have a single vote. In all group meetings, as well as in their teaching that addressed moral matters, teachers used the moral discussion method (Blatt & Kohlberg, 1975) of inviting students to reflect in a critical way on the reasons given pro and con for the proposal under consideration in the meeting (Power, Higgins, & Kohlberg, 1989). The moral discussion method proved to be a helpful tool in stimulating student interaction, common deliberation, and consensus building. The teachers in the just-community approach acted as more than group facilitators, however. They advocated for particular courses of action, made arguments, and held out ideals for what the community could become.

I found in my own experience of starting a just-community program years later in South Bend that the most difficult challenge was to communicate some vision for what the community could offer. If students and faculty have no idea of a "possible community," how can they participate in its establishment? Why would they chose to become something that they cannot even imagine? How can we stimulate their imagination? I have had little success in stimulating students' and teachers' imaginations by presenting them with stories of other just-community programs or impressive research data. There seems to be no real substitute for learning about the just-community approach by experiencing its benefits firsthand, by trying it out.

Participation is vital to the experience of community. One cannot adequately understand or "taste" the joy of community life as an outside observer. The *eudaimonia* of community life is accessible only through participation in the activities of the community (MacIntyre, 1981). I will elaborate this notion and how it influences motivation when I discuss the just-community schools as providing an apprenticeship. Here I simply wish to point out that the just-community approach consists of more than involving students in processes of democratic deliberation. It asks students to devote themselves to a common *moral* project—building a community that exemplifies the values of trust, caring, participation, and shared responsibility. Unlike classes that teach about democracy or about ethics, the just-community approach puts democracy and ethics at the center of its practice.

Research on the just-community schools indicated that much more was happening than moral reasoning development. In fact the research showed that the just-community schools fostered no more moral reasoning development than good moral discussion classes (Power, Higgins, & Kohlberg, 1989). On the other hand the just-community approach succeeded in influencing behavior, such as cheating, fighting, stealing, class attendance, and caring, through the establishment of shared norms based on communal values. At first glance there is nothing remarkable here. There is a wealth of social-psychological research showing that individuals are more inclined to follow rules that they had a role in making than those imposed from above and that individuals will conform to the norms of a group that they value. To this we may add that many students in the just-community program follow the rules out of a sense of reciprocity based in gratitude. The following statement is typical: "Because the community helps us, we have to help the community." How did the just community "help" the students? Self-determination theory provides a partial answer—by meeting their needs for connection (through community), social control (through democracy), and competence (through giving many students in the just-community schools the support to overcome histories of school failure by completing high school and going on to postsecondary schools). I would go a step further, however, by noting that the just-community programs helped students by engaging them as responsible moral agents in the common project of building community. The just-community approach responded to a distinctively moral desire to be oneself while being at one with others.

The moral atmosphere research that we conducted on traditional high schools indicated that students felt little or no responsibility for upholding school rules, even when they believed that violating such rules would be wrong (Power, Higgins, & Kohlberg, 1989). For example, referring to a widely known case in which a radio was stolen from a locker in their high school, students told me that they would not report the thief or even attempt to persuade him to return it because: "You can't put pressure on students [to do] . . . that. The school is responsible [not us]; we are teenagers. The teachers are grown up. . . . They are supposed to control the students in the school" (Power, 1985, p. 235). It is understandable that these students would feel uncomfortable in dealing with the enforcement of school rules, but it is surprising that some students went further and excused the thief: "If someone is dumb enough to bring something like that into school, they deserve to get it stolen. . . . If somebody is going to steal then more power to them" (p. 235). All the students said that stealing was wrong, but none of them felt obliged to intervene in any way to see that the rule was upheld.

In contrast, students in the just-community programs told us that they expected their peers to follow the rules and would be willing in the case of stealing to express their disapproval and even report the thief because "we are a community" and "we are supposed to trust and care for each other." These expressions of the subject *we* figured prominently in our analysis of what we called *collective norms*. What prompted students to say *we* and not *I* in addressing moral concerns? Students in the conventional high schools had not discussed problems, like stealing, even though they were victimized by them. None knew how the others felt. When we asked students from conventional high schools whether they cared about stealing in their school, many said that they did. When asked whether they believed that their peers cared, however, many students responded that their peers were indifferent. This we called a manifestation of *pluralistic ignorance*. Had students simply known more about each other, they would at least have discovered that they all cared as individuals. This would have been the first step in trying to do something about it. The second step follows from the first. Once students agree that something is wrong, they must address it as members of a group. In the just-community programs this typically happened intentionally in the community meetings. It could conceivably happen, however, simply as a function of a tacit group understanding. In any case the expression of the *we* subject in prescribing a norm implies that there is a shared moral consciousness within the community about what ought to be done.

This shared consciousness adds another dimension to moral motivation. Individuals feel obligated to act, not only out of a sense of duty arising in their individual consciences, but also out of a sense of duty arising out of an identification with the community. Not only do students prescribe moral norms in the name of the community and experience accountability for the violation of moral norms to the community, but they also experience collective responsibility. For example, the students in the Cluster School responded to an incident of stealing in which no one admitted to the theft by agreeing to chip in to restitute the victim. They reasoned that they shared responsibility that the stealing occurred in the first place ("it's not her [the victim's] fault that her money got stolen"), and they further shared responsibility for helping the victim ("we should all care that she got her money stolen"). What motivates this expression of a collective responsibility is a sense of attachment with the community as a whole and thus with all those in it.

In addition to the experience of attachment, the just-community approach motivated students to become responsible for their behavior by giving them a sense ownership of or control over their social setting. This was accomplished by cultivating in students a sense of themselves as legislators interacting with other legislators for the purpose of fostering the common good. In other words through the democratic process the just-community approach gives students an experience of autonomy guided by a concern for the good of the whole and not only their individual good. We found through an analysis of interviews that asked students to describe how they went about voting in community meetings that most students initially thought only of themselves and their interests. These same students a year later took a more interactive approach and saw themselves bargaining to balance their interests with those of others. Finally, the students saw themselves as responsible for voting for what would help the community as a whole. From a motivational standpoint students in the just-community programs experienced a far greater sense of personal and collective agency than did their peers in other programs. Students in the just-community schools discovered that they had power, not only as individuals and blocks of individuals, but also as a united community working together toward a common end. The experience of "collective efficacy" may well be important to the development of civic engagement in a democratic society.

MOTIVATION AND APPRENTICESHIP

Having described the just-community approach and some of the ways in which it exerts a moral influence, I would like to reflect more systematically on the educational approach itself. I noted at the outset of my discussion of the just-community approach that the basic insight to educate through a specially constructed environment came from Plato, who proposed that participating in an ideal society was the most effective means of moral education. Plato created the system of moral education presented in the *Republic* in response to the failed philosophical program that eventually led a democratic majority in Athens to vote for Socrates' execution. Kohlberg likened the philosophically oriented moral dilemma discussion approach that he and others vigorously championed in late 1960s and early 1970s to Socrates' dialogic approach. Although he never disavowed the moral discussion approach, after several years of working in the Cluster School he had clearly judged it to be inadequate. He embraced the method of Plato's *Republic* with caution as well as reservations. The just-community approach, Kohlberg conceded, involved faculty advocacy and peer influence that came close to what he regarded as "indoctrination" (Kohlberg, 1981, p. 3). Moreover, the practice of the just-community approach led him (Kohlberg 1981) to reappraise Aristotle's understanding of moral education as habituation. While Kohlberg continued to emphasize the influence of the just-community approach on students' moral reasoning, he took note of the fact that reasoning was "embodied" in dispositions, not unlike Aristotle's virtues.

In my view, the just-community approach comes closer to an apprenticeship model of moral education than Kohlberg, Higgins, or I realized, even after acknowledging Aristotelian features of the approach. In my more recent writing on moral education I have consistently cited Horace Mann's call for American schools to provide an apprenticeship in democracy: "In order that men may be prepared for self-government, their apprenticeship must begin in childhood. . . . He who has been a serf until the day before he is twenty-one years of age cannot be an independent citizen the day after; and it makes no difference whether he has been a serf in Austria or America. As the fitting apprenticeship for despotism consists in being trained for despotism, so the fitting apprenticeship for self-government consists in being trained to self-government" (Mann, 1845/1957, p. 58). Mann emphasizes but one element of the just-community approach—the apprenticeship in self-government. Yet this element is key for the future of democracy in America. It challenges us, as educators, to examine what kinds of apprenticeship schools provide (whether this apprenticeship is conducted consciously or unconsciously). The ultimate test of the just-community approach is how well it prepares students for moral life in society.

The concept of apprenticeship to describe the interactive process of what is typically called *socialization* has been gaining popularity in developmental psychology (e.g., Bruner, 1997; Gardner, 1993; Rogoff, 1995). This model calls our attention to the subtle as well as the overt ways in which social structures influence the child and also to the fact that children are active in the process of adapting to their culture. Children in this model are novices whose development is guided by "masters" or experts in the community. Aristotle (1985) indirectly referred to the model in his analogy between learning a craft and acquiring virtue, and Narvaez (in this volume) has also used the model in her most recent moral education projects.

The motivational framework of the apprenticeship model operates on several levels. At the most obvious level, the level of achievement, the novice desires mastery and is willing to submit to the direction of the expert. This explanation implies, however, a prior acceptance of the standards that constitute mastery. These standards are established by a community of practitioners. The motivation to achieve is thus embedded from the very beginning within a social context. A novice is an initiate who, in the process of becoming a member of a particular community, learns both the standards of judgment and the competencies that will make him or her an expert and full member of the community. The process of moving from novice to expert is self-motivating to the extent that the activities themselves are enjoyable, as is the social participation involved in these activities. The approval of the expert or the "veteran" community members also plays a motivational role insofar as the novice-initiate seeks full membership in the community.

A frequently raised objection to these motivational dynamics is that their influence is context specific; students may be "good citizens" while they are in the just-community school, but the effect may not be lasting. The apprenticeship model suggests that, in addition to whatever development occurs within students' moral reasoning, they develop competencies or habits of the common life that will serve them and society after graduation. Indeed we now have evidence from the Cluster School that the just-community approach has had a thus far lasting influence on many of its graduates.

Grady (1994) interviewed a sample of thirty alumni approximately 10 years after they had graduated from the Cluster School and compared them with a matched group from the regular high school. She found that Cluster graduates were significantly more likely than those in the comparison group to report that their high school experience enhanced respect for women and minorities. The Cluster graduates were also more likely to be interested in politics and national affairs, have voted in local elections, have a concern for local government decisions, and have worked with others in a community to solve community problems. She also reported that 63% of Cluster graduates, in contrast with 5% of their peers, found that their experience in school helped them feel more self-confident, self-directive, and efficacious in sociopolitical situations. Here are two of their comments:

> I learned about democracy, that when I feel strongly about something that I can stand up and state my opinions and not be afraid. I became more confident and had more self-esteem. (p. 145)

> I challenged myself to take control of situations in that program and that helped me in life. Cluster was a microcosm of the world I later entered, so I was prepared for real-life situations. I truly learned to become a responsible leader. (p. 146)

Grady's data suggest that the just-community approach helped its graduates become engaged democratic citizens. From a Durkheimian perspective, we might argue that, having acquired a "taste" for democratic community, and having developed the skills of effective democratic participation, students were both motivated and prepared for life in the wider society. Yet clearly more was involved than that. The just-community approach influenced the ways in which students defined and valued themselves. Students began to identify, not just with the Cluster School in particular, but with its larger ideals and vision. That identification provided a special personal source of moral motivation after the Cluster School.

The Moral Self

I return now to a consideration of the role of the self in the moral life. My own contribution to this emerging area of inquiry has been on the construct of moral self-worth. I have since the beginning seen my own work as a part of a much broader project exploring the developmental and motivational processes involved in the moral self and moral identity (Blasi 1984, 1988, 1995, 1999; Colby & Damon, 1992). By showing how personal responsibility mediates between moral judgment and moral action, Blasi (1980) makes a strong case that the self is integral to the experience of moral motivation. Blasi's argument is a complicated one, and I cannot do it justice within the limits of this chapter. I would like to note, however, two related ways of analyzing the role of the self in his theory. First, one is motivated to act on one's judgments because of the very unity of the self. The subject self who judges is the same self who executes the judgment in action. The tendency to self-consistency is what Blasi (1983) calls a "central tendency in personality organization" (p. 194). The tendency is, in my view, based, not just on the dynamics of personality organization, but on the very unity of consciousness itself. Coming to a decision to act one way but failing to act on the decision violates the original intentionality of the decisionmaking process to guide one's action. Yet Blasi says more than that the unity of personal consciousness leads from judgment to action. He argues that individuals construct identities in which moral values are at the core, such that to violate what one knows to be a moral prescription is to violate one's very sense of self. Responsibility in this second sense follows, not only from the unity of the subject, but also from a relation between one's moral understanding and one's moral self. Of course, in order to experience such a sense of responsibility, one must have moral values at the core of one's identity.

There is a growing body of empirical evidence that substantiates Blasi's observation that individuals vary to the extent that moral concerns are at the core of their self-descriptions (Arnold, 1993; Blasi, 1984; Colby & Damon, 1992; Power & Khmelkov, 1997). In our research, we (Khmelkov, Makogon, & Power, 1995) asked children and adolescents (age 6–16) to describe their "real," "imagined," and "dreaded" selves, and we coded their descriptions according to cognitive-developmental levels described in Power and Khmelkov (1997). Approximately half describe their ideal (52.4%), real (56.6%), and dreaded selves (48.7%) using at least one moral characteristic. The highest percentages of respondents including a moral characteristic in their descriptions of their ideal, real, and dreaded selves are at the highest cognitive-developmental level coded (66.7% of the respondents for the ideal self, 63.2% for the dreaded self, and 58.3% for the real self). Of all the characteristics used to describe the selves, 30.0% of the dreaded self characteristics, 19.6% of the ideal self characteristics, and 17.0% of the real self characteristics are moral. These results only weakly supported our hypothesis that individuals would be more likely to use moral concerns to describe their ideal and dreaded selves. There is a growing body of evidence that, within the United States at least, many individuals form a sense of themselves with little or no moral characteristics. This suggests that, although individuals may develop a relatively high stage of moral knowledge, they may lack a sense of identity-based responsibility to act on their knowledge, especially when more personally relevant concerns are at stake.

Blasi (1993) maintains that, if moral concerns are only peripheral to identity, individuals will not experience the same kind of moral motivation that they would if they had moral identities. They will not be very troubled by an inconsistency between their behavior and their sense of self, although they may still be troubled by inconsistencies between their moral beliefs and their actions. Blasi qualifies this assertion slightly by noting that, however moral very young children describe themselves to be, the self does not have motivating power until preadolescence. Drawing on his own research and that of Nunner-Winkler and Sodian (1988), Blasi (1988) argues that the linkage between moral understanding and the moral self is forged sometime around age 12 and is absent in children from age 6 to age 8. His evidence for this is that, while young children understand that some actions are right and wrong, they do not experience a sense of personal responsibility to act on their understanding, nor does moral wrongdoing arouse guilt and shame. Children around the age of 12 thus appear to integrate their sense of self with their moral understanding, which makes their moral understanding far more effective in motivating them to act.

Most of the current interest in Blasi's theories of responsibility and moral identity focus on the extent to which individuals base their identity on moral as opposed to nonmoral characteristics. However, Blasi's theory of identity goes further than its content. Blasi (1988) has also identified a developmental sequence of four identity types (social-role identity, identity observed, management of identity, and identity as authenticity), which he derived from Erickson's identity theory as well as from his own cognitive-developmental approach to the self. This sequence proceeds in the direction of an identity received from others to an autonomous identity constructed by the self. In the course of this sequence individuals have a far greater sense of agency or personal control of their lives, which would appear to make them all the more responsible for acting on their moral identities. In the course of this sequence, moreover, individuals become more autonomous insofar as they have chosen the moral principles that give direction to their selves. Colby and Damon's (1992) study of moral exemplars underscores the significance of the motivational role of the moral self. In fact, their study so emphasizes the role of the moral self that it calls into question the relevance of moral reasoning development to moral action. What Colby and Damon's exemplars had in common was not that they were at Kohlberg's postconventional moral stages (5 or 6) but that they were personally committed to the service of others. The fact that a substantial number of Colby and Damon's subjects scored below stage 5 on the Moral Judgment Interview suggests only that there are motivational sources for highly committed moral lives in addition to moral understanding. It may also indicate that the motivation to act on one's moral experience may be somewhat different than the motivation to develop to a higher stage of moral understanding. Colby and Damon found many moral exemplars that apparently reached moral equilibrium at conventional moral stages.

In a recent theoretical article, Bergman (2002) presents a model that attempts to integrate Kohlbergian moral judgment theory with Colby and Damon's (1992) and Blasi's (1988) perspectives on the moral self and identity. Bergman, in my view, tends to undermine the motivational efficacy of moral reasoning while overemphasizing the role of the self. Citing Colby and Damon's finding that their sample of moral exemplars was distinctive, not because of the exemplars' high stage of moral reasoning, but because of their moral identities, Bergman speculates that the integration that occurs between morality and the self "seems to be Colby and Damon's alternative to stage six" (p. 118). Bergman, as Anne Colby (2002) notes in her commentary, goes too far in attempting to "replace" postconventional moral reasoning with the moral self (p. 131). Colby does, however, praise Bergman's model as one that "gets to the relationship between moral judgment and moral action in a more direct and satisfying way than Kohlberg's cognitive framework" (p. 130).

In attempting to draw conclusions from the Colby and Damon (1992) study, one should be careful of committing the naturalistic fallacy of deriving an "is" from an "ought." The finding that many moral exemplars reason at stages 3 and 4 does not imply that conventional moral reasoning is an adequate end point of moral judgment development as long as it is accompanied by a moral identity. Heroically devoting one's life to the service of others does not excuse one from the responsibility to make carefully reasoned moral judgments about a number of very difficult moral issues that may lie outside one's particular set of moral commitments. One may, for example, render heroic service to poor and orphaned children while supporting social policies that contribute to rather than ameliorate social inequities.

MORAL SELF-WORTH

Colby and Damon (1992) report that almost all the exemplars in their sample felt good about their lives and their service. They were never defeated by their setbacks or crushed by the suffering that they sought to alleviate. Their sense of self-esteem seemed to follow directly from their living up to their high moral aspirations. They did not pursue self-esteem as an end per se; in fact they avoided many of the ways in which individuals go about enhancing their self-esteem (Colby & Damon, 1992). The exemplars took responsibility for their actions and never blamed others for their failures. The exemplars did not seek social approval, compare themselves to others, or even take credit for what they did. They did not indulge in self-serving distortions, nor did they lower their high moral aspirations when faced with difficulty. Above all they were humble.

These findings suggest that there is something unique about moral self-worth that has eluded the self-esteem models that have dominated psychological research for many years. My colleagues and I have been investigating the puzzling relation of self-esteem to morality for over a decade now. There is little, if any, empirical support for a causal relation between high self-esteem and prosocial behavior (Eisenberg, 1986; Kohn, 1994; Staub, 1986) or between low self-esteem and delinquency (e.g., McCarthy & Hoge, 1984; Wells & Rankin, 1983). In their review Scheff, Ratzinger, and Ryan (1989) note that correlational studies of the relation between self-esteem and crime and violence yield generally weak and inconsistent results. More intriguing are the findings reported by Oyserman and Markus (1990) and others (cf. Gold & Petronio, 1980) that the most delinquent youths report the highest self-esteem. There is, however, more recent research that associates low self-esteem with less extreme antisocial behavior, such as bullying (Hay, 2000; Neary & Joseph, 1994; Paquette & Underwood, 1999).

From a theoretical point of view, it is not surprising that high self-esteem is compatible with delinquency if self-esteem simply represents feelings of positive self-regard without taking into account the sources of those feelings. Such feelings may well be empowering, that is, they may encourage individuals to act on their beliefs, and the absence of such feelings may lead to resignation and passivity. Yet, if feelings of self- regard are in and of themselves morally neutral, why should they be expected to be related positively to moral behavior? Of course the desire to enhance or protect one's sense of self-esteem may motivate individuals to act in ways that are moral. In this sense, self-esteem may be thought of as motivating moral action, but the pursuit of self-esteem may not in and of itself be a moral motive. What count in the determination of whether self-esteem is the source of moral motivation are the criteria that individuals use to evaluate their self-worth. If these criteria are essentially amoral, then self-esteem is not a moral motive. If on the other hand the criteria for determining self-esteem are based on moral principles and values that are seen as "objectively important" (Blasi, 1993), then self-esteem can be a moral motive.

Most theorists, however, think of self-esteem as based (at least in part) on a moral foundation. For example, Schwalbe and Staples (1991) define *self-esteem* as "a positive affective response to the self deriving from beliefs that one is competent and moral" (p. 159). Coopersmith (1967) and Harter (1983) identify *moral self-approval* or *virtue* as one of four basic dimensions (the others are *power*, *competence*, and *social acceptance*) for evaluating self-esteem. The inclusion of moral self-approval or integrity as a dimension in theoretical accounts of self-esteem has not, however, led to any systematic exploration of how moral self-approval comes about or how moral self-approval contributes to global self-esteem in relation to the other sources of self-esteem.

Harter (1983) has restricted her measure of the moral dimension of self-esteem to the assessment of behavioral conduct as one of several competencies, such as academic and athletic achievement. Unfortunately her items do not distinguish between conventional and moral deportment in school (Nucci, 1982; Turiel, 1983). For example, the item "some kids usually act the way they are supposed to" can refer to arbitrary classroom conventions, such as raising one's hand before speaking, or to moral norms, such as no fighting or name-calling. Testing the relation between her scales of perceived behavioral competence and global self-worth with samples of children and adolescents, Harter (1985, 1988b) finds moderate correlations between the two. The strength of this correlation is comparable to the strength of the correlations between her scales of global self-worth and scholastic competence. Bear, Clever, and Proctor (1991), however, report somewhat stronger correlations between Harter's scales of behavioral conduct and global self-worth with a third-grade sample. The Harter (1983) and Bear et al. (1991) studies suggest that moral criteria enter into judgments of global self-esteem as expected, yet the items used to measure the moral domain are too ambiguous and not commensurate with current measures of moral understanding. The question of the relation of the moral domain to global self-worth thus remains unanswered.

Key to understanding the relation of moral self-appraisal to global self-esteem is the self-evaluation process itself. How do we go about the self-evaluation process? William James (1892/1985) gave the classic answer, which has influenced research to the present: Self-esteem is the ratio of one's successes to one's pretensions. This simple claim has been empirically refined, tested, and confirmed by Harter (1988a, 1998). The strategy of examining the gap between one's pretensions or aspirations and the extent to which one actually meets them has informed a number of research programs and led to contradictory hypotheses about the significance of the discrepancy between aspirations and perceived competence. A number of theorists—for example, Higgins (1991), Zigler (see Glick & Zigler, 1985), and Markus and colleagues (Markus & Nurius, 1986; Markus & Wurf, 1987)—have conceptualized the discrepancy between aspirations and competence as a discrepancy between real and ideal (or possible) selves. Some of this research supports James's prediction that discrepancy leads to negative self-evaluation and psychological distress (e.g., Higgins, 1991). On the other hand, Zigler and colleagues (Glick & Zigler, 1985; Rosales & Zigler, 1989) have maintained that the discrepancy may be a function of development as children develop the capacity to make more differentiated judgments about themselves. Rejecting the view that the discrepancy between the ideal and the real self has a negative effect, Rosales and Zigler (1989) advocate the opposite position that the discrepancy can motivate behavior. Bandura (1990) reports that individuals actually create motivational discrepancy by intentionally setting high standards. Markus and Wurf (1987) make a somewhat similar point in noting that hoped-for possible selves and dreaded negative selves can provide a source of direction and motivation.

I believe that the contradiction between the positive, motivating function of the ideal/real discrepancy and the negative, debilitating function of that discrepancy cannot be resolved by simply measuring the ideal/real gap. What the gap does not reveal is the meaning that the gap has for the individual experiencing it. There is a wealth of developmental research that confirms Glick and Zigler's (1985) finding that, the more developed one's self-understanding, the greater the potential for differentiating one's real from one's ideal self. Our research (Power & Khmelkov, 1997) went further in exploring the extent to which individuals engaged in self-criticism in their real self definitions. We found that the capacity for self-criticism is itself a developmental achievement, which occurred at level 2 (generally not until the age of 10). Although there was a small but insignificant negative correlation between the global self-esteem rating used by Harter (1986) and developmental level, we did find a modest but significant relation between self-esteem and self-criticism. We expected that self-criticism might be related to somewhat lower self-esteem but did not find this to be a source of concern. Most of the self-critical individuals in our sample expressed confidence that they could and would change for the better.

James's (1892/1985) self-esteem model offers a possible solution to the negative effects of the ideal/real discrepancy. His model predicts that individuals will have high self-esteem if their aspirations are adjusted to their competencies. Anticipating the multidimensional models prevalent today, James recognized that there were all kinds of possible sources of self-esteem. In his view individuals with high self-esteem would discount the importance of domains in which they lacked competence. Harter (1985, 1986, 1990, 1993, 1998) conducted a number of studies that confirmed the relevance of importance ratings. Children and adults with high self-esteem are thus not necessarily the most successful but manage to discount the importance of domains in which they are not successful.

This leads to the question of whether James's discounting principle works for the moral domain. If morality may be understood as a particular area of competence, is it then possible to discount the significance of moral failure in the interest of self-esteem, or does the nature of morality preclude it from being discounted? Moral duties are categorical; they bind unconditionally. While I may be able to discount aspirations in the athletic domain, I do not have the same freedom to discount aspirations in the moral domain, at least insofar as they are based on moral duties. We (Power & Makogon, 2003) examined this question by asking a cross-sectional sample of children (ages 7–14) to respond to four stories about failure. These stories tap the following areas of competence: (1) athletics; (2) success in school; (3) popularity; and (4) everyday moral behavior. Each story begins with the protagonist (the same sex as the participant) feeling that his or her goals in a particular area of competence are very important. The protagonist then discovers that, in spite of his or her efforts, he or she fails at reaching this goal. In addition to finding level-related differences in participants' responses to failure, we also found story-related differences. Over half (52.6%) of the participants discounted on the popularity story, less than half (44.7%) on the sports story, a third (33.3%) on the academic story, and very few (7.1%) on the moral story. The rarity of discounting on the moral story indicates that goals based on negative moral duties (duties that proscribe harm or unfairness to others) cannot be discounted as readily as can other nonmoral goals.

We limited our investigation of the moral domain to what are sometimes called *negative duties,* which are duties that protect the rights and welfare of others. An interesting area for future investigation would be *positive duties* related to helping others and building a just and peaceful social order. One can in this area have very high and challenging aspirations. Discounting may well play a role in this area of the moral domain. On the other hand there may well be a threshold beyond which one could not in good conscience discount.

EARNED AND INHERENT SELF-WORTH

To this point, I have argued that moral self-esteem is earned through meeting one's moral ideals and aspirations. Within this framework self-esteem constitutes a source of moral motivation. I will leave this topic with a very brief consideration of another source of moral self-worth, one that has a limited but relevant motivational function. There is a tradition of "humanistic psychology" that maintains that one can also experience a sense of unconditional self-worth (e.g., Maslow, 1968; Rogers, 1961). This sense of self-worth may protect the ego in times of failure, when one's sense of self-respect has come under assault from within because one has not achieved one's goals or from without because one has not gained the respect of others. We use the term *inherent self-worth* to refer to this sense of self as having fundamental value simply because of one's humanity or personhood. Moral developmental theory (Kohlberg, 1984) suggests that an understanding of the inherent worth of one's self develops as part of a recognition of the worth of all human beings. Within the moral judgment coding scheme (Colby et al., 1987), a valuing of human life apart from external or instrumental considerations does not appear until the third stage of moral development (criterion judgment 9; p. 20). This understanding of the inherent value of the person continues to develop through the later stages.

We have begun to investigate the notion of inherent self-worth by asking individuals to respond to a protagonist who feels both incompetent and rejected. As we hypothesized, individuals did not appeal to a notion of inherent self-worth until level 3, which has some parallels with stage 3 of moral judgment. At this level, earned and inherent self-esteem are differentiated, as participants recognize the worth of all people no matter what they did nor did not accomplish.

An acknowledgment of one's inherent self-worth, I believe, entails more than self-acceptance. Insofar as inherent self-worth derives from a moral insight into the basic worth of and respect due to all persons, it implies an awareness of one's responsibility to live out what Kant (1788/2002) calls one's *sublime moral vocation*. The insight into one's inherent self-worth derives from the "golden rule" of mutual respect. In the conclusion of his remarkable autobiography, Frederick Douglass (1845/1992) shows how the assertion of one's inherent worth is bound up in a responsibility to others: "Sincerely and earnestly hoping that this little book may do something toward throwing light on the American slave system, and hastening the glad day of deliverance to the millions of my brethren in bonds—faithfully relying on the power of truth, love, and justice, for success in my humble efforts—and solemnly pledging my self anew to the sacred cause,—I subscribe myself, Frederick Douglass" (p. 789). Douglass's self-discovery of his inherent self-worth and the inherent self-worth of his fellow slaves led him to claim his own dignity and to work on their behalf. While achieving great personal success as an author and orator, Douglass did not glory in his accomplishments. To elevate himself would be to denigrate his brethren. Diminishing his efforts as "humble," he acknowledges truth, love, and justice, powers greater than himself, for whatever success may come from his work. Douglass, like Colby and Damon's exemplars, affirms his worth simply by devoting himself to a cause greater than himself—a "sacred cause," which also embodies a sense of the collective.

As I will discuss in the section to follow, Douglass's assertion that his success is due not so much to his own effort as to the powers of "truth, love, and justice" is based on what I will call a *spiritual insight* into the relation between what theologians may call *grace* and *nature*. Of interest in this discussion of self-esteem is that Douglass seems to place a relatively higher value on intrinsic self-worth than on earned self-worth in framing his personal struggle to abolish slavery. The recognition that every person, including Douglass, has worth as a person should be sufficient to motivate the fight for freedom. On the other hand the sense of one's inherent self-worth does not appear to mitigate the importance of honest moral self-evaluation. If Douglass did not devote himself to the "sacred cause" of freeing all slaves, then he surely would have felt a loss of moral self-worth for failing to commit himself to an ideal so fundamental, not just to his moral understanding, but to his very sense of self. What I find worthy of further psychological investigation is the way in which Douglass, like many of the moral exemplars in the Colby and Damon (1992) study, appears to experience a sense of moral self-worth without seeking moral credit from others.

Theonomy: The Role of the Spiritual in Moral Motivation

As I noted, Douglass's appeal to a transcendent moral dimension raises the question of the relation between the spiritual and the moral. Moral and motivational psychologists have generally avoided the exploration of a spiritual or religious dimension of moral experience, probably for reasons that have more to do with the history of the discipline of psychology than with the phenomenon of moral experience itself. There is a growing body of data that points to a relation between religiosity and prosocial behavior (see Ellison, 1992).

Why moral psychology has avoided the study of religion is a topic worthy of historical investigation. There should be no question, however, that religious concerns play a preeminent role in motivating moral and immoral behavior. Martin Luther King, perhaps the best-known moral exemplar in our lifetime, was clearly motivated by Christian beliefs. Yet common people, not only moral heroes, say that they are striving to lead moral lives out of a desire to do God's will, or please God, or be with God in the afterlife. As Durkheim noted, religious beliefs often bring great energy and sense of purpose to moral causes. Yet religious beliefs can also bring great energy and sense of purpose to immoral causes, as can be seen in various expressions of fanaticism, which often lead to intolerance and violence.

The perspective that I take on the question of religious, or what I prefer to call *spiritual*, sources of moral motivation is similar to the perspective that I have taken on the community and on self-esteem. If one's spiritual or religious outlook is basically to be in harmony with one's moral understanding, that outlook can be what I call an *authentic* source of moral motivation. If one's religious or spiritual outlook is opposed to moral understanding, then that outlook is not a source of authentic moral motivation. I am making a distinction here between a spirituality that may transcend moral rationality and a spirituality that contradicts moral rationality. There is a third possibility: one's spirituality may not engage one's moral life at all.

Because spirituality can relate to rational morality in different ways, we need to be very careful about the use of terms like *spirituality, faith,* and *religion*. Because of this I have borrowed Tillich's (1967) term *theonomy* to point to at least one way of integrating morality and spirituality without losing the integrity of either. Tillich (1967) coined the term *theonomy* to describe an inner sense of spirituality that does not contradict but enhances human autonomy. Tillich (1967) distinguishes theonomy from *religious heteronomy*, which constitutes an external source of moral authority over and against human reason. I will leave it to theologians and philosophers to determine whether Tillich's claims for theonomy are, indeed, compelling. For my purposes in this chapter I will confine myself to empirical psychology and consider examples of individuals who appear to be motivated by a religious or spiritual outlook that respects their moral autonomy.

Blasi (1990) and Walker, Pitts, Hennig, and Matsuba (1995) charge that philosophically driven limitations of Kohlberg's cognitive-developmental paradigm constrained Kohlberg and his followers from giving due attention to the role of religious and spiritual concerns in moral judgment. In one of the few psychological studies that explores the role of the spiritual in moral reasoning, Walker et al. (1995) present evidence that the hypothetical dilemmas that Kohlberg used constrained the range of concepts, especially those having to do with religion and spirituality, that informed individuals' actual moral decisionmaking. So, for example, individuals mentioned the importance of prayer, meditation, and reading the scriptures to moral decisionmaking. They also spoke of wanting to please God and to follow Christ's example. Finally, they embedded religious content in their arguments, which Walker et al. (1995) admit had a "stagelike" quality but were absent from the scoring manual (p. 384).

Although Walker et al. (1995) present compelling evidence that many individuals make use of religious and spiritual concepts in their everyday lives, they do not assess what these religious and spiritual concepts really add to the moral domain. The fact that they appear to be "stagelike" suggests that they may be moral concepts in religious disguise. On the other hand, by focusing purely on the moral meaning of spiritual references, we may be missing their deeper significance.

I have been using the terms *faith, religion,* and *spiritual* interchangeably to refer to a transcendent quality of human experience.

Elsewhere (Power, 1992; Power & Kohlberg, 1980) I distinguish implicit faith in a transcendent reality from explicit religious belief in God. This is an old and venerable distinction made by many theologians and religious philosophers. It derives from a traditional definition of *theology* as "faith seeking understanding." People who hold a religious outlook maintain that faith is preconscious. As I am writing this paper I am conscious only of my writing and thinking and of the ideas that I struggle to put into words. I am not conscious of myself as an object, as the *I* who is thinking and writing. Yet, although I am not conscious of myself as an object, I am at least tacitly aware of myself as subject and agent. I experience my writing and thinking as *my* writing and thinking and not as isolated and detached occurrences of writing and thinking. I can make this tacit awareness explicit by reflecting on myself as object and inquiring into who I am, into what William James and Damon and Hart call the *me-self.* This is similar to what believers say occurs when implicit faith becomes objective and is expressed in religious language and institutions.

It should be clear from what I am saying that explicit religious expressions need not be tied to any particular institution or creed. They may not even be theistic in content. I use the term *spirituality* to refer to an outlook or point of view based on an understanding of the self and world that is infused with the presence of a higher, transcendent reality. According to the way in which I am defining *spirituality,* one can invoke a spiritual interpretation of one's situation without adhering to a religion or affirming the existence of God. A theonomous spirituality can act as a source of moral motivation in at least three different ways. First, one's spirituality can lead to a heightened awareness of moral values, especially the worth of others. Second, it can heighten one's sense of agency by bringing hope in the face of indifference and injustice. Third, it can frame one's moral identity as a vocation originating beyond the self.

Kohlberg and I (Kohlberg & Power, 1981; Power & Kohlberg, 1980) argued for a theonomous spirituality in writing about stage 7, which we described a spiritual stage that went beyond justice (which Kohlberg believed was fully realized at stage 6). The best illustration of what we meant by stage 7 comes from our discussion of an interview with Andrea Simpson, whom we regarded as a stage 7 moral exemplar (Kohlberg & Power, 1981). Andrea Simpson spent many years as a devoted mental health worker. She related that she discovered her "vocation" to work in that field in an almost mystical moment when she visited her older brother, who had been hospitalized with a mental illness: "And here was a little old man all bent over sitting there and I got down on my knees in front of him so I could look into his face, and he saw who it was, and I saw a smile right out of heaven, a smile of an angel. He'd found his old sister" (p. 350). She explained that the act of helping others originates beyond the self: "I think it is terribly important not only to give what help we can but not to feel we are doing it. . . . They will be helped because in a sense love is God, and if you give love you give something much more than yourself" (p. 350). Andrea Simpson's spiritual outlook seemed to lead her inexorably to a selfless love (agape) of others. We wrote: "This sense of union [with God and the whole of life] promoted the development of an ethical orientation of *agape* to resolve the gap between the is and the ought" (p. 355).

In the case of Andrea Simpson, and in the examples that follow, it appears that individuals' spirituality creates the perception of a supramoral atmosphere (a world infused with an elevated sense of dignity and purpose) that motivates by calling forth, not only a duty to follow the moral law, but also a desire to serve others. Spirituality also creates a perception of a supramoral self that draws its sense of moral agency from a power beyond the self. By discussing the spiritual dimension within the framework of stage 7, Kohlberg and I may have given the false impression that spirituality was the culmination of moral development and even that spirituality belonged to the final stage of the life cycle (Erikson, Erikson, & Kivnik, 1986). Although I have elsewhere argued (Power, Power, & Snarey, 1988) that spiritual concerns may emerge with a special urgency in old age and at an advanced stage of cognitive development, a spiritual outlook can be found at earlier stages of life.

A spiritual outlook can manifest itself as a source of moral motivation in many ways. As I illustrate below, it can constitute a coherent philosophy of life, or it can provide a source of energy and transforming hope in a time of crisis, transforming in very simple ways the categories of ordinary existence. After graduating from Notre Dame, Lou did what many Notre Dame graduates do—volunteered a year of his life in service to the poor. Lou chose a program serving the poor in a shantytown in Santiago, Chile, amid the cruelties of the Pinochet regime. Lou's classical liberal arts education seemed terribly irrelevant for life under a military dictatorship among the poor and uneducated. Lou wrote about that experience:

> Distant from family and friends, I struggled with health problems as I adjusted to a new language, culture, political situation and economic reality. Loneliness and self-doubt filled the space where pride and self-confidence had recently dwelled. I cried myself to sleep many nights thinking of the profound suffering which surrounded me in our neighborhood. . . . Masses of people who had lost belief in themselves and hope for the future. . . . I soon came to feel that I was as powerless as they to change this unjust reality, even for one lost soul, or so it seemed. While searching in vain for satisfaction I found joy. I found joy in the common-day prophets all around me. People who had transformed suffering into joy. People who had found resurrection in their own crucifixion and shared it with others. (Himes, 1995, p. 46)

Lou became an activist himself, helping the poor, and risking his life to capture the brutalities of the military regime on a hidden camera. He talked about a kind of "restlessness" that led him to leave the comforts of security and wealth in the first place to experience a new reality, which first completely overwhelmed him, but later sustained him in a newfound sense of purpose and joy. Lou named the source of that restlessness the "Holy Spirit" (p. 47). Would Lou have lived differently or felt differently if he had attributed his restlessness to his birth order, his experience of an adolescent moratorium, or the influence of certain features of his personality? Would Lou have lived differently or felt differently if he simply dwelt on the moral realities of the situation—or on the acts of moral heroism as well as the injustices he encountered? Lou's spirituality informed his decision to do a year of service and sustained him in that service. In particular, Lou's spirituality transformed not only his outlook but also his emotions. Lou may well have been paralyzed by his feelings of sadness, moral outrage, and lack of self-confidence. Instead he felt a contagious sense of joy and moral purpose.

Lou's spirituality helped direct his quest for an identity in a very challenging situation. A spiritual outlook can have a more direct and immediate influence by stimulating the moral imagination and by pointing to a source of transcendent power. A small group of Latina women from East Los Angeles met weekly for scripture reading and prayer (Himes, 1995). During one of their meetings, they had begun to ask themselves what they could do to protect their children from the violence of the drug dealers, who had installed a reign of terror over their housing project. One night, as they read the gospel stories of Jesus calming the storm (Matt. 8:22ff.) and calling Peter to walk on the water (Matt. 14:22ff.), they saw their neighborhood as the story's sea and came to believe that Jesus had the power to calm those seas and support them if they had the faith to leave the security of their "boat." These women ventured out to meet gang bangers and drug dealers, whom they began to call their *prodigal sons*. Welcoming them into their hearts, these "powerless" women subdued those who had once terrified them and reclaimed their neighborhood. These women had a desire to change their world; in order to change it they had to reenvision and rename it. The process of spiritual reenvisioning and renaming suggested not only a plan of action (confronting the drug dealers and gang bangers) but also a way of confronting them (as wayward sons). Moreover, the process served to embolden the women by making them aware of a power strong enough to calm the sea.

The three examples that I have given suggest that spirituality motivates moral action by changing the way in which individuals perceive themselves, their world, and their sense of agency. In all these cases, a spiritual outlook led neither to a specifically religious moral principle nor to a moral justification that depended on divine revelation. Rather a spiritual outlook fostered both a sense of moral urgency and a sense of agency.

I will conclude this discussion of the role of a spiritual outlook on moral motivation by discussing very briefly some research that a colleague, Susan Aarestad, and I have been conducting on the development of forgiveness judgments (Aarestad, 2004; Aarestad & Power, 2004; Power, 1995). Forgiveness is a complex response to injury that combines aspects of supererogation and justice. Enright and the Human Development Study Group (1994) claim that forgiveness is a supererogatory and unilateral act of love that cannot be obligated and that the logical basis for this act rests on the acknowledgment that the injured and injuring parties share the same humanity. I (Power, 1994) have taken a somewhat different view and maintained that forgiveness should be understood within a larger framework of reconciliation. Forgiveness involves considerations of justice insofar as injustice has been done and the victim feels entitled to retribution. Forgiveness also involves a release from desires that may be immoral (e.g., from revenge) and from feelings that may be burdensome (e.g., from resentment).

The sequence of developmental levels that Aarestad and I identified (Aarestad & Power, 2004) indicates that the development of forgiveness is closely tied to the dynamics of friendship and to the cognitive operation of reciprocity. Piaget (1932/1965) was right; forgiveness is a product of reason and does not require an appeal to God or to any spiritual concepts. Yet Piaget (1932/1965) oversimplified the matter by focusing only on forgiveness as the renunciation of retaliation. Piaget did not take up the more troublesome issue of whether forgiveness as an act of love is an act of supererogation or obligation. We found that children and adults frequently referred to religious beliefs in establishing forgiveness as an obligation and in justifying the moral superiority of forgiveness over retaliation. For example, 9-year-old John says that it would be wrong not to forgive because: "You should always forgive, like what God said to the soldiers." Twelve-year-old Mary also says that it would be wrong not to forgive: "Because in the Bible it says, 'forgive everyone.'" Asked why the Bible says that, Mary replies: "Because if you can't forgive anyone, you won't have any friends because everyone does wrong. If you keep track of wrongs, it's like you're just criticizing that person and not looking for anything good about the person." Both John and Mary make reference to religious authority to establish the obligation to forgive. Yet both also offer nonreligious arguments in support of forgiveness. Earlier in his interview John said that one ought to forgive an injury in order to maintain a friendship. John's reference to God's example thus underscores his norm, based on purely relational considerations, that one ought to forgive. Mary's response indicates that she believes that there is a consistency between the biblical injunction to "forgive everyone" and a prudential approach to relationships: "If you can't forgive anyone, you won't have any friends." These two examples suggest that religious appeals do not supplant the role of reason but add motivational weight to what is reasonable. Yet John's and Mary's reference to a religiously based obligation to forgive also appears to transform a supererogatory into an obligatory act.

In her seminal social-psychological study of forgiveness, Trainer (1980) recounts the autobiographical account of Jay Meck. One afternoon, as Meck's son was crossing the street in front of his school bus, he was run over by Frank, a policeman on vacation with his wife, Rose Ann. Searching for an explanation for their son's death, Jay and his wife, Ruth, arranged to meet Frank and Rose Ann over dinner. Their conversation was awkward and labored. Jay and Ruth felt sorry for for Frank and Rose Ann, as they had obviously suffered a great deal and stood to suffer more if Frank were laid off the police force. At the meal, Jay and Ruth noticed their guests looking at a picture of Jesus and the lost sheep. Ruth explained how their son loved that picture and how much their faith meant to their son and themselves. After the couples had parted, Jay and Ruth decided not to press charges. Jay explained that he felt for Frank, whose mistake was only human: "Jesus Christ was a man too—the perfect man—and through Him I could see that hatred or vengeance was not the way to handle that mistake—certainly not if Ruth and I professed to live out our faith every day" (Meck as quoted by Trainer, 1980, p. 10).

The Mecks' decision to forgive was prompted by attending to a picture of Jesus based on the parable of the lost sheep. In that story the owner of a hundred sheep leaves the herd of ninety-nine to find the one sheep who strayed. This parable of extravagant love reminded the Mecks of their commitment as Christians to act as Jesus did. The Mecks were moved by Jesus' humanity, a humanity that united them with Frank and Rose Ann, and a humanity that prompted them to forgive in spite of great pain. In this particular case, religious awareness facilitated a process of discovery in which the Mecks became aware of a duty to forgive: "Through Him [Jesus] I could see that vengeance was not the way to handle a mistake—certainly not if Ruth and I professed to live out our faith every day" (p. 10). This insight—that vengeance is not the way to handle a mistake—is grounded on role taking: "He [Frank] had made a mistake that anyone could have made" (p. 10). The religiously based decision to forgive as an act of love built on that moral insight and went beyond it.

The Mecks' decision to forgive thus had a moral basis. To have taken the opposite course of action—to have sued—would have needlessly hurt Frank and Rose Ann and brought little solace to the Mecks. On the other hand the generous act of forgiveness freed both parties from the psychological burdens of guilt and resentment and, in fact, led to an ongoing, mutually supportive relationship. Forgiveness accomplished far more for both parties than the mere renunciation of retaliation. The point of this story is to illustrate the power of the spiritual, not only in initiating, but also sustaining the process of forgiveness. It is particularly noteworthy that, prior to meeting Frank and Rose Ann, the Mecks felt powerless to overcome their anger and desire for revenge. They experienced forgiveness as a grace that freed and enabled them to act in a way that had seemed impossible.

The story of the Mecks suggests that the real function of spirituality is to offer a way of seeing and understanding that goes beyond the ordinary. While I regard the spiritual dimension as a domain that can be distinguished from the moral domain, theonomous spirituality is not an alternative to the moral domain. Spiritually based moral arguments are subject to moral evaluation, as are any other kinds of arguments. In my view, the spiritual permeates the moral but does not supplant it. As we have seen with forgiveness, a spiritual outlook may transform a supererogatory act of love into an obligatory act of love. Theonomous spirituality constitutes a source of moral motivation by offering an outlook or an interpretive framework that engages one's sense of moral duty and moral agency. Theonomous spirituality, moreover, also involves a joining of duty and desire. Many individuals experience a profound sense of joy in sacrificing themselves for others.

Conclusion

In this chapter I have discussed sources of moral motivation from the perspectives of the just-community approach to moral education, the development of a moral self, and theonomous spirituality. The sources of moral motivation that I have identified do not reduce morality to an instrument of self-interest or self-protection. Group solidarity, self-worth, and a sense of spiritual well-being are sources of moral motivation insofar as they support individuals' commitment to live a moral life. They can, however, undermine the moral life by becoming heteronomous forces undermining moral judgment and personal freedom. My aim in this chapter has been to point out that there can be a distinctively autonomous moral dimension to communal participation, self-worth, and spirituality. This dimension easily gets lost in conventional psychological discussions of group conformity, self-esteem, and religiosity. We need, I believe, to develop an approach to these constructs that indicates how they can foster as well as subvert the moral life.

Key to my understanding of moral motivation is the role of second-order moral desires in the formation, not only of individuals' life plans, but also of their sense of identity. Although the forces of group conformity, self-interest, and spiritual connection can operate below the level of conscious reflection and free choice, they can and from a moral point of view should be subjected to careful scrutiny. The link that Blasi (in press) forges between second-order desires and moral judgment moves moral psychology beyond the narrowly Kantian focus on duty that so dominated Piaget and Kohlberg's theories. This concept of second-order desires provides a way of taking into account the motivational role of desire that takes into account moral duty. I have tried to illustrate how the pursuit of certain objects of second-order desires—such goods as group attachment, self-worth, and spirituality—can motivate the moral life. As we develop a comprehensive theory of moral motivation, we need, not only to take into account the perspectives of society, self, and spirituality, but also understand how they inform each other in the moral life.

References

Aarestad, S. L. (1994). *The moral development of forgiveness.* Unpublished senior thesis, University of Notre Dame.

Aarestad, S. L., & Power, F. C. (2004). *The development of forgiveness.* Manuscript in preparation.

Aristotle. (1985). *Nicomachean ethics* (T. Irwin, Trans.). Indianapolis: Hackett.

Arnold, M. L. (1993). *The place of morality in the adolescent self.* Unpublished doctoral dissertation, Harvard University.

Bandura, A. (1990). Conclusion: Reflections on non-ability determinants of competence. In R. J. Sternberg & J. Kolligan Jr. (Eds.), *Competence considered* (pp. 316–352). New Haven: Yale University Press.

Bear, G. G., Clever, A., & Proctor, W. A. (1991). Self-perceptions of non-handicapped children and children with learning disabilities in integrated classes. *Journal of Special Education, 24,* 409–426.

Bergman, R. (2002). Why be moral? A conceptual model from developmental psychology. *Human Development, 45,* 104–124.

Blasi, A. (1980). Bridging moral cognition and moral action: A critical review of the literature. *Psychological Bulletin, 88,* 1–45.

Blasi, A. (1983). Moral cognition and moral action: A theoretical perspective. *Developmental Review, 3,* 178–210.

Blasi, A. (1984). Moral identity: Its role in moral functioning. In W. M. Kurtines & J. L. Gewirtz (Eds.), *Morality, moral behavior, and moral development* (pp. 128–139). New York: Wiley.

Blasi, A. (1988). Identity and the development of the self. In D. K. Lapsley & F. C. Power (Eds.), *Self, ego, and identity: Integrative approaches* (pp. 226–242). New York: Springer.

Blasi, A. (1990). How should psychologists define morality? or, The negative side effects of philosophy's influence on psychology. In T. Wren (Ed.), *The moral domain: Essays on the ongoing discussion between philosophy and the social sciences* (pp. 38–70). Cambridge: MIT Press.

Blasi, A. (1993). The development of identity: Some implications for moral functioning. In G. G. Noam & T. E. Wren (Eds.), *The moral self* (pp. 99-122). Cambridge: MIT Press.

Blasi, A. (1995). Moral understanding and the moral personality: The process of moral integration. In W. M. Kurtines & J. L. Gewirtz (Eds.), *Moral development: An introduction* (pp. 229–253). Boston: Allyn & Bacon.

Blasi, A. (1999). Emotions and moral motivation. *Journal for the Theory of Social Behavior, 29,* 1–19.

Blasi, A. (in press). Moral character: A psychological approach. In D. Lapsley & C. Power (Eds.), *Character psychology and character education.* Notre Dame IN: University of Notre Dame Press.

Blatt, M., & Kohlberg, L. (1975). The effects of classroom discussion programs upon children's level of moral judgement. *Journal of Moral Education, 4,* 129–161.

Bruner, J. (1997). *The culture of education* (2d ed.). Cambridge: Harvard University Press.

Carlo, G., Eisenberg, N., & Knight, G. P. (1992). An objective measure of adolescents' prosocial reasoning. *Journal of Research in Adolescence, 2,* 331–349.

Colby, A. (2002). Moral understanding, motivation, and identity. *Human Development, 45,* 130–135.

Colby, A., & Damon, W. (1992). *Some do care: Contemporary lives of moral commitment.* New York: Free Press.

Colby, A., Kohlberg, L., Speicher, B., Hewer, A., Candee, D., Gibbs, J., & Power, C. (1987). *The measurement of moral judgment: Vol. 1. Theoretical foundations and research validation.* New York: Cambridge University Press.

Coopersmith, S. (1967). *The antecedents of self-esteem.* San Francisco: Freeman.

Damon, W. (1977). *The social world of the child.* San Francisco: Jossey-Bass.

Douglass, F. (1992). Narrative of the life of Frederick Douglass, an American slave. In M. Mack (Ed.), *The Norton Anthology of World Masterpieces* (6th ed., vol. 2, pp. 7277–7789). New York: Norton. (Original work published 1845)

Durkheim, E. (1973). *Moral education: A study in the theory and application of the sociology of education*. New York: Free Press. (Original work published 1925)

Eisenberg, N. (1986). *Altruistic emotion, cognition, and behavior*. Hillsdale NJ: Erlbaum.

Eisenberg, N., & Fabes, R. A. (1998). Prosocial development. In W. Damon (Series Ed.), N. Eisenberg (Vol. Ed.), *Handbook of child psychology: Vol. 3. Social, emotional, and personality development* (5th ed., pp. 701–778). New York: Wiley.

Ellison, C. G. (1992). Are religious people nice people? Evidence from the National Survey of Black Americans. *Social Forces, 71*, 411–430.

Enright, R. D., & the Human Development Study Group. (1994). Piaget on the moral development of forgiveness: Identity or reciprocity? *Human Development, 37*, 63–80.

Erikson, E., Erikson, J., & Kivnik, H. (1986). *Vital involvement in old age*. New York: Norton.

Frankfurt, H. (1988). *The importance of what we care about*. New York: Cambridge University Press.

Frankfurt, H. (1993). On the necessity of ideals. In G. G. Noam & T. E. Wren (Eds.), *The moral self* (pp. 16–27). Cambridge: MIT Press.

Gardner, H. (1993). *The unschooled mind: How children think and how schools should teach*. New York: Basic.

Glick, M., & Zigler, E. (1985). Self-image: A cognitive developmental approach. In R. Leahy (Ed.), *The development of the self* (pp. 17–56). New York: Academic.

Gold, M., & Petronio, R. J. (1980). Delinquent behavior in adolescence. In G. Adelson (Ed.), *Handbook in adolescent psychology* (pp. 495–535). New York: Wiley Interscience.

Grady, E. A. (1994). *After Cluster School: A study of the impact in adulthood of a moral education intervention project*. Unpublished doctoral dissertation, Harvard University.

Harter, S. (1983). Developmental perspectives on the self-system. In P. H. Mussen (Series Ed.), E. M. Hetherington (Vol. Ed.), *Handbook of child psychology: Vol. 4. Social and personality development* (4th ed., pp. 275–385). New York: Wiley.

Harter, S. (1985). *Manual for the Self-Perception Profile for Children*. Denver: University of Denver.

Harter, S. (1986). Processes underlying the construction, maintenance, and enhancement of the self-concept in children. In S. Suls & A. Greenwald (Eds.), *Psychological perspectives on the self* (Vol. 3, pp. 137–181). Hillsdale NJ: Erlbaum.

Harter, S. (1988a). The construction and conservation of the self: James and Cooley revisited. In D. K. Lapsley & F. C. Power (Eds.), *Self, ego, and identity: Integrated approaches* (pp. 43–70). New York: Springer.

Harter, S. (1988b). *Manual for the Self-Perception Profile for Adolescents*. Denver: University of Denver.

Harter, S. (1990). Issues in the assessment of the self-concept of children and adolescents. In A. LaGreca (Ed.), *Childhood assessment: Through the eyes of a child* (pp. 292–325). New York: Allyn & Bacon.

Harter, S. (1993). Causes and consequences of low self-esteem in children and adolescents. In R. F. Baumiester (Ed.), *Self-esteem: The puzzle of low self-regard* (pp. 87–116). New York: Plenum.

Harter, S. (1998). The development of self-representations. In W. Damon (Series Ed.), N. Eisenberg (Vol. Ed.), *Handbook of child psychology: Vol. 3. Social, emotional, and personality development* (5th ed., pp. 553–618). New York: Wiley.

Hartshorne, H., & May, M. A. (1928–1930). *Studies in the nature of character: Vol. 1. Studies in deceit; Vol. 2. Studies in service and self-control; Vol. 3. Studies in organization of character*. New York: Macmillan.

Hay, I. (2000). Gender self-concept profiles of adolescents suspended from high school. *Journal of Child Psychology and Psychiatry, 41*, 345–352.

Heckhausen, H. (1991). *Motivation and action*. New York: Springer.

Hickey, J., & Scharf, P. (1980). *Toward a just correctional system*. San Francisco: Jossey-Bass.

Higgins, E. T. (1991). Development of self-regulatory and self-evaluative processes: Costs, benefits, and tradeoffs. In M. R. Gunnar & L. A. Sroufe (Eds.), *Self processes and development* (Minnesota Symposia on Child Development, Vol. 23, pp. 125–126). Hillsdale NJ: Erlbaum.

Himes, M. J. (1995). *Doing the truth in love: Conversations about God, relationships, and service*. New York: Paulist.

James, W. (1985). *Psychology: The briefer course*. Notre Dame IN: University of Notre Dame Press. (Original work published 1892)

Kagan, J. (1987). Introduction. In J. Kagan & S. Lamb (Eds.), *The emergence of morality in young children* (pp. ix–xx). Chicago: University of Chicago Press.

Kant, I. (2002). *Groundwork for the metaphysics of morals* (Alan Wood, Ed. & Trans.). New Haven: Yale University Press. (Original work published 1788)

Khmelkov, V. T., Makogon, T. A., & Power, F. C. (1995). *The development of self-esteem in adolescence: A moral perspective*. San Francisco: American Educational Research Association.

Kohlberg, L. (1968, September). The child as moral philosopher. *Psychology Today*, 25–30.

Kohlberg, L. (1970). Education for justice: A modern statement of the Platonic view. In T. Sizer & N. Sizer (Eds.), *Moral education: Five lectures* (pp. 57–83). Cambridge: Harvard University Press.

Kohlberg, L. (1971). Cognitive developmental theory and the practice of collective moral education. In M. Wollins & M. Gottesman (Eds.), *Group care: The educational path of youth Aliah* (pp. 342–379). New York: Gordon & Breach.

Kohlberg, L. (1981). *Essays on moral development: Vol. 1. The philosophy of moral development*. San Francisco: Harper & Row.

Kohlberg, L. (1984). *Essays on moral development: Vol. 2. The Psychology of moral development*. San Francisco: Harper & Row.

Kohlberg, L., & Power, F. C. (1981). Moral development, religious thinking, and the question of a seventh stage. *Zygon, 16*, 203–260.

Kohn, A. (1994, December). The truth about self-esteem. *Phi Delta Kappan*, 272- 283.

Latané, B., & Darley, J. M. (1970). *The unresponsive bystander: Why doesn't he help?* New York: Appleton-Century-Crofts.

LaVoi, N. (2002). *Examining relationships in sport contexts*. Unpublished doctoral dissertation, University of Minnesota.

MacIntyre, A. C. (1981). *After virtue: A study in moral theory*. Notre Dame IN: University of Notre Dame Press.

Mann, H. (1957). *The republic and the school: The education of free men*. New York: Teachers College, Columbia University. (Original work published 1845)

Markus, H., & Nurius, P. (1986). Possible selves. *American Psychologist, 41*, 954–969.

Markus, H., & Wurf, E. (1987). The dynamic self-concept. *Annual Review of Psychology, 38*, 229–337.

Maslow, A. H. (1968). *Toward a psychology of being*. New York: Van Nostrand Reinhold.

McCarthy, G. D., & Hoge, D. R. (1984). The dynamics of self-esteem and delinquency. *American Journal of Sociology, 90*, 396–410.

Munzel, G. F., & Power, F. C. (in press). Immanuel Kant's influence on Jean Piaget's and Lawrence Kohlberg's approaches to moral education. In W. Willis & D. Fasko (Eds.), *Philosophical and psychological perspectives on moral development and education*. Cresskill NJ: Hampton.

Neary, A., & Joseph, S. (1994). Peer victimization and its relationship to self-concept and depression among schoolgirls. *Personality and Individual Differences, 16*, 183–186.

Nucci, L. (1982). Conceptual development in the moral and conventional domains: Implications for values education. *Review of Educational Research, 52*, 93–122.

Nucci, L. P., & Nucci, M. (1982). Children's social interactions in the context of moral and conventional transgressions. *Child Development, 53*, 403–412.

Nunner-Winkler, G. (1993). The growth of moral motivation. In G. G. Noam & T. E. Wren (Eds.), *The moral self* (pp. 269–291). Cambridge: MIT Press.

Nunner-Winkler, G., & Sodian, B. (1988). Children's understanding of moral emotions. *Child Development, 59*, 1323–1328.

Oyserman, D., & Markus, H. R. (1990). Possible selves and delinquency. *Journal of Personality and Social Psychology, 59*, 112–125.

Paquette, J., & Underwood, M. (1999). Gender differences in young adolescents' experiences of peer victimization: Social and physical aggression. *Merrill-Palmer Quarterly, 45*, 242–246.

Piaget, J. (1965). *The moral judgment of the child*. New York: Free Press. (Original work published 1932)

Power, A. M. R. (1999). *Getting involved and getting ahead: Participation in extracurricular activities and the educational attainment process*. Unpublished doctoral dissertation, University of Notre Dame.

Power, F. C. (1985). Democratic moral education in a large high school: A case study. In M. Bekowitz & F. Oser (Eds.), *Moral education: Theory and application* (pp. 219–240). Hillsdale NJ: Erlbaum.

Power, F. C. (1992). Hard versus soft stages of faith and religious development: A Piagetian critique. In K. E. Nipkow, F. Schweitzer, & J. Fowler (Eds.), *Stages of faith and religious development: Implications for church, education, and society* (pp. 116–129). New York: Crossroads.

Power, F. C. (1994). Commentary. *Human Development, 37*, 81–85.

Power, F. C. (1995, April). *Children's judgments of retaliation and forgiveness: A developmental approach*. Paper presented at the conference "Encuentro Mundial de Investigatores Profesionales y Estudiantes de Psicologia," Puebla, Mexico.

Power, F. C. (2002). Building democratic community: A radical approach to moral education. In W. Damon (Ed.), *Bringing in a new era in character education* (pp. 129–138). Stanford: Hoover Institution Press.

Power, F. C., Higgins, A., & Kohlberg, L. (1989). *Lawrence Kohlberg's approach to moral education*. New York: Columbia University Press.

Power, F. C., & Khmelkov, V. T. (1997). The development of the moral self: Implications for moral education. *International Journal of Educational Psychology, 27*(7), 539–551.

Power, F. C., & Kohlberg, L. (1980). Faith, morality, and ego development. In J. Fowler & A. Vergote (Eds.), *Toward moral and religious maturity* (pp. 343–372). Morristown NJ: Silver Burdett.

Power, F., & Makogon, T. A. (2003, July). *The distinctiveness of the moral self: Maintaining moral self-worth*. Paper presented at the meeting of the Association for Moral Education, Krakow.

Power, F. C., Power, A. M., & Snarey, J. (1988). Integrity and aging: Ethical, religious, and psychosocial perspectives. In D. K. Lapsley & F. C. Power (Eds.), *Self, ego, and identity: Integrative approaches* (pp. 130–151). New York: Springer.

Reed, D. R. C. (1997). *Following Kohlberg: Liberalism and the practice of democratic community*. Notre Dame IN: University of Notre Dame Press.

Rogers, C. (1961). *On becoming a person: A therapist's view of psychotherapy*. Boston: Houghton Mifflin.

Rogoff, B. (1995). Observing sociocultural activity on three planes: Participatory appropriation, guided participation, and apprenticeship. In J. V. Wertsch & P. del Rio (Eds.), *Sociocultural studies of mind* (pp. 139–164). New York: Cambridge University Press.

Rosales, I., & Zigler, E. F. (1989). Role-taking and self-image disparity: A further test of cognitive-developmental thought. *Psychological Reports, 64,* 41–42.

Ryan, R. M., & Deci, E. L. (2001). On happiness and human potentials: A review of the research on hedonic and eudaimonic well-being. *Annual Review of Psychology, 52,* 141–166.

Scheff, T. G., Ratzinger, S. M., & Ryan, M. T. (1989). Crime, violence, and self-esteem: Review and proposals. In A. M. Mecca, N. J. Smelser, & J. Vasconcello (Eds.), *The social importance of self-esteem* (pp. 165–199). Berkeley and Los Angeles: University of California Press.

Schwalbe, M. L., & Staples, C. L. (1991). Gender differences in sources of self-esteem. *Social Psychology Quarterly, 54*(2), 158–168.

Shields, D., Bredemeier, B., & Power, F. C. (2002). Character development and children's sport. In F. Smoll & R. Smith (Eds.), *Children and youth sport: A biopsychosocial perspective* (2d ed., pp. 537–564). Indianapolis: Brown & Benchmark.

Shulman, M. (2002). How we become moral. In C. R. Snyder & S. L. Lopez (Eds.), *Handbook of positive psychology* (pp. 499–514). Oxford: Oxford University Press.

Smetana, J. G. (1995). Preschool children's conceptions of transgressions: Effects of varying moral and conventional domain-related attributes. *Developmental Psychology, 21,* 18–29.

Staub, I. (1986). Altruism and aggression. In C. Zahn-Waxler, E. M. Cummings, R. Ianotti, et al. (Eds.), *Altruism and aggression: Biological and social origins* (pp. 135–164). Cambridge: Cambridge University Press.

Tillich, P. (1967). *Systematic theology.* Chicago: University of Chicago Press.

Trainer, M. (1980). *Forgiveness: Intrinsic, role-expected, expedient, in the context of divorce.* Unpublished doctoral dissertation, Boston University.

Turiel, E. (1983). *The development of social knowledge, morality, and convention.* New York: Cambridge University Press.

Walker, L. J., Pitts, R. C., Hennig, K. H., & Matsuba, M. K. (1995). Reasoning about morality and real-life moral problems. In M. Killen & D. Hart (Eds.), *Morality in everyday life: Developmental perspectives* (pp. 371- 407). Cambridge: Cambridge University Press.

Wells, L. E., & Rankin, G. H. (1983). Self-concept as a mediating factor in delinquency. *Social Psychology Quarterly, 46*(1), 11–22.

White, R. (1959). Motivation reconsidered: The concept of competence. *Psychological Review, 66,* 297–333.

Contributors

Gustavo Carlo is a professor in developmental psychology at the University of Nebraska–Lincoln. His main scholarly interests are individual, parenting, and cultural correlates of positive social and moral behaviors in children and adolescents. He received his Ph.D. from Arizona State University and was recipient of a John Templeton Foundation and American Psychological Association Award for Excellence in Research on Positive Psychology. He has several publications in distinguished research journals. He coedited (with Richard Fabes) a two-volume special issue on "Prosocial and Moral Development" in the *Journal of Early Adolescence* and is currently coediting (with Daniel Hart) a special issue on "Moral Development in Adolescence" in the *Journal of Research on Adolescence*. Currently he serves as an associate editor for the *Journal of Research on Adolescence* and serves on the editorial boards of *Developmental Psychology* and the *Journal of Early Adolescence*.

Carolyn Pope Edwards is Willa Cather Professor and Professor of Psychology and Family and Consumer Sciences at the University of Nebraska–Lincoln. She received her BA in anthropology and Ed.D. in human development from Harvard University. She has been an invited fellow at the Norwegian Centre for Advanced Study in Oslo and a visiting professor at the National Research Council in Rome and has also taught at the University of Massachusetts (1977–1990) and the University of Kentucky (1990–1996). She is the author or editor of *Promoting the Social and Moral Development of Young Children: Creative Ideas for the Classroom* (1986), *Children of Different Worlds: The Formation of Social Behavior* (1988), *The Hundred Languages of Children: The Reggio Emilia Approach to Early Childhood Education* (1993), *The Hundred Languages of Children, 2nd Edition: The Reggio Emilia Approach, Advanced Reflections* (1998), *Bambini: The Italian Approach to Infant-Toddler Care* (2001), and *Ngecha: A Kenyan Village in a Time of Rapid Social Change* (2004).

Nancy Eisenberg is Regents' Professor of Psychology at Arizona State University. She has published numerous books and papers on social, emotional, and moral development. She has been a recipient of Research Scientist Development Awards and a Research Scientist Award from the National Institutes of Health. She was president of the Western Psychological Association, has been associate editor of the *Merrill-Palmer Quarterly* and the *Personality and Social Psychology Bulletin*, and has just finished a term as editor of the *Psychological Bulletin*. She also has been on the governing council of the American Psychological Association and the governing council and publications committee of the Society of Research in Child Development, and she is a member of the U.S. National Committee for the International Union of Psychological Science (a committee of the National Academy of Science). Her books include *The Roots of Prosocial Behavior in Children* and *The Caring Child*; she was editor of volume 3 (*Social, Emotional, and Personality Development*) of the *Handbook of Child Psychology* and a volume editor (for entries on social, personality, and developmental psychology) for the *International Encyclopedia of the Social and Behavioral Sciences*.

Daniel Hart is a professor of psychology at Rutgers University. He received his Ed.D. from Harvard University in 1982. Hart's research focuses on the development of identity, personality, and morality in childhood and adolescence. In recent years, his research has focused on urban America as a context for development in these different areas. Hart is also cofounder of the Sports Teaching Adolescents Responsibility and Resiliency (STARR) Program and the Healthy Future for Camden Youth Initiative. He is the author of "Personality and Development in Childhood: A Person-Centered Approach," in the series *Monographs of the Society for Research in Child Development* (2003), and many research articles and chapters.

Jerome Kagan is a research professor emeritus at Harvard University. He has been nominated by peers as one of the most influential and respected psychologists of the 20th century. He earned his BA at Rutgers University and his Ph.D. at Yale University. He has held teaching and research positions at Ohio State University, West Point Army Hospital, and Fels Research Institute in Yellow Spring, Ohio. In 1964 he joined the faculty at Harvard University, where he became Daniel and Amy Starch Professor of Psychology as well as director of the Mind/Brain/Behavior Interfaculty Initiative. Dr. Kagan has received many honors, including Distinguished Scientist awards from the American Psychological Association and the Society for Research in Child Development. He is a member of the Institute of Medicine and the American Academy of Arts and Sciences. He has authored and edited numerous monographs, textbooks, collections, and articles, including *Surprise, Uncertainty, and Mental Structures* (2002), *Three Seductive Ideas* (1998), *Unstable Ideas: Temperament, Cognition, and Self* (1992), *Galen's Prophecy: Temperament in Human Nature* (1994), *The Emergence of Morality in Young Children* (1987), *The Nature of the Child* (1984), *The Second Year: The Emergence of Self-Awareness* (1981), *Infancy: Its Place in Human Development* (1978), and *Birth to Maturity: A Study in Psychological Development* (1962).

Darcia Narvaez is an associate professor of psychology at the University of Notre Dame. She is the director of EthEx: Center for Ethical Development at the University of Notre Dame. She earned her Ph.D. in educational psychology from the University of Minnesota, where she also taught (1993–2000) and was executive director of the Center for the Study of Ethical Development. She also earned a master of divinity degree from Luther Northwestern Seminary. She received a Carey Senior Fellowship at the Erasmus Institute at the University of Notre Dame. She is coauthor or coeditor of *Moral Development in the Professions: Psychology and Applied Ethics* (1994), *Postconventional Moral*

Thinking (1999), and *Moral Development, Self, and Identity* (2004). She has also written many journal articles and book chapters on moral development, character education, and the influence of moral development on moral story comprehension. She has published various curriculum materials and was the leader of the design team for the Minnesota Community Voices and Character Education Project, which she reported on at a Whitehouse conference.

F. Clark Power is a professor of psychology at Notre Dame University. He is a fellow of the Institute for Educational Initiatives and associate director of the Mendelson Center for Sports, Character, and Culture. He received his Ed.D. from Harvard University in 1979, MA from Washington Theological Union in 1974, and BA from Villanova University in 1970. Power's areas of interest include moral development and education, democratic education, the psychology of religious development, and sports and character education. He cofounded the Community Extension Program in the Program of Liberal Studies for the South Bend Center for the Homeless. He is a past president of the Association for Moral Education and a recipient of the Kuhmerker Award for his contributions to the field of moral education. He is a coauthor of *The Measurement of Moral Judgment: Vol. 2. Standard Issue Scoring Manual*; *Lawrence Kohlberg's Approach to Moral Education*; *Self, Ego, and Identity: Integrative Approaches*; *The Challenge of Pluralism: Education, Politics and Values*; and *Character Psychology and Education*.

Ervin Staub is a professor of psychology at the University of Massachusetts, Amherst, and director of the Ph.D. specialization on "The Psychology of Peace and the Prevention of Violence." He has taught at Harvard and been visiting professor at Stanford, the University of Hawaii, and the London School of Economics and Political Science. His books include *Positive Social Behavior and Morality: Vol. 1. Social and Personal Influences*; *Vol. 2. Socialization and Development*; *The Roots of Evil: The Origins of Genocide and Other Group Violence*, and two forthcoming books, *The Psychology of Good and Evil* (Cambridge) and *A Brighter Future: Raising Caring and Nonviolent Children* (Oxford). He also edited and coedited a number of volumes, the most recent *Patriotism in the Lives of Individuals and Groups*. Among his awards are the Otto Klineberg Intercultural and International Prize of the Society for the Psychological Study of Social Issues and the Award for

Life-Long Contributions to Peace Psychology from the Society for the Study of Peace, Conflict, and Violence: Peace Psychology Division of the American Psychological Association. He is past president of the latter organization as well as of the International Society for Political Psychology.

Subject Index

Page numbers in italics refer to figures or tables.

adolescents: and domain theory, 123; and moral identity, 174–187, *186*, 191–192; moral reasoning of, 90–92; moral schemas of, 125–128; predicting prosocial behavior of, 85, 86; research on, xxiii; self-worth of, 229; and social categories, 14; spirituality of, xx. *See also* children
adultery, 10
affection, 40
aggression, 8–9, 37–40, 42, 43, 45–50, 92–95, 108. *See also* bullying; violence
altruism: and basic human needs, 38–40; born of suffering, 34, 57–64; context of, 4; definition of, xiv, xvi, 76–77; promotion of, 40–47, 51; sources of, 35–36
amygdala, 22–26, *24*
anger, 99
animal behavior, 19–20
ANOVA, 122–124
antisocial behavior, xiv, 92–97, 108, 129
anxiety, 21, *26*
apprenticeship, 211, 221–224
Argentina, 52
Aristotle, 166, 171, 172, 208, 221
attribution error, 12
Australian aboriginals, 4
autonomy, 38, 56, 220, 226, 235

bad. *See* good
beliefs, xiv, 181
Bell, Mary, 8–9
bigotry, 10
biographical analyses, 173
bullying, 47–48, 228. *See also* aggression
bystandership, xiv, 33, 48, 55, 57

California Adult Q-Sort, 175
care reasoning, 90, 121

caring: development of, 33, 49–50; inclusive, xiv, xxiii, 33, 50–52; and moral identity, 178–180; promotion of, 40–48; study of, 174–178. *See also* empathy; empathy-related responding
character education: day-to-day, 152–155; deliberative, 138–155; need for, 191–192; promotion of, xii; structure of, 148–152; teaching traits in, 137–138. *See also* education
Character Education Partnership grant, 138
children: in apprenticeship model, 222; connections among, 59–60; emotional regulation of, 100–101; empathy of, 21, 77–83, 102–109; and ethical obligations, 16–17, 201–202; on forgiveness, 240; healing from victimization, 61–62; influence of environment on, 209; knowledge of right and wrong, 205–206; moral development of, x–xi, 5–16, 122; and moral identity, 174–187, *186*; moral judgment of, 134–135, 177–178, 201–202; moral knowledge of, 202–203; and moral motivation, 225–226; moral reasoning of, 88–91; moral schemas of, 125; prosocial behavior of, 77–78, 84–87, 108–109; research on, xxi, xxiii; and self, 229–231; social competence of, 94–97; socialization of, 40–48, 54–55, 102–107; temperaments of, 21. *See also* adolescents; character education; infants
citizenship, 141–142
Citizenship Education Policy Study Project, 141–142
civic engagement, 210, 220
civic obligation, 188–190. *See also* moral duties
civil rights, 54, 180
club membership, 186–187, *188*
Cluster School, 216, 220, 221, 223–224
cognitive-developmental stage theory: criticism of, 121; formulation of, xi; influence of, 119–120; limitations of, 130; and moral discourse processing, 132–133; and moral identity of children and adolescents, 177; and moral motivation, 226, 227; and self-worth, 232; and spirituality, xix–xx, 236; and validity of Defining Issues Test, 128. *See also* Kohlberg, Lawrence; stages
cognitive science, xiii, 89, 130–132, 199–200
coherence, 167–168, 176–177, 224–225
collective norms, 219, 220
collectivist cultures, 55–56, 216
community, 141, 213–215. *See also* community service; groups; just-community approach
community service, 180–187, 189, 192
competence, 92–97, 231
connection, human, 38, 39, 41, 42, 46, 50–52, 59–61
constraint attunement hypothesis, 137
continuity. *See* coherence
control, 38, 39, 41, 56
conventional standards, 10, 122–124, 127, 156n2
corticotrophin-releasing hormone, 22
critical consciousness, 56–57
culture, xvii–xviii, 2, 52, 55–56, 123–124, 216–217

decisionmaking, xv

Defining Issues Test, xi, xvii–xviii, 120, 122, 125–132, *126*, 134
democracy, 211, 217–218, 220–223
deontological theories, 166–167
desire, 202–208, 243
discipline, 42–44, 213–215
discrimination, 52
distress: alleviation through sympathy, 76–77; altruistic responses to, 35–37; and antisocial behavior and social competence, 94–96; and empathy-related responding, 75, 76, 78–83; individual tendencies toward, 97–98; in infants, 21–23; and moral reasoning, 91; and parental influence, 105–106; and predicting prosocial behavior, 85, 88, 108; regulation of, 99–101; in research methodology, xxi, xxii
dopamine, 22

education, xxi–xxiii, 52, 124, 129, 207–210, 213, 215–221. *See also* character education
EEG activation, 25–26
effortful control, 98
effortful emotion related regulation, 98
emotion: expression of, 104–107, 143; and moral norms, 205–206; and moral standards, 10, 30–31; and motivation, xiii; and reflection, 172; regulation of, 97–102; and research methods, xxi, xxii; and social categories, 11
empathy: and altruism, 35–37, 59; in children, 21, 77–83, 102–109; definition of, 75, 76; and definition of morality, 5; development of sense of, 6–7; and evolution of self, 49–50; and moral motivation, xiii–xiv, 203; and passive bystanders, 48; promotion of through guidance, 43–44; in research methodology, xxi; and socialization process, 41. *See also* empathy-related responding; sympathy
empathy-related responding: and antisocial behavior and social competence, 92–97; behaviors motivated by, 73; conceptual and methodological issues of, 74–78; and emotional regulation, 97–102; empirical findings on, 78–83; and moral reasoning, 88–92, 108; predicting influences on, 107–109; and prosocial behavior, xxi–xxii, 83–88; and socialization, 102–107; types of, 75–76
environment, xix, 129, 149–150, 198, 205–206, 209–210. *See also* moral atmospheres
ethical expertise model, 139–141, 148–152, *149*
ethics, 1–2, 15–21, *139*
eudaimonic well-being, 208–209, 217
expertise: in apprenticeship model, 222; and Defining Issues Test, 128; model of ethical, 139–141, 148–152, *149*; and personality formation, 136–137; and schemas, 130, 133, 142–148; social-cognitive view of, 135–138

facial expressions, 44, 78–79, 82, 91, 93, 96, 101, 103, 106
fairness, 11, 30
faith, 236. *See also* spirituality
fear, 21, *25*
focus. *See* moral motivation
forgiveness, 239–242
formal operations, 14

GABA, 22

Gandhi, Mohandas, 171
gender, 11, 13, 46, 55
generosity, 43
genocide, xxiii, 45, 60, 62, 170–171
Genovese, Kitty, 154
good, 1–2, 7–8, 30, 139, 142, 197–201, 204–209
Greece, 3
groups, 55–57, 210–213. *See also* community
guidance. *See* socialization
guilt, 9, 10, 14, 20, 21, 27–31, 89, 205–206, 215

harsh treatment, 41–44
healing, 61–63
heart rate (HR), 79, 80, 81, 97, 101, 105
helping, 34–38, 40–50, 85, 188–190
Holocaust, 51, 52, 56, 58–60, 177, 180
human flourishing, 139–142
Hutcheson, Francis, 19
Hutus, 170–171, 179

ideals, 127
identity: consolidation of, 171–172; and culture types, 55–56; definition of, 165, 167–169; positive, 38, 39, 41, 43, 46, 49–50. *See also* moral identity
ideology, 39–40, 129–130
ihuma (reason), 7
individualist cultures, 55–56
Indonesia, 101, 106, 107
infants, 23–27, 30, 42. *See also* children
inference, 7
inferior colliculus, 25–26
information processing, 132, 133, 136–137
inhibited temperament, 22–24, *28*, 30
INRC group, 121
integration, 9–10, 167–168
Iraq war (2003), 56–57

Japanese culture, 2
just-community approach: and apprenticeship, 221–223; description of, 208–209; to moral education, xxii, 208–210, 215–220; to punishment, 214–215. *See also* social relations
justice, 11, 35, 207–209. *See also* just-community approach
justice-related reasoning, 90

Kant, Immanuel, 5, 15, 30
Keynes, John Maynard, 17
King, Martin Luther, 171, 234
knowledge, 147–148. *See also* moral knowledge
Kohlberg, Lawrence: criticism of, 120–130; influence of cognitive model of, 119–120. *See also* cognitive-developmental stage theory

laws, 127. *See also* rules
learning, 45–47, 49, 52, 150–151. *See also* education
life satisfaction, 38
locus ceruleus, 25–26

maintaining norms schema, 126–127, 132
Mandela, Nelson, 171
Meck, Jay, 241–242
me-self, 236
metacognitive skills, 155
Midlife in the United States Survey (MIDUS), 187–189, *191*
Milgram obedience study, 38
Minnesota, xxiii
Minnesota Department of Education, 138
moral action, xiv; definition of, 121, 135; expertise in, 137, 138; and moral identity, 174, 179, 180, 192–193; and moral self, 224–227; and reflection, 172, 192–193; skills and subskills,

145–146, 147; specificity of, 171–172
moral agents, xviii–xix, 5–16
moral atmospheres, 216, 218–219. *See also* environment
moral behavior, xiii, 121, *144–146*
moral collapse, 169–171
moral consciousness, 219–220
moral courage, xiv, xxiii, 33, 53–57
moral development: in children, x–xi, 5–16, 122; and desire, 204–207; judgment as key to, 120–124; methods of investigating, xx–xxi; motivation for, 199–201; over time, 191; and personality, 188, 190; and self-worth, 232
moral dilemmas, 10, 88, 90, 169–170, 221
moral discourse processing, 132–135
moral discussion method, 217, 221
moral domain, xi, 122–124, 166–167, 199, 201, 229, 231–232
moral duties, 203, 231–232, 243. *See also* obligations
moral goals, 167, 190
moral identity, 165–193; in adulthood, 187–190; background to, 169–173; in childhood and adolescence, 174–187, *186*, 191–192; components of, 190; formation of, 178–190, *179*; and moral action, 174, 179, 180, 192–193; and moral self, 224–227; research on, xxiii, 173–174, 181; sources of, xiv; types of, 226. *See also* identity
moral imagination, 146
morality: concept of, 29–30; definition of, 124; developmental stages of, 5–16; marketing of, 152–154
moral judgment, xiv; in childhood and adolescence, 134–135, 177–178, 201–202; and Defining Issues Test scores, 128; definition of, 121; and desire, 243; development of, 129–130, 133–134; expertise in, 137, 138; interviews on, xi; as key to moral development, 120–124; and moral identity, 179–180; and moral self, 224–227; and self-worth, 232; and sense of good, 204–205; skills and subskills, *144–145*, 146–147
Moral Judgment Interview, 226, 227
The Moral Judgment of the Child (Piaget), 206, 209
moral knowledge, 131, 201–204, 208
moral luck, xvi, xix, 178–179, 190
moral, meanings of, 3–5
moral motivation: definition of, 121, 135; and desire for good, 199–201; and environment, 198, 209–210; expertise in, 137, 138; and group attachment and experience, 210–213; and knowledge, 201–203; research in, x–xiv; and self, 198, 224–234; skills and subskills, *145*, 147; and spirituality, 198, 234–242. *See also* desire; just-community approach
moral orientation, xiv
moral reasoning, 88–92, 108, 128, 135, 226–227, 235
moral sensitivity, xiv, 121, 135, 137, 138, *144*, 146. *See also* sensitivity
moral standards, 2–4, 9–10, 30–31
moral theories, 166–167
moral values, 224
Mothers of the Plaza del Mayo, 52
mutual exclusivity bias, 13–14

narrative elaboration, 154–155

National Household Educational Survey (NHES-99), 184–185
National Longitudinal Survey of Youth (C-NLSY), 181, 182, 186–188
needs: and altruism, 38–40, 58–59; emphasis on basic human, xiv; and evolution of self, 49–50; and optimal human functioning, 63–64; and socialization process, 41–48; societal role in fulfilling, 64–65
neglect, 41
neo-Kohlbergian perspective, 120–130
nonaggression, 40–47
norepinephrine, 22
nurturance, 40, 49

objectivity, xiv–xvi
obligations, 16–17, 188–190, 201–202. *See also* moral duties
optimal human functioning, 63–64

parents, 43, 102–107, *104*, *105*, 177, 181, 183
patriotism, 36, 55, 56
peers, 47–48
personal interests schema, 125–126
personality: formation of, 136–137; and moral development, 188, 190; and moral identity, 177–178, 181–183, *183*, 185, 187, *188*, *189*, 191, 192; in research methodology, xxi; social-cognitive view of, 135–138
perspective taking, xi, 85, 86, 92, 108
philosophy, 124, 140, 169–173, 201, 207–208
physiological predisposition, xxi
Piaget, Jean, 14, 47, 206, 209
Plato, 137, 140, 207–208, 216, 221
pleasure, sensory, 1–2
pluralistic ignorance, 219
postconventional thinking, 122, 124, 127, 132–133, 156n2
poverty, 64, 174–175, 184, 185
principlism, 124
prisons, xi, 215–216
prohibited actions, 6, 7, 30
prosocial behavior: in character education, 152–155; in children, 77–78, 84–87, 108–109; conceptual and methodological issues of, 74–78; context of, 4; definition of, xvi; and empathy-related responses, xxi–xxii, 83–88; empirical findings on, 78–83; inherited predisposition to, 102; and moral reasoning, 88–92, 108; motivations for, 73–74, 76; predicting, xiv, 83–88, 108–109, 129; and self-esteem, 228; and socialization process, 41, 43; and spirituality, 234
prosocial value orientation, xiv, 36–38, 42, 55
psychological courage, 53
psychological reactance, 46
psychology, 120, 121, 140, 141, 169–174, 199–201, 209, 232, 235
psychopathic tendencies, 96
Public Agenda surveys, 192
punishment, 214–215

Rabbit Proof Fence, The, 30–31
rationality, 89, 199–202
reactivity, 23–30
reading comprehension, 134–135
reality, comprehension of, 38
reciprocity, 34, 35, 47, 240
reflection, 172–173, 192–193, 215
relational class, 14–16
religion, xv, 13, 129–130, 186–187, *189*, 198, 202, 211, 235. *See also* spirituality
Republic, The (Plato), 137, 140, 216
resilience, 58–59
right and wrong, 205–209
rules, 43, 49. *See also* laws

Rwanda, xxiii, 62, 170–171

sadness, 30–31, 91, 99, 101, 105, 106
schemas: in character education, 142–147, 152, 154, 155; development and application of, 136, 155–156; explanation of, 130–132; levels of knowledge in, 147–148; measurement of, 125–128, *126*; and moral discourse processing, 132–135; structure for teaching, 148–152
security, 38, 41, 42
self: and cost of prosocial behavior, 84–85; evolution of, 49–50; helping, 188–190; ideal, 175–177, 225, 230; and moral knowledge, 202–204; and moral motivation, 198, 224–234; relation to group, 55–57; and social categories, 13, 18–20; transcendence of, 38–39
self-awareness, xiv, xix, 7, 167, 179, 181, 190, 192–193
self-conception, 173–174
self-esteem, 228–232
self-evaluation process, 229–230
self-focus, 97
self-interest, 35, 202
self-motivated morality, 200
self-reinforcement, 43
self-report, 78–79, 85–87, 90–93, 95, 96, 99–100, 102, 103, 106
self-worth, 227–234
sensitivity, 29–30, 40–41, 49. *See also* moral sensitivity
September 11 attacks, 56–57
serotonin, 22
sexual abuse, 8–9
shame, 7, 9, 21, 205–206, 215
sharing, 84–87
Simpson, Andrea, 236–237
skin conductance (SC), 79, 80–82, 97, 106
slavery, 54, 233
Smith, Adam, 19
social categories: attitudes toward, 11–13; awareness of, 30; and ethical obligations, 16–17; and loss of moral persuasion, 17–21; types of, 14–16
socialization: and apprenticeship, 222; and empathy-related responding, 102–107; and evolution of self, 49; of moral courage, 54–55; and moral judgment, 129; natural, 45–47; peer, 47–48; and promotion of altruism, 51; for promotion of caring and nonaggression, 40–47; self, 50; and sympathy and distress, 98, 103–107
social relations, 168, 189–190, 206, 209. *See also* just-community approach
social structure, 183–185, 191, 222
society, 64–65, 125–127
sociobiology, 19–20
Socrates, 221
spirituality, xvii, xix–xx, 198, 233–242. *See also* religion
sports activities, xxii, 211–213, 231
Sports Teaching About Responsibility and Respect (STARR) program, xxii
stages, 11, 13, 122. *See also* cognitive-developmental stage theory
strategies, 136
Studies in the Nature of Character (Hartshorne and May), 200
subjectivity, xiv–xvi, 3
sublime moral vocation, 233
sympathy: and altruism, 36–37, 59; and antisocial behavior, 92–95; definition of, 75–76; and empathy-related responding, 73–74, 78–83; and moral reasoning, 88–92; motivation for feeling, 76–77; and predicting prosocial behavior, 84–88,

sympathy (*cont.*)
108; regulation of, 98–101; in research methodology, xxi; and social competence, 95; and socialization, 44, 98, 103–107; tendencies toward, 97–98, 102. *See also* empathy
Symposium (Plato), 208

tasks, 136
temperament, 21–24, 27–30, 40, 59, 98, 101, 108
theonomy, 235–242
trauma, 57–63
truth, xiv–xv, xvii–xviii
Turing, Alan, 12
Tutsis, 170–171, 179

uninhibited temperament, 22–24, *28*
universalism, xvii–xviii, 3
Utku Eskimo, 7

vakayalo, 7
verbal expressiveness, 122
victimization, 57–63
violence, xxiii, 33, 45, 228. *See also* aggression; nonaggression
violentization, 42
virtue, 17–20, 31, 135, 147, 166–167, 172, 208, 229
volunteering, 189–192, *191*

Wave 5, 25–26, *27*, 29
wealth, 13, 18

Author Index

Aarestad, Susan L., 239–240
Abelson, R., 136
Abernathy, C. M., 151, 152
Ackerman, P., 74
Adelson, J., 125–126
Afflerbach, P., 133
Ahn, R., 83, 87
Ainsworth, M. D. S., 41
Allport, G. W., 51
American Psychiatric Association, 93
Appleby, S., 130
Aquino, K., 169, 173
Argyris, C., 150
Aristotle, 222
Armitsu, K., 2
Arnold, M. L., 204, 224
Aronson, E., 52
Arthur, M. W., 43
Atkins, R., 175, 178, 181, 183, 184, 185, 187, 192

Baldwin, James Mark, x
Bandura, A., 230
Bargh, J. A., 151, 153, 154, 172
Barnett, M. A., 105
Barnett, R., 129
Bartlett, F. A., 133, 134
Basinger, K. S., xi
Bates, J. E., 98
Bates, S. E., 41
Batson, C. D., 36, 73, 74, 75, 76–77, 78, 80, 82, 89, 102
Battistisch, V. A., xii, 152
Baumeister, R. F., 165
Baumrind, D., 43, 54, 56
Beall, S. K., 62
Bear, G. G., 229
Beauchamp, T. L., 124
Bebeau, Mickey J., xxiii, 120, 125, 128, 129, 130, 156n1
Belenky, M. F., xi
Bell, S. M., 41
Bennett, William, 134
Bentley, J., 134
Bergman, R., 169, 171, 209, 226, 227
Berkowitz, L., 34, 37
Bernzweig, J., 80, 81, 82, 101, 107

Birch, K., 75
Black, A., 123
Blair, R. J. R., 96
Blaney, N., 52
Blasi, A., 88, 121, 123, 139, 201, 202, 224, 225–226, 228, 235, 243
Blatt, M., 217
Block, J., 175
Blum, L. A., 73
Bock, T., 129
Bolen, M. H., 80
Bradley, M. M., 96
Bredemeier, B., 211, 212
Brehm, J. W., 46
Bretherton, I., 41
Bridges, D., 81
Brooks-Gunn, J., 7, 183, 184
Bruner, J. S., 154, 222
Bryant, B. K., 87, 90
Buckley, T., 74
Burton, J. W., 38
Buss, A. H., 45
Butler, K., 58, 59

Cacioppo, J. T., 79
Callero, P. L., 174
Call, V. R. A., 174
Cameron, E., 83, 85
Candee, L., 37
Cantor, N., 135, 136
Carlo, Gustavo, ix, xvii, xviii, 36, 75, 81, 82, 88, 90, 91, 97, 205
Carlson, M., 34
Carroll, J., 77, 93
Caspi, A., 182
Ceci, S. J., 133
Champion, C., 102
Chapman, C., 184
Charness, N., 151
Chartrand, T. L., 154, 172
Chase, W., 151
Chi, M. T. H., 133, 136
Chiesi, H., 134
Childress, J. F., 124
Chrisjohn, R. D., 87
Cialdini, R. B., 46
Clark, F., 96
Clever, A., 229
Clouser, K. D., 124
Cogan, J., 141
Cohen, D., 92
Cohen, J. D., 10
Coie, J. D., 40, 41, 43, 47
Colby, A., xi, xx, 64, 88, 89, 135, 169, 171, 173, 175, 224, 226–227, 232, 233, 234
Cole, P. M., 81, 94
Coopersmith, S., 41, 43, 229
Coy, K. C., 21
Crafton, L. K., 134
Crick, N. R., 37
Crisp, V. W., 104
Crocker, J., 131, 132
Cross, J. A., 81
Cumberland, A., 90, 102
Cummings, E. M., 102

Damon, W., xi, xx, 64, 135, 171, 173, 201, 204, 224, 226–227, 233, 234, 236
Dann, S., 59
Darley, J. M., 10, 209
Da Silva, M. S., xvii, 88
Davidson, A., 141
Davidson, P., 123
Davies, P. T., 102
Davis, M. H., 87, 94
Davis, R. W., 45
Deci, E. L., 208, 212
DeGrazia, D., 124
Derry, S. J., 136, 152
Deutsch, M., 51
de Waal, F. B. M., 75
Dewey, John, x
DiLalla, L. F., 43
Dodez, R., 83
Dodge, K. A., 37, 40, 41, 42, 43
Donnelly, T. M., 181, 185, 187, 192
Doris, J. M., 171
Douglass, Frederick, 233–234
Dovidio, J. F., 36
Duffett, A., 192

Duncan, B., 74
Durkheim, Emile, xi, 210–211, 213–215, 234

Eaton, K. L., 104
Edelstein, W., 124, 133, 182
Edwards, Carolyn Pope, ix, xi, xvii, xviii, 2, 47
Egeland, B., 42
Ehlstein, J., 52
Eisenberg, Nancy, x, xi, xiii, xvi, xvii, xix, xxi, 36, 38, 40, 43, 44, 46, 73, 74, 76, 77, 78–79, 80, 81, 82, 83, 85, 86, 87, 88, 89, 90, 91, 92, 93, 94, 95, 97, 98, 99, 100, 101, 102, 103, 104, 105, 106, 107, 121, 205, 228
Eisenberg-Berg, N., 73, 76, 77, 84, 88, 89, 91
Eisenbud, L., 80
Elliott, J., 168
Ellison, C. G., 234
Emde, R. N., 102
Endicott, L., 129, 132
Enright, R. D., 239
Epstein, N. A., 92
Erickson, M., 42, 226
Ericsson, K. A., 133, 151
Erikson, E. H., 38, 167, 168, 237
Erikson, J., 237
Erkut, S., 36
Eron, L. D., 41, 42
Etzioni, A., 139
Eysenck, H. J., 102

Fabes, R. A., 36, 38, 40, 43, 75, 78–79, 80, 81, 82, 95, 97, 98, 100, 101, 102, 103, 105, 106, 107, 205
Farber, E. A., 41, 102
Farkas, S., 192
Farr, M. J., 136
Fegley, S., 135, 174, 181
Feinberg, J. K., 36
Fekken, G. C., 87
Feltovich, P. I., 136
Ferguson, M. J., 154
Feshbach, N. D., 37, 73, 92, 93, 94
Feshbach, S., 37, 73, 92
Field, N. P., 176
Fiske, S. T., 50, 136, 153, 154
Fivush, R., 155
Flanagan, Owen, 140, 166, 169, 176
Ford, D., 178
Forman, D. R., 21
Fowles, D. C., 21
Fox, N. A., 81, 94
Frankfurt, H., 203
Freud, A., 59
Frick, P. J., 93
Frohlich, C. B., xvii, 88
Fulker, D. W., 102
Fuller, D., xi
Furman, W., 60

Garcia-Coll, C. T., 64
Gardner, H., 222
Garfinkle, J. R., 176
Gernsbacher, M. A., 132
Gershoff, E. T., 103
Gert, B., 124
Getz, I., 129
Gewirtz, Jacob, x
Gibbs, J. C., xi, 88, 121
Gielen, U. P., 124
Gijselaers, W. H., 147
Gilbert, D. T., 151
Gilligan, C., xi, 90, 119
Gilligan, J., 58
Glaser, R., 136
Gleason, T., 121, 134
Glick, M., 230
Glover, J., 169, 170, 171, 173
Gold, M., 228
Goldberg, L. R., 175
Goldsamt, L. A., 97
Goldstein, J. H., 45
Gourevitch, P., 170
Grady, E. A., 223
Greenberg, M. T., 109
Greene, J. D., 10
Grief, E. B., xi
Grodman, S. M., 36

Gross, J. N., 9
Gruber, C., 23
Grusec, J. E., 42, 45, 46
Gubin, A., 34
Guthrie, I. K., 95, 101

Hagengimana, A., 34
Haidt, J., 89, 172
Halberstadt, A. G., 104, 105
Halberstam, D., 180
Hamm, R. M., 151, 152
Hand, M., 84, 85, 89
Hare, R., 124
Harkness, S., xviii
Harlow, H. F., 60
Harris, J. D., 103
Harris, R. J., 134
Hart, Daniel, xiv, xvi, xvii, xix, xx, xxi, xxii, xxiii, 135, 165, 167, 172, 174, 175, 176, 178, 181, 182, 183, 184, 185, 187, 192, 204, 236
Harter, S., 229, 230, 231
Hartshorne, H., x, 200
Hartup, W. W., 60
Hastings, P. D., 81, 96
Hay, I., 228
Heckhausen, H., 200, 209
Hennig, K. H., 235
Hensley, D. L., 134
Hepburn, M. A., 184
Herman, D., 45
Herman, J., 39, 58
Hewer, A., 121
Hickey, J., 215, 216
Higgins, A., xi, 210, 215, 216, 217, 218, 221
Higgins, E. T., 132, 153, 230
Himes, M. J., 238
Hoffman, J., 64
Hoffman, M. L., 36, 40, 43, 73, 75, 89, 93, 97, 102
Hofmann, V., 182
Hogarth, R. M., 149, 151, 153
Hoge, D. R., 228
Holmgren, R. A., 81, 82
Horn, J., 102
Huessman, L. R., 41, 42
Hull, J. G., 94
Human Development Study Group, 239
Hume, D., 73, 89
Hunter, J. D., 130, 141

Independent Sector, 189
Inhelder, B., 121

Jacobs, M., 47
James, William, 167, 229–230, 236
Jaquette, D., 36
Jasper, J. M., 173
Jennings, M. K., 192
Jensen, L. A., 123
John, O. P., 182
Johnson, J., 192
Johnson, L. G., 82
Johnson, M. L., 140
Jones, L., 96
Joseph, S., 228

Kagan, Jerome, xiii, xv, xvii, xix, xxi, xxii, 1, 6, 7, 9, 205
Kant, Immanuel, xv, 89, 166, 206, 233
Karbon, M., 80, 81, 82, 95, 107
Karylowski, J., 35
Kaufman, J., 58
Kegan, R., xi
Keil, F. C., 122
Kekes, J., 150
Keller, M., 182
Kelman, H. C., 38
Kestenbaum, R., 41, 102
Khmelkov, V. T., 224–225, 230
Killen, M., 172
King, R. A., 7, 103
Kivnik, H., 237
Knight, G. P., xviii, 75, 82, 91, 108, 205
Kochanska, G., 9, 21
Kohlberg, Lawrence, x, xi, xviii, xix–xx, xxii, 37, 47, 88, 89, 119, 120, 121, 124, 125, 128, 129, 169,

175, 199, 200–201, 206–208, 209–210, 215, 216, 217, 218, 221, 232, 236, 237
Kohn, A., 228
Koller, S. H., xvii, xviii, 88, 90, 91
Krauss, R. M., 79
Krettenauer, T., 124, 133
Kruglanski, A. W., 132
Kuczynski, L., 45
Kurtines, W. M., x, xi
Kusche, C. A., 109

Ladewig, B., 129
LaGasse, L., 23
Lagerspetz, K., 41
Lamb, S., 6
Lang, P. J., 96
Lapsley, D. K., 136, 153
Lasky, B., 153
Latané, B., 184, 209
LaVoi, N., 211, 212
Lazarus, R. S., 79
Lee, D. J., 134
Lee, L., 174
Lefkowitz, M. N., 41
Leichtman, M., 9
Lennon, R., 77, 93
Levenston, G. K., 96
Leventhal, T., 183, 184
Levine, C., xi, 121
LeVine, R. A., xviii
Lewis, M., 7
Lickona, T., x
Lieberman, M., 88
Liebert, R. M., 44
Liew, J., 95, 96, 101, 103, 106, 107
Lin, M., 9
Lipsitt, L. P., 23
Loken, E., 9
London, P., 177
Losoya, S., 79
Lourenço, O., 123
Lykken, D. T., 41
Lynam, D. R., 93

MacDowell, K. A., 79
Machado, A., 123
MacIntyre, A. C., 217
Mahapatra, M., xvii, 2, 124
Makogon, T. A., 224, 231
Malone Beach, E., 129
Mandler, G., 79
Mann, Horace, 221–222
Markey, P., 183
Markoulis, D. C., 124
Markus, H. R., 228, 230
Marshall, S. P., 122, 131, 142–148, 152, 153
Marty, M., 130
Maslow, A. H., 38, 64, 232
Masten, A. S., 58
Matsuba, K. M., 187
Matsuba, M. K., 235
Matthews, K. A., 102
Mauss, M., 34
May, M. A., x, 200, 209
McAdams, D. P., 155
McCann, I. L., 58
McCarthy, G. D., 228
McClelland, J. L., 151
McCreath, H., 83, 87
McKinnon, C., 140
McLoyd, V. C., 40, 64
McNalley, S., 82, 106
McNeel, S. P., 124, 127
Mead, George Herbert, xi
Mehrabian, A., 92
Meilaender, G., 137
Merkl, P. H., 53
Midlarsky, E., 38
Miller, J. G., xvii, 124
Miller, N., 34
Miller, P. A., 73, 74, 78, 79, 80, 81, 82, 86, 90, 91, 92, 93, 94, 97, 106, 108
Miller, S. M., 77
Miller, V., 34, 50
Mischel, W., 44, 135, 155
Mitchell, C. M., 43, 134
Moffitt, T. E., 182
Moore, B., 74, 77, 88, 94

Moore, G. E., 7
Morris, A. S., 98
Moshman, D., xviii
Much, N. A., 2
Munzel, G. F., 206
Murphy, B. C., 82, 95, 100
Murray, H. A., 38
Murray, K. T., 21
Mussen, P., 73, 76, 91

Nagel, Thomas, 178–179
Narvaez, Darcia, xi, xiv, xv, xvii, xix, xxi, xxii, xxiii, 119, 121, 124, 125, 127, 128, 129, 130, 132, 133, 134, 136, 152, 156n1, 156n3, 222
Neale, J. N., 97
Neale, M. C., 102
Neary, A., 228
Neisser, U., 137, 151
Nelson, K., 155
Neuringer-Benefiel, H. E., 81
Nias, D. K. B., 102
Nichols, K. E., 9
Niemi, R. G., 184
Noddings, N., xii, 73
Norman, D. A., 148
Nowak, M. A., 170
Nozick, Robert, 156n2
Nucci, L. P., 201, 229
Nucci, M., 201
Nunner-Winkler, G., 121, 202, 204, 225
Nurius, P., 230
Nystrom, L. E., 10

O'Connell Higgins, C., 58, 62, 64
Oh, W., 64
Okun, M. A., 99, 100
Oliner, P. M., xx, 51, 52, 177, 180
Oliner, S. P., xx, 51, 52, 177, 180
Olweus, D., 47
Operario, Don, 42
Opotaw, S., 50
Oyserman, D., 228

Page, K. M., 170
Pagliococca, P. M., 43
Paquette, J., 228
Park, L., 2
Pascarella, E. T., 127
Pasternack, J. F., 85
Patrick, C. J., 96
Pearlman, L. A., 34, 38, 39, 50, 58, 62
Pennebacker, J. W., 62
Penner, L. A., 36
Petronio, R. J., 228
Pettigrew, T. F., 51
Pettit, G. S., 41
Piaget, Jean, xi, 119, 121, 122, 131, 169, 206–207, 209–210, 240
Pidada, S. U., 95, 101, 103, 106, 107
Piliavin, J. A., 36, 174
Pitts, R. C., 176, 235
Power, A. M. R., 211, 212, 237
Power, F. C., xi, xiv, xvi, xvii, xix, xxi, xxii, 119, 197, 206, 210, 212, 215, 216, 217, 218, 219, 224–225, 230, 231, 236, 237, 239–240
Powers, S., 170, 171
Pressley, M., 133
Preston, S. D., 75
Proctor, W. A., 229
Putnam, L. E., 79

Quart, A., 152
Quattrone, G. A., 151

Rachmiel, T. B., 97
Radke-Yarrow, M., 7, 40, 43, 103
Rahe, D. F., 60
Rankin, G. H., 228
Ratzinger, S. M., 228
Rawls, John, xv, 89, 124, 156n2
Reed, A., 169, 173
Reed, D. R. C., 207
Reimer, K., 169, 178
Rest, J. R., xi, xvi, xxiii, 89, 120, 121, 124, 125, 127, 128, 129, 130, 135, 156n1, 201
Reykowski, J., x
Rhodes, R., 42, 58

Richburg, K., 170
Robins, R. W., 182
Robinson, J. L., 81, 102
Roesch, S. C., xviii
Rogers, C., 232
Rogoff, B., 154, 222
Rorty, A. O., 169
Rosales, I., 230
Rosenhan, D., 54, 176
Rosenman, R. H., 102
Ross, D., 47
Ross, S., 47
Rothbart, M. K., 98
Rummelhart, D. E., 131, 148
Rushton, J. P., 45, 87, 102
Rutter, M., 58, 59
Ryan, M. T., 228
Ryan, R. M., 208, 212

Saakvitne, K. W., 38, 39
Saltzberg, J. A., 97
Sampson, E. E., 55
Samuels, J., 134
Sandman, C. A., 79
Saucier, G., 175
Schaller, M., 79, 81, 97, 105, 106
Schank, R. C., 136, 154, 155
Schaps, E., xii
Scharf, P., 215, 216
Schatz, R. T., 36, 55
Scheff, T. G., 228
Schiller, R., 129
Schiro, K., 102
Schlaefli, A., 128
Schmitz, S., 102
Schoen, L. M., 134
Schwalbe, M. L., 228
Scott, P. M., 41
Seligman, Martin, 141
Selman, R. L., xi
Sereny, G., 9
Shae, C. L., 75, 76, 82
Shaffer, D. R., 41, 42
Shell, R., 80, 82
Shepherd, S. A., 95, 99
Shields, D., 211, 212–213
Shroeder, D. A., 36
Shulman, M., 209
Shuttleworth, F. K., x
Shweder, R. A., xvii, 2, 123, 124
Siegler, R. S., 122
Sigmund, K., 170
Sikes, J., 52
Simon, H., 151
Simutis, Z. M., 45
Singer, J. L., 176
Skinner, B. F., xix
Skoe, E., 90
Slote, M., 73
Smetana, J. G., 201
Smith, J., 133, 151
Smith, M., 96
Smith, R. S., 58, 59
Snapp, M., 52
Snarey, J., xi, 124, 237
Sodian, B., 202, 225
Solomon, D., xii, 152
Solomon, J., xii
Sommerville, R. B., 10
Speer, A. K., 36
Speer, A. L., 80
Spielman, D., 38
Spilich, G., 134
Spinrad, T. L., 79, 102, 103
Sroufe, L. A., 41, 102
Staples, C. L., 228
Staub, Ervin, x, xi, xiv, xv, xvi, xvii, xviii, xix, xxi, xxii, xxiii, 33, 35, 36, 37, 38, 39, 40, 41, 43, 44, 45, 46, 47, 48, 50, 51, 52, 53, 54, 55, 56, 57, 58, 60, 62, 63, 64, 65, 73, 76, 102, 154, 169, 170
Staub, I., 228
Stayton, D. J., 41
Stephan, C., 52
Sternberg, R., 136, 150
Stone, A. A., 97
Stouthamer-Loeber, M., 182
Strayer, J., 92
Strike, K. A., 124, 130
Suomi, S. J., 60

Super, C., xviii
Surrey, J., 55
Switzer, G., 36, 80, 81, 82, 95

Taylor, Charles, 165, 168, 172–173, 190
Taylor, S. E., 50, 131, 132, 136, 153, 154
Tec, N., 56
Terenzini, P., 127
Thoma, Steve J., xxiii, 120, 125, 128, 129, 130, 132, 156n1
Thompson, R. A., 41
Thompson, W. R., 42
Thrash, T. M., 168
Tietjen, A., xvii
Tillich, P., 235
Tisak, M., 123
Tjebkes, T. L., 21
Toch, H., 37, 49
Tompkins, S., 54
Toulmin, S., 124
Trainer, M., 241
Triandis, H. C., 55
Tropp, L. R., 51
Troy, M., 41
Troyer, D., 36, 80, 81, 82, 95
Turiel, E., xi, 122–123, 124, 128, 201, 229
Tyron, K., 83, 85

Uleman, J. S., 151
Underwood, B., 74, 77, 88, 94
Underwood, M., 228
Usher, B. A., 81, 94

Valent, P., 58
Valiente, C., 102, 106, 107
Van Court, P., 82
Vesonder, G., 134
Vicente, K. J., 137
Voss, J., 134
Vygotsky, L. S., 154

Walder, L. O., 41
Walker, L. J., 176, 235
Walzer, Michael, 156n2
Wang, J. H., 137
Warren, G. G., 94
Waters, E., 41, 102
Watson, G., 167
Watson, M. S., xii, 152
Weiss, B., 41
Wells, L. E., 228
Welsh, J. D., 81, 94
Wentzel, M., 103
Werner, E. E., 58, 59
White, R., 200
Whitehead, A. N., 139
Whiting, B. B., xvii, 45, 47
Whiting, J. W. M., 45
Widom, C. S., 41, 58
Williams, B., 166, 167, 172
Wilson, G., 135
Wilson, R. A., 122
Winton, W. M., 79
Wippman, J., 41, 102
Woltjer, G., 147
Wong, D. B., xvii
Wood, J. V., 97
Wurf, E., 230

Yarrow, M. R., 41
Yates, M., 126, 135, 167
Young, R. D., 94
Youniss, J., 126, 183, 192

Zahn-Waxler, C., 6, 40, 43, 81, 94, 102, 103
Zajonc, R. B., 153
Zakriski, A., 47
Zhou, Q., 90, 91, 95–96, 103, 105, 106
Zigler, E. F., 58, 230

www.ingramcontent.com/pod-product-compliance
Lightning Source LLC
Chambersburg PA
CBHW030922150426
42812CB00046B/491
* 9 7 8 0 8 0 3 2 1 5 4 9 8 *